# Anatomy of a Song

Also by Marc Myers

*Why Jazz Happened*

# Anatomy of a Song

The Oral History of 45 Iconic Hits
That Changed Rock, R&B and Pop

## Marc Myers

Grove Press
*New York*

A version of each chapter first appeared in *The Wall Street Journal* as part of the column "Anatomy of a Song," 2011–2016.

First Grove Atlantic hardcover edition: November 2016

*Published simultaneously in Canada*
*Printed in the United States of America*

FIRST EDITION

ISBN 978-0-8021-2559-0
eISBN 978-0-8021-8965-3

Library of Congress Cataloging-in-Publication Data is available for this title.

Grove Press
an imprint of Grove Atlantic
154 West 14th Street
New York, NY 10011
Distributed by Publishers Group West
groveatlantic.com

16 17 18 19    10 9 8 7 6 5 4 3 2 1

For Alyse and Olivia

My melody and harmony

# Contents

# Contents

# Acknowledgments

On Friday, September 23, 2011, I was grabbing a late lunch with my wife on New York's Upper West Side when Rich Turner, *The Wall Street Journal*'s music editor, e-mailed an idea for a fast turnaround: "We're wondering about whether there are stories to be done about individual songs, an Anatomy of a Song, classic songs that resonate today and have backstories behind them, anecdotes surrounding them, huge histories of what happened to them after they came out. They're like people and we could profile them. To start, how about 'My Girl' by Smokey Robinson?"

And so began the newspaper's "Anatomy of a Song" column and my ongoing odyssey to gather the dramatic stories behind the writing and recording of some of America's most iconic rock, soul, country, R&B, gospel, reggae, and disco songs. Originally, the mandate was to treat the column as a "write-through"—an article on the song with the songwriter's quotes spread throughout. But by the third column, on the Righteous Brothers' "You've Lost That Lovin' Feelin'," I faced a problem. There were two accessible songwriters —Cynthia Weil and Barry Mann—instead of one. That's when I realized the column would be better served as an oral history, with the stories told through my edit of the songwriters' and artists' own words. The new format would be flexible enough to include as many sources as were needed to tell the story, and would also allow me to capture the sound of a subject's voice.

When I proposed the new format idea to Rich and Eben Shapiro, *The Wall Street Journal*'s global arts editor, in July 2012, they agreed, and it worked perfectly. In the years that followed, the three of us routinely batted around artist and song ideas, and the process has been wonderfully collaborative and fruitful. My heartfelt thanks to Eben and Rich for their initial vision and guidance and for giving me the opportunity to preserve music history. A special thanks to the Anatomy of a Song team over the past five years—Lisa Bannon, Emily Gitter (now editor of the Mansion section), Michael Boone, Brenda Cronin, Catherine Romano, and photo editor Ericka Burchett. I also want to thank *Wall Street Journal* senior deputy managing editor Michael W. Miller for his critical eye and support for the column.

I am especially grateful for the friendship and sage guidance of Glen Hartley, my literary agent, and Lynn Chu, my literary attorney. I had the good fortune to meet both of them several years ago when author, critic, and playwright Terry Teachout introduced us at his book party for *Duke: A Life of Duke Ellington*.

I would like to thank legendary editor Morgan Entrekin, CEO and publisher of Grove Atlantic. Morgan's wisdom, love of music, and passion were huge motivating factors for me. I also was lucky to work with Morgan's brilliant and devoted team, particularly Allison Malecha, Julia Berner-Tobin, Sal Destro, Tom Cherwin, Charles Rue Woods, Deb Seager, and John Mark Boling.

A big hug for my wife, Alyse, a wonderful memoirist whose love, sharp editing eye, and support never flagged, even during my eight-day weeks. And hugs for my fabulous daughter, Olivia, who shares my adoration of music and respect for musicians.

A big thanks to Dion and Susan DiMucci for use of their photo (I can hear the music drifting across the rooftops); to Cary Raditz for use of his loving photo with Joni Mitchell in Crete; to Cathy Sherrill Lale, who kindly allowed me to use the photo of Tammy Wynette and her father—songwriter and producer Billy Sherrill; to Lloyd Price for use of his image; and to Patsy Lynn Russell for use of the photo of her mom, Loretta Lynn, with her family.

And finally, a big thanks to all of the publicists who understood that preserving musicians' stories is a noble enterprise and worked hard to make top artists available to me. And most of all, to the artists in this book who opened their hearts and shared their recollections.

# Introduction

At its heart, this book is a love story—a five-decade oral history of rhythm & blues, rock, and pop as told to me by the artists who wrote and recorded the forty-five songs in these pages. Through their narratives, we hear the composers' original motives for writing the songs as well as the emotions that artists poured into their recordings. We also learn about the discipline, poetry, musicianship, studio techniques, and accidents that helped turn these songs into meaningful generational hits that still endure today. Over the decades covered in this book, the sound of R&B, rock, and pop changed repeatedly along with the statements musicians were trying to make in response to their times and the desires and dreams of record-buyers. To put these songs in perspective, I thought I'd provide a sense here of how R&B and rock emerged in the first place, a back story that sets the stage for the book's opening oral history of "Lawdy Miss Clawdy" (1952).

Unlike popular music of earlier eras, R&B wasn't written for Broadway musicals, movies, or crooners. Instead, R&B originated as dance music by African-Americans for the African-American market in the years just after World War II. During this period, dance music was at an impasse. The tightening post-war economy had forced many large Swing Era dance bands to fold while jazz musicians began playing a new improvised style intended to be heard in club and theater seats rather than on ballroom dance floors. To fill the void, several African-American bandleaders including Lionel Hampton and Louis Jordan merged the blues with boogie-woogie rhythms and dance beats to extend

the Swing Era just as jazz was becoming more esoteric and popular music was growing increasingly saccharine and bland.

The merging of blues and dance tempos was largely the result
of a sizable demographic shift that took place shortly after America's entry into World War II in 1941, when round-the-clock
defense plants in Southern California, the Midwest, and other
parts of the country needed as many workers as they could hire.
As word reached the South in early 1942, a mass migration of
African-Americans to cities such as Los Angeles, Detroit, and
Chicago began. The newly arrived brought with them a passion
for music from back home—the blues of the Mississippi Delta. By
war's end in 1945, the demand for blues-flavored dance music in
many of these urban African-American neighborhoods gave rise
to blues shouters, saxophone honkers, and guitarists backed by
foot-tapping arrangements influenced by jazz, boogie-woogie
piano, and the rocking rhythms of trains and factory machinery.
At first, the new up-tempo genre was called "jump blues."

Most jump-blues recordings were initially released on major
labels such as Decca and the so-called "race record" subsidiaries
of Columbia and RCA. These three companies dominated the
record industry up until the late 1940s, when a pair of recording
bans by the American Federation of Musicians allowed small independent labels such as King, Aladdin, Apollo, Specialty, Imperial,
and many others to gain footholds in urban markets, creating
opportunities for African-American blues singers and jump-blues
musicians. By 1949, beat-driven blues records had become so
numerous and varied that *Billboard* writer Jerry Wexler convinced
the magazine to drop the pejorative "Race Records" title from its
charts and use "Rhythm & Blues" instead. Wexler, who went on to
become a partner at Atlantic Records and one of the most important R&B and soul record producers of the 1950s and '60s, wrote in
the *Saturday Review* of June 1950 that the new name was appropriate for "more enlightened times."

The popularity of R&B records among adults in African-American
communities continued to grow in the early 1950s, thanks largely to

the proliferation of bar jukeboxes and independent radio stations. But the music also began to inspire younger listeners who discovered R&B stations while cruising radio dials at night. Their growing interest in R&B singles recorded by artists such as Fats Domino, Jackie Brenston, Joe Turner, and Big Mama Thornton led artists to record songs that specifically addressed adolescent aspirations and anxieties. As younger fans gravitated to R&B in the early 1950s, white disc jockeys such as Alan Freed in Cleveland and those in other major urban markets championed R&B records. They referred to the music as "rock 'n' roll" for dramatic effect and to make the music more acceptable to white households.

Eventually, white artists figured out how to sing and play the music authentically. Chief among them in the early 1950s was Bill Haley & His Comets, whose "Rock Around the Clock" in 1954 was featured during the opening credits of the feature film *Blackboard Jungle* a year later. The movie helped the song become the first rock 'n' roll single to hit No. 1 on *Billboard*'s pop chart, turning the music into a national sensation. The film—a noir morality drama about an urban high school overrun by rock 'n' roll–crazed juvenile delinquents—added a new defiant dimension to the music. Up until "Rock Around the Clock," music aimed at young audiences had largely been an audio experience. You clicked on the radio, fed coins into a jukebox or placed a stylus on vinyl, and used your imagination as the music played. The release of the film added dramatic visual imagery and, by doing so, inadvertently glamorized rebellion against teachers and other authority figures. The rudeness and recalcitrance by students in the film against "uncaring" and "disinterested" authority figures remains a mainstay of rock to this day.

The popularity of "Rock Around the Clock" not only excited young imaginations in markets across the country but also paved the way for electrifying performers like guitarists Chuck Berry and Bo Diddley, and white rockabilly musicians in the South and Southwest, including Elvis Presley, Carl Perkins, and Buddy Holly, who combined the twang of country and energy of R&B.

The result of this fusion was a new, impatient form of rock 'n' roll with a rural feel that emphasized the electric guitar rather than the saxophone. With the rising sales of portable phonographs and family television sets nationwide in the late 1950s, the popularity of R&B and rock 'n' roll expanded again, helping the music make up an ever-growing slice of record-company profits. In the decades that followed, R&B and rock proved resilient as the music divided into subgenres. But over time, most songs released did not remain artistically important or even interesting. In fact, only a small percentage of songs recorded have managed to retain their power and transformative significance while the majority have been long forgotten.

This book is concerned with the songs that have endured. Although all of the songs featured in this book appeared originally in the "Anatomy of a Song" column for *The Wall Street Journal,* the material here is framed a bit differently. The forty-five columns now appear in chronological order by year so they tell a collective story about the music's evolution and the role each song played. Each song begins with a new introduction to explain its historical significance. In addition, many entries feature new material added from fresh reporting or from my original interview tapes. In some cases, only one interview was conducted with the primary artist who wrote and recorded the song. In other cases, when multiple perspectives were needed, I included sources who could shed light on different phases of the song's development and recording.

Each song appears as an oral history, which not only lets artists tell you the story behind their songs but also provides a rare opportunity to hear the artist's voice, thinking, and process. In this regard, each oral history shares the immediacy of an audio podcast, since it enables you, the reader, to feel as if the artist is speaking directly to you. In each case, I carefully edited these oral histories from interviews to ensure a story's seamless narrative and flow. For example, if an artist talked about a guitar solo and ten minutes later returned to the solo to flesh out a point, that material was united in the same section about the solo. Or if an artist stopped talking about the song to go into lengthy remarks about something unrelated to the song's history, that material was edited out.

This collection of forty-five songs does not purport to be a list of the best songs ever recorded nor do the songs chosen claim to cover every major event in music history. Together, they simply are a subjective collection of music milestones that I believe provide us with a greater understanding of the songs, the artists, and the music's history. Some readers might argue that other songs belong on the list. Maybe so. But I don't believe their inclusion would have dramatically altered the book's larger story about the music's development. Ultimately, these forty-five songs are stand-ins for the music's major turning points, presenting us with a starting point for conversation and debate about other worthy songs.

As for the time span covered, the book begins in 1952 with Lloyd Price's "Lawdy Miss Clawdy," a song critical to the development of both R&B and rock 'n' roll, and ends in 1991 with the release of R.E.M.'s "Losing My Religion"—arguably alternative rock's biggest hit and the song that primed the pump for grunge rock's rise. Certainly, there have been songs recorded after 1991 that seem to have all the ingredients of an iconic work. Only time will tell. In my mind, a song is not iconic until it has stood the test of a generation—twenty-five years. There's no question that there are songs recorded as recently as last year that seem destined for iconic status. But the truth is we simply don't know that to be the case yet. In my role as a historian, I decided that 1991 was as good a cutoff date as any, since it gives us at least twenty-five years to evaluate a song's merits free from the gravitational pull of fads and music trends that existed when they were released.

Some of the songs in the book may not be as familiar to you as others, but that's part of the fun. Once you've read about the thinking behind a particular song, I urge you to listen to the songs, preferably before and after reading about them. You also may want to listen to them in chronological order, so you can hear the same audio history of R&B and rock that I heard and see how the music's branches split off into other genres.

After conducting the in-depth interviews for these forty-five songs, I found that fascinating nuggets of information emerged. Some of my favorites include:

- The Doors' lead vocalist Jim Morrison often listened to Frank Sinatra's *Strangers in the Night* album in 1966, while the Latin rhythm that drummer John Densmore used on "Light My Fire" was inspired by the 1964 bossa nova hit "The Girl From Ipanema."
- The Four Tops' "Reach Out I'll Be There" was inspired by Bob Dylan's "throw-down" style of singing.
- Keith Richards' "Street Fighting Man" was inspired by the sound of French police-car sirens.
- John Fogerty based the opening of "Proud Mary" on Beethoven's Fifth Symphony.
- Janis Joplin cowrote the lyrics to "Mercedes Benz" at a bar while the Beatles' "Hey Jude" was blasting on the jukebox.
- "Midnight Train to Georgia" was originally based on Farrah Fawcett telling the song's composer that she was catching a midnight flight to Houston.
- Steven Tyler wrote the lyrics to "Walk This Way" on the wall of a New York recording studio.

Throughout the interview and writing process, I viewed myself as a storyteller and the custodian of artists' recollections, reputations, and legacies. I've always felt that interviewing celebrated artists about their work is a sizable responsibility and privilege.

Without exception, those who participated in these oral histories expressed gratitude that the stories behind their work were being preserved accurately, sensitively, and with enormous care. Now I'm passing their stories on to you. Please think of this book as an oral-history jukebox.

Singer-songwriter Lloyd Price, whose "Lawdy Miss Clawdy" in 1952 featured an early rock 'n' roll backbeat.
*Courtesy of Lloyd Price*

# 1 : Lawdy Miss Clawdy
**LLOYD PRICE**
*Released: April 1952*

Up until the early 1950s, records were marketed primarily to adults who could afford phonographs. Pre-teens and teens had radios and jukeboxes, but much of the music they heard reflected adult tastes. The turning point came in 1949, when RCA introduced the 45—a virtually unbreakable vinyl disc with a large hole in the center. At first, RCA used the 45 to compete against Columbia's 33 1/3 album, which had been unveiled a year earlier. To take on its rival, RCA sold multiple 45s for each album and manufactured a special phonograph that could drop a stack of 45s individually onto the turntable, each one playing in turn. But by 1951, RCA realized that its efforts on behalf of the 45 were impractical compared with the ease of Columbia's LP, a format that quickly became the industry's preferred standard for albums. But the 45 had a bright future. In 1952, the jukebox industry announced it would begin replacing the heavy 78 with the lighter and more durable 45. Since most R&B recordings were heard on jukeboxes, that genre soon rolled over onto the 45.

R&B was also greatly helped by a second innovation—the magnetic-tape recorder, which began replacing the clunky "cutting" stylus and wax disc in recording studios in 1948. Tape improved fidelity; lowered the cost of recording, since music could be recorded, erased, and rerecorded on the same reel; and made musicians' mistakes easier to fix through splicing. As a result, less accomplished musicians were able to record, boosting the number of R&B recording artists in the early 1950s. Tape also enabled executives at small independent labels to travel the country with portable recorders in search of new talent. One of those executives was Art Rupe, owner of Specialty Records, a Los Angeles R&B and gospel label.

In early 1952, Rupe arrived in New Orleans, home of pianist Fats Domino, who had already recorded three R&B hit singles. Rupe traveled to New Orleans hoping to find other musicians with Domino's magic but instead wound up auditioning a nineteen-year-old singer named Lloyd Price, who was introduced to him by local bandleader and arranger Dave Bartholomew. In March, Rupe recorded Price singing an original song—"Lawdy Miss Clawdy"—with Domino on piano. The song became one of the first R&B recordings to dryly emphasize the second and fourth beats without the more common boogie-woogie jump-blues flourish found in songs such as "Rocket 88" (1951). After "Lawdy Miss Clawdy" was released in April 1952, it spent seven weeks at No. 1 on *Billboard*'s R&B chart, becoming an early template for teen-directed rock 'n' roll.

## Interviews with LLOYD PRICE (singer), DAVE BARTHOLOMEW (producer and arranger), ART RUPE (Specialty Records owner)

**LLOYD PRICE:** I grew up in Kenner, Louisiana, a rural suburb of New Orleans. As a child, I took a few trumpet lessons, but taught myself to sing and play piano. By the time I was seventeen, in 1950, I had a band and was singing at local clubs. We covered R&B jukebox hits, like "Blue Moon," "Good Rockin' Tonight," and "Honey Hush."

My mother was a great cook and owned a popular sandwich shop in Kenner called Beatrice's Fish 'n' Fry. I went there to eat and play the beat-up old piano she kept there. I was hoping to write and record a song that she could put in her jukebox. I hoped that fame would be my bus ticket out of town. The bigotry down there was unbelievable then.

One day, I was listening to WBOK and heard a black radio announcer named James "Okey Dokey" Smith, who had his own twenty-minute show. Okey Dokey's appeal was his funny way of grabbing your ear. He'd say things like, "Lawdy, Miss Clawdy, eat your mother's homemade pies and drink Maxwell House instant coffee." Maxwell House was his only sponsor.

I liked that line—"Lawdy Miss Clawdy." Days later, I was with my band at Morgan's, a club in Kenner, when I began fooling around on the piano with Okey Dokey's line. At some point, Okey Dokey came into the club and wandered over to where I was playing. He said, "Hey, you're doing my thing from the radio." He gave me a pat on the head and walked off.

Around this time, my girlfriend, Nellie, broke up with me. I was crushed. At my mom's sandwich shop, I was playing the piano and working on my song, "Lawdy Miss Clawdy," with pitiful sorrow in my voice. Halfway through, I just stopped in frustration. A customer asked what I was playing. I told him without turning around. He told me to play it again and sing all the words. When I finished, I looked up. Dave Bartholomew was standing next to me. I nearly fell off my chair.

Dave was one of the most important musicians in New Orleans back in the late 1940s and early '50s. He was a trumpeter, composer, arranger, and bandleader. He played all the black proms and big clubs. He also was a huge figure in the recording studios as an R&B producer.

**DAVE BARTHOLOMEW:** I had dropped in to get a sandwich when I heard Lloyd playing that piano. The feeling in his voice caught me. It was completely original. Art Rupe, the owner of Specialty Records, a gospel label in Los Angeles, was holding an audition in a few weeks in New Orleans for young singers. I thought Lloyd should come by and sing his song.

**PRICE:** When Dave told me I had a shot at recording, I couldn't believe it. Dave had cowritten, arranged, and played on Fats

Domino's "The Fat Man," a big R&B hit in 1950. "Lawdy Miss Clawdy" sounded like it, but with a younger feel.

Weeks later, Dave called and told me to come down the next day to Cosimo Matassa's J&M Recording Studio on New Orleans' Rampart Street. That was like telling me to get on a plane and fly someplace. I had never been to the French Quarter. Fortunately I knew a bus driver who let me ride for free, and he directed me to the studio. At J&M, seven or eight musicians were there, and Dave was explaining how my song would go. Art was there, too. He loved gospel growing up in Pittsburgh and was trying to bring gospel singing together with an R&B beat.

**ART RUPE:** I had gone out to Hollywood in the early 1940s with hopes of becoming a writer for radio and film. I started my first R&B record label, Juke Box, in 1944, but changed the name to Specialty in 1946. By 1948, Specialty also was recording gospel, which soon had a big influence on R&B.

I went to New Orleans in '52 because I liked the Creole sound down there, particularly on Fats Domino's recordings. I wanted to emulate the sound. Cosimo owned the big R&B studio in town and put me in touch with Dave [Bartholomew]. At the audition, Lloyd was the only one who impressed me, based on the commercial potential of "Lawdy Miss Clawdy." Lloyd's voice and the way he sold it had gospel's intensity. Lloyd was nervous and shy, but he sang with such sincerity and passion that I decided to record him.

**PRICE:** When it was time to record "Lawdy Miss Clawdy," Fats Domino arrived and took over the piano. He started playing a boogie-woogie, but Dave stopped him. He wanted something different. So instead of playing boogie-woogie, Fats played the introduction like a tinkling piano roll. To this day, nobody has ever played that intro like Fats did that day.

Then drummer Earl Palmer came in and I started singing, with the horns and rhythm section behind me. Earl's beat was complex.

He was hitting the second and fourth beats hard on the snare but also adding a 6/8 figure on the cymbal, picking up on Fats's piano triplets. The rest of Dave's band included Ernest McLean on guitar, Frank Fields on bass, Herbert Hardesty on tenor sax, Joe Harris on alto sax, and Jack Willis was on trumpet. There was no sheet music—it was all in their heads. We called it "padding"—the horns playing held notes behind me while I sang.

**BARTHOLOMEW:** Before Lloyd arrived for the audition, the band did a few run-downs to polish and tighten it up. We had a great time recording "Lawdy," but it was work to get it done just right.

**PRICE:** After the first take, Dave decided I needed a second verse, to turn the song into a story. I quickly wrote: "Because I gave you all my money/Girl, but you just won't treat me right/You like to ball in the mornin'/Don't come back till late at night." It wasn't hard. That's what my friends and I did all day—we'd make up lyrics. After we recorded this section, it was spliced in on the tape to lengthen the song.

When we finished, Art said, "Sounds great. What's the B-side?" I didn't know I needed to write a song for the record's other side. So I had to come up with something. With Fats playing a boogie-woogie, I wrote the lyrics for "Mailman Blues," which was really a jam session with solos. I was expecting my draft notice any day, so the lyrics related to that.

**RUPE:** I recorded Lloyd's songs on a two-track Magnecord tape recorder. Dave's arrangement and the musicians gave Lloyd's vocal greater urgency. Lloyd's soulful singing style had authenticity and would connect with teens who listened to the growing number of R&B radio stations.

**PRICE:** When we were done, there was no playback of the tape. That was it. The first time I heard myself on the record was four weeks later. I was helping my father and brother install a septic tank in our backyard. The radio was playing, and Okey Dokey announced my song. My brother looked up and said, "Hey, don't you have a song like that?" At the end, Okey announced my name. I felt like I was flying.

Even more remarkable was what Art did for me. If you wrote a blues or R&B song back then, you were lucky if you got credit for it. If you did, you often shared the credit with others who had nothing to do with it. They were on there just to feed off the royalties.

Art was different. He listed me as the sole writer, which is amazing when I think back on it. He had published the song, so he kept the publishing rights, but everything else on the writing side was mine.

**RUPE:** It never occurred to me to put my name on Lloyd's composition or that of any other songwriter. To do so would have been theft. My contribution was my role as record producer, publisher, and manager of the creative process. That's it.

**PRICE:** When the record came out, my mother opened her jukebox, moved all the records down one, and put "Lawdy Miss Clawdy" in the A-1 button spot. After that, every girl in Kenner wanted to ride in my car.

Singer-pianist Little Willie Littlefield (c. early 1950s) was first to record "Kansas City," known initially as "K.C. Loving."

*Gusto Records*

# 2: K.C. Loving
## LITTLE WILLIE LITTLEFIELD
*Released: Late 1952*

In the summer of 1952, about 40 percent of all R&B records sold in Southern California were being bought by white teens, thanks largely to the region's growing number of independent radio stations. Teens cared little about the race or ethnicity of artists and more about a song's beat and feeling. They also were attracted to the energy and endurance of R&B instrumentalists such as saxophonists "Big Jay" McNeely, Red Prysock, Paul Williams, and Joe Houston. As television caught on faster than expected in the early 1950s, the Federal Communications Commission began issuing a greater number of radio licenses to independently owned stations to ensure that radio remained competitive. Many of these new, smaller radio stations played R&B records.

Few songs better illustrate the fickle R&B market in the early 1950s than "K.C. Loving." As Los Angeles became an R&B recording center, songwriters Jerry Leiber and Mike Stoller found themselves with plenty of opportunity. R&B recording sessions needed not only songs but also musicians, arrangements, and overall management to ensure efficiency. Late in the summer of '52, Leiber and Stoller wrote "Kansas City," a bluesy coming-of-age song. At the last minute, Federal Records decided to change their title to "K.C. Loving," thinking it would better connect with African-American record buyers than just the name of the city. But when the single by Little Willie Littlefield was released at the end of '52, it failed to chart and soon faded away.

Seven years later, in 1959, little-known singer-pianist Wilbert Harrison recorded the song as a relaxed stroll with a shuffle beat.

Retitled "Kansas City," the single featured finger-popping vocal phrasing by Harrison and a twangy electric guitar solo. The single shot to No. 1 on *Billboard*'s pop and R&B charts, and it was followed by several additional cover versions, illustrating how timing and tweaking could turn a forgotten R&B song into a sensation. "Kansas City" was inducted into the Grammy Hall of Fame in 2001 and though it may have been the bigger hit, it's hard to beat Maxwell Davis's tenor saxophone solo on "K.C. Loving."

**Interviews with MIKE STOLLER (cowriter), BILLY DAVIS (guitarist with Hank Ballard and the Midnighters), and ALFRED "PEE WEE" ELLIS (saxophonist and arranger with James Brown)**

**MIKE STOLLER:** I was still living at home in L.A. with my parents when Jerry [Leiber] and I wrote "K.C. Loving." We were both nineteen and had been writing together since 1950. Los Angeles back in '52 was a frenzy of R&B artists. Small record companies like Federal constantly needed songs. The guy who ran Federal was Ralph Bass, and he had us write for artists like Little Esther and Etta James. We'd teach them our songs and then they'd record them. Everything happened fast.

One day, Bass asked us to write a song about Kansas City for Little Willie Littlefield. Kansas City was the home of swing, jazz, and the blues—music that Jerry and I loved. It also was known as a pretty wild place. So Jerry and I set to work at my folks' house at 1444 South Norton Avenue. Off the living room they had a separate alcove with a sliding door and an upright piano. Jerry would come over and write lyrics while pacing back and forth, and I'd experiment with melodies to go with them.

We asked a bunch of R&B musicians for the names of big streets in Kansas City. When we heard that 12th Street and Vine was a hot part of town, we used it. After Jerry finished the lyrics, I wrote a blues with a melody. Jerry wanted the blues to be more traditional—the kind a blues shouter might sing. I wanted a recognizable melody so if it was recorded as an instrumental, it would still be identified as ours.

We argued about the music until I finally said, "Who's writing the music, you or me?" Jerry gave in. After we finished, we played "Kansas City" for Bass. He loved the song and told us to teach it to Little Willie Littlefield. We already knew saxophonist-arranger Maxwell Davis, so we all met at his house in South Central L.A. In those days, Max ran recording sessions for Federal, Modern, Aladdin, and lots of other independent R&B labels—before the title "producer" was even invented.

When Jerry and I arrived at his house, Little Willie was already there. I sang and played the song for him. Usually, Jerry showed artists how to phrase the lyrics, but in this case I wanted to make sure Willie heard how we wanted the music to wrap around the words. Then Willie and I sang and played the song at the same time until he had it down.

We cut the single at Radio Recorders with Federal's engineer Val Valentin. Little Willie was on piano and Max was on tenor sax. Max's boogie-woogie arrangement had a great groove, like a train heading for Kansas City. He didn't really need our help in the studio, but Jerry and I went anyway to make sure Little Willie got the melody and lyrics right. Just over a minute into the record, Little Willie shouted, "All right, Max!"—signaling to Max to take his sax solo. It was a great touch.

Jerry and I had originally called the song "Kansas City," but Federal had the publishing rights. Bass said, "You know what's hip? 'K.C.' is hip. I'm going to change the title." So Bass renamed it "K.C. Loving." There wasn't much we could do. We thought changing the title was dumb since there was no change in the music or lyrics. I also thought the new title was too obscure and probably would keep the song from being recorded by other artists. I was right—for seven years.

By 1959, Jerry and I had relocated to New York to write and produce the Coasters and other artists. One day, tenor saxophonist

King Curtis came into the studio to record on a session and said to us, "Hey, y'all got a hit. It's 'Kansas City.'" Curtis had been the session leader at Fury Records on Wilbert Harrison's recording, even though he didn't play on it. Apparently Harrison had been singing it in clubs for years.

Harrison changed part of Jerry's lyrics from "They've got a crazy way of loving there and I'm gonna get me some" to "They got some crazy little women there and I'm gonna get me one." Maybe Fury Records' Bobby Robinson thought our lyrics were too risqué. The new lyrics didn't rhyme perfectly and Jerry and I liked perfect rhymes. But in the history of the blues, messing around with lyrics was common, so we let it go. But there was another problem.

While we liked that Fury used our original title—"Kansas City"—the initial release didn't credit us. They apparently didn't know who had written the song, and didn't care. We showed them Little Willie's single, and the songwriting credit was fixed. Within weeks, six new singles of "Kansas City" came out—including versions by Hank Ballard and the Midnighters and Little Richard.

**BILLY DAVIS:** I was playing rhythm guitar in 1959 for Hank Ballard. We recorded "Kansas City" in Cincinnati for the King label. Hank really wanted Harrison's boogie-shuffle feel but we couldn't get it. Jimmy Johnson, King's studio pianist, was a great player but he was a jazz guy and couldn't come up with that same R&B feel. A hit is always a result of the musicians and how a song is arranged. It's impossible to predict what the winning formula is. You can get close but there's always something special about a hit version that nobody could predict. Little Richard's version came out after ours.

**STOLLER:** When Jerry and I heard Little Richard's recording, we were surprised. He was only singing part of our song—as if he had forgotten the words or was pushing them aside. Instead, he added "Hey, Hey, Hey, Hey," which wound up on the flip side. In 1964, when the Beatles recorded his version, they added Richard as the cowriter. Since Jerry and I thought of Richard as the real king of rock 'n' roll, we let it slide and shared the royalties on that one. By the late '60s, hundreds of artists were recording our song.

**ALFRED "PEE WEE" ELLIS:** James Brown wanted to perform "Kansas City" during a concert at New York's Apollo Theater in June 1967, so I wrote an extended arrangement. I've always been a jazz and big-band fan, and I wanted to get that feel—but with a funky groove. We rehearsed, and James really got into it. The song took us back to R&B at its height—with James slipping between jazz, soul, and funk. He liked operating between the backbeat and the horns to create a dialogue. It's funny, most versions of "Kansas City" sound so innocent—like the singer is heading to a city he knew about only from others. On ours, James sounded like he invented the place and was going back for more.

The Isley Brothers in 1962, from left—O'Kelly Isley, Ronald Isley, and Rudolph Isley.

# 3: Shout

## THE ISLEY BROTHERS
*Released: August 1959*

Jackie Wilson's influence on R&B and rock 'n' roll in the late 1950s was significant. Known as "Mr. Excitement," Wilson introduced electrifying body language to the performance of R&B just as a greater number of young African-American artists began appearing on television. Audiences watching Wilson's live shows in theaters and on TV waited for his rhythmic arm and hand motions, seductive eye-rolling, nimble dance steps (including the first "moonwalk"), and seemingly effortless splits. Elvis Presley, who first saw Wilson perform in 1956 in Las Vegas as a member of the Dominoes and can be heard talking about him during the so-called Million Dollar Quartet session at Sun Records later that year, admired Wilson's relaxed, yet transfixing, moves. So did Ronald Isley and his brothers, who for a time in the late 1950s, were on the same bill as Wilson.

In 1959, the Isleys were appearing in R&B revues booked into regional theaters in the Northeast. Before long, show producers began putting the Isley Brothers on last to ensure that audiences left the theater on a high note. The Isley Brothers loved to close shows, since departing audiences were more likely to buy their records. The Isley Brothers typically ended shows with a cover of Wilson's 1958 hit "Lonely Teardrops."

During one Isley Brothers finale, audiences got so worked up over Ronald Isley's vocal performance that he sensed they weren't going to sit down. So he kicked off an improvised extension to "Lonely Teardrops" that he called "Shout," a song that involved a call-and-response with the audience. Word of the frenzied performance reached New York, and the Isley Brothers recorded the song for RCA, their new label. Released in late August 1959, "Shout" reach No. 47 on *Billboard*'s pop chart and recharted at No. 94 in 1962 after Joey Dee and the Starliters had a No. 6 hit with it. The song also turned up in *National Lampoon's Animal House* in 1978. The single was inducted into the Grammy Hall of Fame in 1999.

## Interview with RONALD ISLEY (lead singer and cowriter)

**RONALD ISLEY:** From the time I was a baby, my mother taught me to sing. She was a pianist and choir director at the First Baptist Church in downtown Cincinnati. Our church was an emotional, physical place. On Sundays, the congregation worked itself up, with people screaming "Hallelujah!" and collapsing on the floor. My mother put me and my five brothers in the front row of a pew while she played piano and organ and sang. I wasn't frightened by everything going on around me. I was more captivated by the minister and how he was able to hold on to so many people for the entire service.

At home in Lincoln Heights, just outside Cincinnati, my mother often played records and rehearsed me. In 1944, when I was three, she entered me in a singing contest at our church. I stood on a chair and sang "I Trust in God." I won, and the prize was a $25 war bond. My brothers and I formed a gospel group in the early 1950s, but in '57, after my father, O'Kelly Sr., died of a heart attack, my brothers, O'Kelly Jr. and Rudolph, and I began singing doo-wop to earn money. A lot of young gospel groups were doing that then. It was a natural move. Vocal harmony was at the heart of both forms.

In 1958, my brothers and I moved to New York, where we met [talent scout] Richard Barrett, who brought us to George Goldner, the owner of Teenage, Gone, and other independent record labels. We recorded a handful of songs for him, including "I Wanna Know" and "My Love" and that kind of stuff. Then we began performing at East Coast theaters. By early 1959, larger labels wanted to sign us. We liked producers Hugo Peretti and Luigi Creatore best, and they signed us to RCA. But our first record, "I'm Gonna Knock on Your Door," didn't do much. We needed a hit.

In July 1959, we were booked into the Uptown Theater in Philadelphia as part of a soul revue hosted by local disc jockey Georgie Woods. There were about fifteen other acts on the bill, like the Flamingos and the Dells. I loved Jackie Wilson then—everyone did. Jackie had a powerful church voice, but it was more than that. He had this easy, natural way of being on stage—taking off his jacket in one move, dancing smoothly, rolling his eyes, and using his entire body to illustrate song lyrics. All of this knocked out audiences.

"Lonely Teardrops" was a big hit for Jackie in 1958, so I sang it with my brothers during our performances. It became such a strong number for us that the promoters put us on last to close the shows. Which was great, since audiences left the theater thinking of us on their way to record stores, not the other groups. Jackie's "Lonely Teardrops" had this part at the end where he'd sing, "Say you will," and his backup singers would respond in kind. Then Jackie would ad-lib, "Say it right now, baby, yeah, come on, come on." That was straight out of gospel.

During one of our performances at the Uptown Theater, I was singing "Lonely Teardrops" when I saw that everyone in the audience was standing up and really getting into it. The place was packed and the audience was yelling their approval, like at church. The energy level was so strong that I didn't want to end the song yet.

I began to ad-lib, the way Jackie did—"You know . . . you make me wanna shout"—and the band picked right up on it with that galloping beat. The people standing went crazy, and I began to ad-lib more lines, like "Kick my heels up" and "Throw my hands up." I'd wait a second at the end of each line so my brothers and the audience had a chance to answer me with "Shout!" That song just took over.

But "Shout" didn't end there. We had ten more days to go on our revue, and audiences were coming to the theater and waiting for the song at the end. As our run continued, I began developing the song. Ray Charles's 1954 recording "I Got a Woman" was a big inspiration. He had opened his song with a big drawn-out "We-eee-ll," and at the end he'd go into these gospel chord changes and a call-and-response thing with the band. He'd sing, "And don't you know she's all right, yeah." We went along with that on "Shout," with me singing "Don't forget to say you will" and my brothers answering me with "Say you will" and "Say it." Then I sang "Come on, now" over and over. We really got everyone going.

When the revue's run ended, my brothers and I returned to New York and told Hugo and Luigi about what had happened in Philadelphia. They already knew, having read about us in the papers. They said, "Why don't you guys record 'Shout'—without 'Lonely Teardrops'? Invite all your friends to the studio so we have a live audience there, like at the theater."

On the night of July 29, we recorded "Shout" at RCA's Studio B in New York. I sang it as close to the way we had been performing it as possible, with all of our friends in the booth and along the studio walls. Hugo and Luigi chose all the musicians—except organist Herman Stephens, who I knew from church in Cincinnati. Herman understood "Shout" from the start.

When the single came out in August 1959, it was spread over two sides—Parts 1 and 2. As we performed "Shout" at concerts to support the record, I came up with a dance, treating the audience like a congregation. When I sang, "Shout—a little bit softer, now," people would dance down low, rising slowly only when I sang "a little bit louder now."

Church groups weren't happy with "Shout." We turned a song with a gospel feel into an R&B hit, and church groups began writing disc jockeys asking them to stop playing our record. They felt "Shout" should have been a church record.

In 1978, the song wound up in the movie *Animal House*. I only found out about it after the movie came out. In the '60s, the Isley Brothers had played at so many colleges it was pathetic. You can't name a college we didn't play. My guess is that whoever had the idea to put "Shout" into the movie had first heard us perform it on their campus.

We didn't mind that the movie's fictional band, Otis Day & the Knights, sang it and not us. They were cast to sing the song, and after the movie came out, they began touring, singing "Shout" and our other hits. By then, we were too big to play smaller clubs, so they took all the jobs we turned down. They made a living off of that song.

Back in late '59, after "Shout" came out, my brothers and I began working with Jackie Wilson. We were fans of his when he was with Billy Ward and His Dominoes, and he became one of our best friends. He was crazy about us, though he was a little jealous, since we'd always tear up the show at the end.

In fact, we had followed him to Englewood, New Jersey, in late 1959. He was living there, and we wanted to live there, too. First we were in an apartment and then we bought a house where we could live along with our mom. She was crazy about "Shout." Today, when we perform, we always end with "Shout." I tell everyone in the audience to stand up, and they know what's coming. Once we jump into it, most of the people try to re-create the *Animal House* thing all over again.

The Marvelettes (c. 1964), from left—Gladys Horton, Wanda Young, Georgeanna Tillman, and Katherine Anderson.
*Michael Ochs Archives/Getty Images*

# 4: Please Mr. Postman

## THE MARVELETTES

*Released: August 1961*

R&B and rock 'n' roll were built on envelopes of cash. Throughout the 1950s, record promoters slipped disc jockeys sizable gifts in exchange for the frequent airplay of their clients' records. The hope was that through repeated play, those singles would become addictive to the ear and wind up as hits. In fact, many of them did. But by the fall of 1959, the practice was rampant, and with a major election looming the following year, Congress decided to hold "payola" hearings. By the time the hearings ended in June 1960, rock 'n' roll had been linked to tax evasion, prostitution, and criminal conspiracies. While Congress didn't legislate on the results of its hearings, congressmen demanded that radio change its practices and that record companies do something to dial back the delinquent and suggestive nature of the music.

Radio was quick to respond, cutting back on the airing of rock and R&B records and making sure disc jockeys were no longer the ones who decided which records aired and when. That job went to the newly created position of program director, who would use a methodology based on surveys of regional record stores and sales sheets from record companies rather than on whims or payoffs.

Once brazen gifts could no longer influence the airplay of R&B and rock records, labels were forced to rely on songs that would appeal to the widest possible audience in order to wind up high in the Top 40 rankings. To give sales a boost, music publishers in New York immediately hired dozens of young songwriting teams to craft songs about the romantic interests and desires of young girls, who were avid consumers of records.

Rock 'n' roll's shift to a gentler, less suggestive form of pop in 1960 greatly helped Motown, a new Detroit label eager for its African-American artists' records to cross over to the more lucrative pop charts. Motown's first crossover coup was the Marvelettes' "Please Mr. Postman," which in December 1961 became the label's first No. 1 hit on *Billboard*'s pop chart. From its explosive instrumental opening and vocal pleas ("Wait, whoa yes, wait a minute, Mr. Postman/Wai-ai-ai-ait, Mr. Postman") to the hoarse sound of the lead singer's voice, the Marvelettes eagerly asked their mailman to search his sack for a boyfriend's love letter. The record helped launch pop rock and codified the girl-group era, which would last until roughly 1966. The song was inducted into the Grammy Hall of Fame in 2011.

## Interview with KATHERINE "KAT" ANDERSON SCHAFFNER (Marvelettes singer)

**KATHERINE "KAT" ANDERSON SCHAFFNER:** Back in the day in Inkster, Michigan, I lived in the Carver Homes projects that Henry Ford had developed to attract people from the South to move north and work for his car company. These projects weren't apartment buildings, like in New York or Chicago. They were duplex houses and subdivided homes. As soon as you stepped outside, you could hear music coming from every apartment. I listened to all kinds of music back then, on the radio or at friends' houses. I couldn't afford records and didn't start buying them until after I was a Marvelette.

My father was a cement finisher. His job was to make sure that cement was even and smooth as it poured out of the mixer onto a construction site. My mother was a housekeeper and then went to work as a nurse's aide at Wayne County General Hospital in Westland, Michigan. Inkster wasn't rural, as most people have said, but we didn't have much industry. It was more of a village, and people who lived there had to travel outside of town to find work.

In high school, I sang with the glee club and chorus. I also sang with some church gospel groups. In 1960, a few friends and I formed a vocal quintet to compete in a talent contest. Our group included Gladys Horton, Georgia Dobbins, Georgeanna Tillman, Juanita Cowart, and me. Gladys, Juanita, and Georgeanna sang alto. Georgia and I sang soprano.

Once we started rehearsing, we began thinking up names for the group just before the talent show. Gladys pointed out that we couldn't really sing as a group yet because we had just gotten started. That's when it hit her: She said, "We should call ourselves the Cansinyets—because we can't sing yet." We fell out laughing, but decided to keep it because we needed a name for the contest.

The prize for the top three finalists was an audition at a new record company about a half hour away in Detroit called Motown. I can't remember what we sang, but I know we didn't win. We finished fourth. But that didn't stop us. We asked one of the school's guidance counselors to see if she could get us an audition anyway. Motown agreed.

At the time, Motown didn't have that many acts. They had Mary Wells, Smokey Robinson and the Miracles, and the Satintones. So they were hungry for new acts. When the five of us auditioned at Motown as the Cansinyets, we sang two or three numbers. I think one was a Shirelles song—hey, we had to pattern ourselves after someone.

I didn't sing lead because I was a soprano and my voice wasn't commercial enough. I didn't have the sound they were looking for. Gladys, on the other hand, had a high alto sound, which was perfect. After our audition, Motown said they liked us but wanted us to bring in original material. This was before they could afford staff writers and all that.

When we left Motown's studio that day, Georgia said she knew this guy named William Garrett, who lived near us. He was a blues guitarist. When she went to see him, he had an unfinished blues song about a nice postman in our projects. Georgia asked if she could have it. He gave it to her, provided he'd get cocredit if everything worked out. It was called "Please Mr. Postman." Overnight, Georgia reworked it as a group song, and we rehearsed it.

When we went back to Motown to audition the song, producers started to fool around with it. The tempo was increased, and [coproducer] Brian Holland came up with the line "Deliver the letter, the sooner the better." [Coproducer] Robert Bateman also had a hand in fine-tuning the song. We sang it a cappella, and after we did, Motown wanted to sign us but said we first had to change our name.

We didn't mind, since the Cansinyets was really just an inside joke. They tossed names around. At some point, someone came up with "the Marvels," and Berry Gordy, the head of Motown, made it "the Marvelettes," which sounded more feminine and elegant. We all left excited, with contracts for our parents to sign. I never thought my mother would sign, but she did. My father told her, "This could be Kat's golden opportunity." He didn't want to block it. He said to my mother, "Don't worry, you can trust her." They could and did.

Georgia was so talented. In school, she played trombone and sang in the chorus. She was very knowledgeable about music. But her father refused to sign the contract. Days after we returned, her mother had become seriously ill and her father wanted her at home, since she was the only girl in the family. She was so brokenhearted—and she stayed that way for some time, especially after the group became famous. She was replaced by Wanda Young, who had already graduated from high school. The rest of us were going into our senior year.

When we went in to record, I remember it was an extremely long session. Everyone recorded together in those days—the musicians and the singers in the same studio. Later, instrumentals were recorded first with vocals added next. Georgia wasn't there when we recorded her song. She was so hurt by that. Instead, Gladys sang lead. The poor thing—they worked her until she became hoarse. That's the version they liked and the one you hear on the record.

For some reason, my voice never felt the strain. I sang from my diaphragm instead of my throat. When you sing from your diaphragm, you hold in your stomach and project out. Most people when they talk use their throat. But when you sing, it comes from your diaphragm and you push the song up.

We were out on the road when we found out that "Postman" had become a hit. We were so excited when we heard that. The charts didn't mean anything to us. We didn't even know there *were* charts. The song's words clearly had connected with girls, which made sense. Motown wanted a No. 1 pop hit, but I don't think they expected that five girls from Inkster were going to give it to them. I think they wanted a Detroiter to get the first No. 1 pop hit. They kind of viewed city people as better than country people. That way of thinking lasted for some time there. We may have been from Inkster, but we kicked the door open for everyone else at Motown to walk through.

Dion DiMucci on the roof of 201 E. 63rd St. in Manhattan, c. 1961.

*Susan DiMucci*

# 5: Runaround Sue
## DION DIMUCCI
*Released: September 1961*

Urban markets produced dozens of male singers who fronted vocal harmony groups in the 1950s, but few combined swagger and vulnerability as deftly as Dion DiMucci. From his earliest hit, "I Wonder Why" in 1958, Dion sang of love's unpredictability and the inevitability of heartbreak. Singing from the perspective of a sensitive male teen, Dion "cried a tear" ("A Teenager in Love"), was "seventeen and still alone" ("Lonely Teenager"), and grappled with being dumped ("Lovers Who Wander" and "Donna the Prima Donna"). Most of Dion's hits during this period blended anguish with elation, as his songs were crafted to both commiserate with and cheer up the lovelorn listener.

Dion's mass-market appeal in 1958 was instant, turning him into a teen idol. He was the fourth headliner on the Winter Dance Party revue in February 1959, a rock 'n' roll concert tour that featured Buddy Holly, Ritchie Valens, and J. P. Richardson (the "Big Bopper"). But Dion, who had never forgotten his parents' bitter fights over raising the $36 needed for rent money each month, balked at the $36 flight fare Holly wanted to charge him, giving up his plane seat to Richardson. Later that night, all three rockers on board and the pilot would die in an air crash. As for Dion's influence and status, he's one of only two American rock stars celebrated on the cover of the Beatles' *Sgt. Pepper*. Bob Dylan is the other.

When "Runaround Sue" was released in September 1961, the song about a girl who "goes out with other guys" became Dion's sole No. 1 *Billboard* pop hit, though he would have 33 hits in all. The swinging "sad but true" fable hit two male hot buttons—sexual humiliation and a desire for revenge. "Runaround Sue" also marked a turning point in rock's treatment of the urban male and how he coped with hurt feelings: In the song, the protagonist deals with his embarrassing predicament by spreading the word about his love interest's dalliances. The song was inducted into the Grammy Hall of Fame in 2002.

## Interview with DION DIMUCCI (singer-songwriter)

**DION DIMUCCI:** We used to have these parties in the Bronx in the late 1950s and early '60s. They were held in the basement of an apartment building at 2308 Crotona Avenue, where a friend was the superintendent. He had turned space near the boiler room into a living room, with couches and chairs. One night in 1960, about thirty guys and girls from the neighborhood got together there to celebrate the birthday of a friend—Ellen.

We had a portable phonograph, but we soon turned it off and began making up our own songs. I was twenty-one and had recorded a few hits with the Belmonts, like "I Wonder Why" and "A Teenager in Love." We didn't have instruments in the basement, so we had to improvise. It was a kick singing for friends at parties.

A lot of the people I knew growing up were there—Tony Gariano, Danny D., Jackie Serra, Joe Zinzi, Joe "B.B. Eyes," Frankie "Yunk-Yunk," as well as Linda, Carol, Susan, Marian, Judy, Ellen, and others. That night, I got everyone to lay down a beat on boxes and bottles and to clap hands rhythmically in time.

I then came up with background vocal harmony parts and had everyone sing them over and over. It went like this [Dion sings]: "Hape-hape, bum-da hey-di hey-di hape-hape." With this going on, I made up a melody and lyrics about Ellen. People were dancing, drinking beer, and having fun.

When I left the party that night, I couldn't let go of that riff and melody. They were firmly ingrained in my head. I didn't know how to write lyrics too well then. None of us did. But I knew that the melody and rhythmic line everyone sang had something special going on.

The next morning I called my friend Ernie Maresca, who was writing songs then. I told him about Ellen's party and asked him to meet me at my label—Laurie Records, on 54th Street and Seventh Avenue in Manhattan. I wanted to see if we could do something with the music in one of their rehearsal rooms.

The bones of the song were already in place when Ernie got there. I had the song's sound and breaks as well as some of the lyrics: "She likes to travel around / She'll love you then she'll put you down. / People let me put you wise / Sue goes out with other guys." After Ernie heard where I was going with the song, we went to work on the melody and lyrics. I had my guitar and Ernie was banging on the desk with his palms.

I wanted the song to be about a girl we knew from the neighborhood who had broken every guy's heart. Not Ellen or anyone else at the party. This girl had dated everyone—that sort of thing. What can I tell you, we were kids. But even though the girl had inspired the song, Ernie and I didn't want to use her real name. Instead, there was this girl named Sue we had admired from a distance at the Harwyn Club in Manhattan. Her name fit the lyric line perfectly.

When we finished, I needed a solid vocal group behind me, since the Belmonts and I had already split up. They wanted to sing smooth pop, like the Four Aces or the Four Lads. Mood stuff. I didn't want to do that, so they took a walk and we split up in 1960. One night around this time, I was up in the Yorkville section of Manhattan and ran into these five guys singing on the street. They sounded great. I introduced myself and said I wanted to use them on a record. They called themselves the Del-Satins.

When they came down to Laurie Records, I showed them how to sing "Hape-hape, bum-da hey-di hey-di hape-hape." They thought I was nuts at first, but that's when "Runaround Sue" really started to rock. As we rehearsed, they got it and gave me this flexible vocal support that let me bounce around on the song and weave in and out.

We didn't have to rehearse much. The Del-Satins got what I wanted right away. Great doo-woppers were like jazz musicians. You didn't have to say a word. The Del-Satins sang a lot together and knew how to jump right in behind me.

As we sang, I studied the Del-Satins. I could tell they were the real deal. Their singing wasn't frantic or forced. It all came naturally. They even picked up on the pronunciations of what I was singing and the attitude of the syllables. They were street—and the best I had heard.

When we had the song in shape, I called in [Laurie's co-owner] Gene Schwartz, and we ran it down for him. Gene thought the song had something. He liked hooks, since hooks sold records. The "Runaround Sue" recording session was held in the summer of '61 at Bell Sound on West 54th Street near Eighth Avenue. There, I gave the musicians rough parts. I didn't know what I was doing musically then, but I knew what felt right.

Fortunately, Gene had brought in some of the city's best studio musicians. We had Teacho Wiltshire on piano, Milt Hinton on bass, Panama Francis on drums, Buddy Lucas on tenor sax, Mickey "Guitar" Baker on lead guitar, and Bucky Pizzarelli on rhythm guitar.

After the guys looked over the music, they made suggestions. Bucky said, "Dion, should I play in this position or inverted in the higher register?" which would give him a different sound. I told him to go for it. I let the guys come up with great stuff. There were timpani drums in the corner of the studio covered in canvas. Panama played on top of those, giving the drum a thud factor and primitive vibe. He also put his wallet on the tom-tom so it would have a deeper sound.

My grandfather used to take me to see opera as a kid at a theater on Fordham Road in the Bronx. Like those operas, I wanted "Runaround Sue" to start slow and sort of pained. It opened with Baker's guitar chord and the Del-Satins' street harmony. Then I started with, "Here's my story, it's sad but true." People listen harder when you tell them you're gonna tell them a story.

Then Panama took a few sharp shots on the snare and the arrangement became pure street rock 'n' roll, like at Ellen's party, with hand-clapping by the Del-Satins. The shift from ballad to attitude, with a New Orleans party sound, gave the song lift.

Chuck Berry used school and cars as song themes. For me, it was stuff like love and broken hearts. I was an introverted James Dean type who was seeking love and writing about it, almost like a diary. My songs were about the journey to find love and the discovery along the way.

After Gene and I mixed and mastered the record, I listened back and knew we had something. I took a promo copy up to the Bronx and played it for my friends. But when the 45 ended, there was complete silence. Everyone looked at me, and someone said, "Dion, what did you do to it? You really fucked it up." They were remembering that night at Ellen's party and the spontaneity of what we had done.

I never thought I had screwed up the song, but I knew what they meant. I had had those feelings before—a record not quite capturing what I had intended. But with "Runaround Sue," I knew I had nailed it, even though that didn't come across for my Bronx friends.

After "Runaround Sue" came out in September '61 and hit No. 1, I went to the old neighborhood for a party. My friends said, "You know, we couldn't really hear how good the record was at first, but it sounds good now." Ellen gave me a big hug and said, "Wow, what a birthday gift to watch that song come together." By then, the song's attitude had grabbed everyone's spirit. But you know, as great as that song sounds on the record, it was even better at Ellen's party. Sad but true.

The Dixie Cups—Barbara Ann Hawkins, front; Rosa Lee Hawkins, rear; and Joan Marie Johnson, right—in 1964 with songwriters Ellie Greenwich and Jeff Barry.

*Alan Betrock / Shake Books, Courtesy of Wayne Betrock*

# 6: Chapel of Love
## THE DIXIE CUPS
*Released: April 1964*

Two weeks before the Beatles' first visit to the U.S., in February 1964, not one of the top 10 song titles on the *Billboard* pop chart included the word "love." The lineup, in descending order, was "There I've Said It Again," "Louie Louie," "Popsicles and Icicles," "Forget Him," "Surfin' Bird," "Dominique," "Hey Little Cobra," "The Nitty Gritty," "Out of Limits," and "Drag City." Shortly after the Beatles performed in the U.S. and returned to Britain in late February, the pop chart began to fill up with "love" songs. By June 6, the chart looked like this, in descending order: "Chapel of Love," "Love Me Do," "My Guy," "Love Me With All of Your Heart," "Hello, Dolly!," "A World Without Love," "Walk on By," "Little Children," "(Just Like) Romeo and Juliet," and "P.S. I Love You." Eight of the 10 (excluding "Hello, Dolly!" and "Walk on By") were innocent puppy-love expressions that stirred up images of exchanged keepsakes, notes passed under desks in class, and holding hands.

But one of those eight songs had gone a little further: the Dixie Cups' "Chapel of Love," which bumped the Beatles' "Love Me Do" out of the No. 1 spot. The chirpy love song was different, focusing on a far bigger commitment than going steady. Its lyrics raised the stakes on the Beatles' obsession with love—or at least redefined what love meant from the female perspective. Marriage, not dating, was the endgame, with the song insisting that the word "love" meant "until the end of time" and that marriage offered the promise of "never being lonely anymore." In this regard, the lyrics became an unintended manifesto that stated what many young women wanted from a serious relationship. Love had strings attached.

But the song's gleeful celebration of marriage—or the idea of marriage—as a natural next step would be short-lived. By 1965, 6.5 million American women were on the pill, all but eliminating the need to exchange vows to enjoy living together and everything else that such an arrangement entailed. In the years following "Chapel of Love," love songs such as Laura Nyro's "Wedding Bell Blues" (1966), the Brooklyn Bridge's "The Worst That Could Happen" (1968), and Tammy Wynette's "D-I-V-O-R-C-E" (1968) began to reflect the reality of their times. But in June 1964, when roughly 75 million baby boomers were eighteen or younger, going to the chapel seemed like the thing to do—at least for young girls. For three straight weeks in June, "Chapel of Love" remained at No. 1, becoming a wedding-season anthem and a female ultimatum.

**Interviews with JEFF BARRY (cowriter),
DARLENE LOVE (singer), MIKE STOLLER (producer),
BARBARA and ROSA HAWKINS (Dixie Cups singers),
and ARTIE BUTLER (musician)**

**JEFF BARRY:** The concept of marriage was very much in my head in 1963. Ellie [Greenwich] and I had married a year earlier, and I had already worked marriage into several hit songs, including "Tell Laura I Love Her" and "Not Too Young to Get Married." Back then, Ellie and I were writing with Phil Spector for whichever artist was due to record next on his Philles label. In the case of "Chapel of Love," we wrote it originally for Darlene Love and the Crystals. Ellie and I didn't have a title initially. We just started writing a song about marriage, without any advance discussions.

The lyrics came first. I wrote them on a yellow legal pad in our penthouse apartment at New York's Mayfair Towers on West 72nd Street. It wasn't a complicated song. There was a chorus about going to the chapel of love and two verses that told the story. Then Ellie went to the piano and started developing a cool chord progression for it. After we got the song in enough shape, we took it over to Phil's penthouse apartment near York Avenue the next day to finish it with him. But after recording the song with Darlene Love, Phil never released the single, and he wasn't happy with the Ronettes' version a short time later, either.

**DARLENE LOVE:** Phil Spector at the time was going through changes with Ronnie Spector and the Ronettes and his other groups, so I wasn't his focus. Even though he recorded me first on "Chapel of Love," he didn't think it was a great record for me. The arrangement didn't quite match the lyrics or the approach, even though he liked playing against type.

**MIKE STOLLER:** At the time, Jeff and Ellie were signed to a publishing company that Jerry [Leiber] and I had started some years earlier. Phil [Spector] liked to write with them, so we cut a deal with him to copublish the songs the three of them wrote together. Around this time, Jerry and I had struck a distribution deal with United Artists. We would pay for studio time to produce and record artists, and UA would reimburse us once we delivered the finished singles. Sometime in early '64, Joe Jones, a New Orleans musician and manager, came to New York with a handful of artists he wanted us to hear. Among them were three young female singers that he called the Mel-tones.

**BARBARA HAWKINS:** In 1963, my sister, Rosa, Joan Marie Johnson, and I sang in a talent contest in New Orleans. Even though we didn't win, Joe Jones told us he wanted to bring us to New York to see if we could get a record deal. We rehearsed a couple of songs for three months and then Joe drove us up—and seven other artists —in a station wagon. The goal was to spend a month singing for different music-publishing companies to see if he could get something going.

None of us had any money, so two of the artists checked into the Hotel Bryant on Broadway and 54th Street. The rest came up later and stayed for free—with five of us to a room. After we checked in, we started pounding the pavement. We sang for Jerry and Mike at their Brill Building office, and they chose us over everyone else Joe had brought along.

Joe left us there because Jerry and Mike wanted us to start working immediately with Jeff and Ellie, who had space in the building. Ellie played and sang "Chapel of Love" for us on the piano. When she finished, there was silence. I asked her if we had to sing it like that. She asked how we'd prefer to sing it. Rosa, Joan, and I huddled in the corner. I said, "Let's start it off together—Rosa, you take the bottom note, Joan, you take the middle, and I'll take the top." We began snapping to set the tempo and sang while holding the lyric sheet. When we finished, Jeff and Ellie looked shocked. We thought we had messed up.

**ROSA HAWKINS:** Jeff asked us to sing it again. He sat at the piano and played along with us, following our lead and giving us a little more oomph. When we were done, Ellie had a big smile on her face. She knew a hit when she heard one. They gave us a couple more songs to sing for the B-side, including "Ain't That Nice," an Earl King Johnson song.

**BARBARA HAWKINS:** The next day, Joe took us to meet with [producer/arranger] Wardell Quezergue [pronounced ka-ZAIR]. We already knew Wardell from New Orleans, where he had arranged all the songs we rehearsed prior to going to New York. We sang "Chapel of Love" for him, the way we had for Jeff and Ellie. Right away, Wardell knew how he wanted the arrangement to sound.

**ROSA HAWKINS:** Wardell had a pad and pencil. As we sang, he knocked on his desk with his hand, creating the rhythm for the horns or bass drum. Then we left. A couple of days later, we went into Mira Sound on West 47th Street. Wardell had written this fantastic arrangement.

**STOLLER:** When the girls arrived to record, Jeff and Ellie rehearsed them in the studio. Jerry wasn't there that day, just Brooks Arthur— the engineer—and me. While Wardell's horn riffs were good, they were just pumping away throughout the song. I felt they needed something to hold the ear on the break between the chorus and the verse, right after the line "Going to the chapel of love." I wrote out a two-bar line that I felt would enhance the record. Then I handed out parts to the horn players.

I also played celeste, starting with the second chorus. The keyboard's bell-like tones helped build the song's wedding-day drama and sweetened the arrangement a little. It just seemed like the obvious thing to do. But at some point I wanted something more obvious for the second verse, beginning with "Bells will ring, the sun will shine." Just a touch. As luck would have it, a set of tubular symphonic chimes had been left behind in the studio from the last recording session. I took a shot at playing them, but I couldn't strike the chimes properly with the little wooden hammer. Then Artie Butler walked into the studio.

**ARTIE BUTLER:** Jerry and Mike were my mentors, so it wasn't unusual for me to drop in on their sessions. In addition to writing songs and arranging, I also played percussion. When I came in, Mike, with his sense of humor, said, "Artie, hello, how are you? Pick up a hammer." Mike had written out the musical part, and I added the tubular chimes you hear in the second verse.

**STOLLER:** When the record was finished, we had a problem. The head of A&R at United Artists, with whom we had our verbal agreement, had a falling-out with the company, and UA said it wasn't going to reimburse us for "Chapel of Love." So they didn't get the record. I'm sure they spent years kicking themselves after that decision.

When the UA deal fell through, Jerry and I realized we had to start our own label. At the time, we had a publishing company called Yellow Dog, so we called our new label Red Bird. We also had to change the Mel-tones' name. It wasn't hip for the time—and it had been the name of Mel Tormé's vocal group in the 1940s. Since the girls were from the South, "Dixie" seemed appropriate, and "Dixie Cup," for me, was always synonymous with ice cream. So I renamed them the Dixie Cups.

But what did Jerry and I really know about running a record company beyond writing songs and producing records? We needed help, especially on the promotion side. Fortunately, George Goldner, who had owned and run record companies, was looking for a job. Jerry and I had a ten-minute conversation with him and decided to give George a third of the label if he came aboard. We hadn't selected a single yet for our first release. It was now George's job to figure out which record would be first. Jerry gave him the keys to our Brill Building office so he could listen to the dozen or so acetates of unreleased singles we had recorded.

When Jerry and I got to the office the next morning, there was George holding up an acetate disc. He said, "I'd bet my life on this record. This is our first release. It's a hit." When we asked which one it was, George said, "Play it." When we put it on, Jerry let out a groan and said, "Oh God, I hate that record." It was "Chapel of Love." George protested, saying, "Who's going to make these decisions, you or me?" Jerry conceded, and "Chapel of Love" became Red Bird's first release—and a No. 1 hit.

**ROSA HAWKINS:** One Saturday in the late spring of '64, I was downstairs in my family's New Orleans home doing chores, with the radio tuned to WTIX. I was dusting when a song came on that sounded familiar. I was sort of humming along until I realized it was our song, "Chapel of Love." I ran upstairs screaming for my mother to listen. She said, "Calm down, what's the matter?" I said, "They're playing our song on the radio. That's us, that's us!" My mother said, "Yes, I know dear. And we're going to hear it many more times." To this day, the feeling of hearing our voices harmonizing on the radio has never left me.

The Kinks in 1965, clockwise from top left—Ray Davies, Mick Avory, Dave Davies, and Pete Quaife at London's Wembley Studios.

*GAB Archive/Getty Images*

# 7: You Really Got Me

**THE KINKS**

*Released: August 1964*

The predictability of pop rock—with its formulaic structure, three-minute length, and labels' demands for a polished sound—didn't sit well with all bands in 1964. Many British working-class groups weaned on gritty American blues recordings were particularly resistant to conformity. Eclipsed by British pop bands that had already made the leap to the U.S., U.K. groups such as the Rolling Stones, the Yardbirds, the Animals, and the Kinks pushed to create a sound that would set them apart. In 1964, the popularity of the Beatles and the Dave Clark Five left little room for another cheery boy band. In fact, prior to their first American tour in June 1964, the Stones positioned themselves as the anti-Beatles—with their manager starting a British media frenzy by encouraging the headline, "Would You Let Your Daughter Marry a Rolling Stone?"

Competitive, impatient, and aggravated by the upbeat tidiness of pop music, the Kinks decided to leverage the rawness of their live club performances to the recording studio. When the band recorded "You Really Got Me" in July 1964, they wanted the song to have an edge, complete with power guitar chords and fuzzy distortion. They wanted the record to have the same coarse sound they projected while performing at London clubs that had poor sound systems. Though their label, Pye Records, tried to clean up their first attempt, the Kinks demanded to go back into the studio to "dirty" up the sound by rerecording it.

After "You Really Got Me" was released in August 1964, the single went to No. 1 in Britain and No. 7 in the U.S. The band's fondness for distortion would influence the Rolling Stones ("Satisfaction"), the Beatles ("Think for Yourself"), the Yardbirds ("Heart Full of Soul"), and other groups in 1965 and beyond. The song, with its fuzzy power chords, also became an inspiration for hard-rock and garage bands later in the decade. "You Really Got Me" was inducted into the Grammy Hall of Fame in 1999.

**Interviews with RAY DAVIES (Kinks lead singer and songwriter), DAVE DAVIES (lead guitarist and Ray's brother), and SHEL TALMY (producer)**

**RAY DAVIES:** Shortly after I formed the Ravens in 1963 with my brother Dave and bassist Pete Quaife, we began wearing colorful outfits we had bought in boutiques on London's Carnaby Street. Dressed in these flamboyant clothes at a pub with our manager, Larry Page, I loudly insisted we needed an edgier name than the Ravens. A drunk who had been watching us remarked that we looked more like kinks to him—short for "kinky," or "weird." Larry picked up on that and said, "The Kinks! That's perfect!"

Before the Ravens, while I was still at college, I played in the Dave Hunt Blues Band, a gritty R&B-jazz crossover group. Around this time I wrote "You Really Got Me" on my guitar at my sister's house in North London. My influences were country and blues—something that [American blues guitarist] Big Bill Broonzy might play.

The inspiration for the lyrics and title came to me one night while playing with Dave Hunt at the Scene Club in Soho. During our set, I looked out in the darkness about ten feet from the stage and saw what appeared to be a seventeen-year-old girl moving better than anyone else on the dance floor. She had ash-colored hair set in a beehive style that was popular then. When we finished, I went off to find her, but she was gone and never returned to the club. She really got me going.

When I first played the song for Pete, our bassist, he didn't care for it. It didn't sound commercial enough for him—not pop enough. He thought it was too basic to grab teens. Then I played it for the rest of the band in the front room of my family's house in London. Everyone liked it. I deliberately wanted it to sound coarse, the way we came across through club speakers that couldn't handle the volume. Then I set the song aside.

In 1964, after we changed our name to the Kinks, we were under a lot of pressure to come up with a hit for Pye Records, our label. Our first two singles—"Long Tall Sally" and "You Still Want Me"—hadn't charted. So I pulled out "You Really Got Me" and went to work on it. I played the riff on the piano at my parents' house. Dave learned the song and played the chords on his guitar. I wanted the song to sound like a repetitive Gregorian chant over a blues, so I pushed for a dirtied-up guitar sound.

I also wanted a distorted bass sound with an echo effect, the way Ray Charles's electric piano sounded on "What I'd Say" coming through the bad speaker of my parents' record player. To try to emulate that sound, I punched a few holes in Pete's preamp speaker with my mother's knitting needle.

**DAVE DAVIES:** I always liked how our band sounded at clubs—coarse and sort of stripped down. Months earlier, I had passed a radio shop a few doors up from my parents' house on Denmark Terrace. In the window I saw a small teal space-age Elpico amp for 10 quid. I bought it, but when I got home, I was alone and had a moment of teenage inspiration or rage. I had just learned to shave, so I took one of my razor blades and slashed up the amp's speaker cone. I had no idea whether what I had done would work, but when I plugged in the guitar, I was blown away by the raucous sound that came out. It was gritty. Up until then, rock guitars in London had sounded very clean and polished, except for blues players. But the blues sound wasn't what I had in my head then. It was just rage.

**RAY DAVIES:** Our first recording of "You Really Got Me" was a demo we made at Regent Sounds on London's Denmark Street. Shel Talmy, an American independent record producer who was working in London at the time, liked what he heard.

**SHEL TALMY:** When I arrived in London in 1962, I expected to stay only a few weeks. But after I met with A&R chief Dick Rowe at Decca, he hired me to bring in new artists and record them. A year later, I was visiting some friends at a music publisher on Denmark Street when Robert Wace, the manager of some band called the Kinks, came into reception and asked if anyone wanted to hear a demo. I volunteered. After we listened in my friend's office, I thought the demo had a number of potential hits. By then, I was ticked at Decca for turning down two bands I had brought in to be signed—Manfred Mann and Georgie Fame. So after I met the Kinks, we went into Pye in '64 to record their first two singles. When those didn't chart, we recorded "You Really Got Me." Pye executives loved the playback, but two days later, Ray said he didn't like it and wanted to record the song again.

**RAY DAVIES:** It was too slow, and the engineers had cleaned up our distortion, adding echo and made it sound perfect, which was exactly what I didn't want. I wanted the single to sound live and raw, the way we sounded at clubs. After some back-and-forth, the label agreed to let us rerecord—provided we paid for it. So I borrowed 200 pounds from our managers, Grenville Collins and Robert Wace. A few weeks later, we rerecorded "You Really Got Me" at London's IBC Studios. I thought about adding a specific girl's name to the lyric but decided against it. I had sung "Girl, you really got me goin'" at most of our gigs and stuck with that.

**DAVE DAVIES:** I was quite an angry kid and got my aggression out through my music. For the opening chords at IBC, I used bar chords—holding down three strings and strumming hard and then shifting my fingers to a different place on the neck. I picked that up from listening to the Ventures' "Walk, Don't Run." Their rhythm guitarist, Don Wilson, wasn't playing the full chords—he was just hitting the bottom three notes. I thought that was great—I could do that and not worry about fifths and sixths and things I didn't know yet.

**TALMY:** At IBC, I placed Ray in an isolation booth so the instruments wouldn't bleed into his vocal. For the drums, instead of using four mikes, which was standard then, I used twelve, to isolate all of the various percussive sounds. I used three mikes for Dave—one in front of his amp, another on a boom at a distance, and one pointed at his guitar strings. Each mike picked up different parts of what he was playing, and I combined them later to get the sound you hear on the single. The mike on Dave's strings picked up the tinny sound that, when mixed with the other two, gave his guitar a nice top. The Kinks didn't have a drummer yet, so I hired Bobby Graham, the best English session drummer at the time for rock. I played the tambourine. I also overdubbed background vocals to enhance Dave's riff. Dave, Pete, Ray, and Rasa—Ray's wife at the time—sang the background track at one mike. Then I had everyone switch positions and I double-tracked the vocals so there would be more dimension.

**RAY DAVIES:** To me, the sheer power of Dave's hands combined with the anger and aggression with which he played the riff of my song counted more than any distorting speaker. After we recorded at IBC, we went on Britain's *Ready Steady Go!* TV show in July '64, just before the single's release. Once teens saw us and heard our metallic sound, the excitement built and the single took off after its release the following week.

Part of what the audience was responding to was the song's key shift from G to A. The more natural and melodic place for the song to go was from G to C or D. But I wanted it to go to A, which was quite revolutionary then. There's something about that full step up that feels like acceleration and raises the excitement level. The progression actually made me shudder when I originally came up with it.

It's funny, the song began as a way for me to reach out to that girl at the Scene Club, to let her know how I felt. I never found her or met her later, but I sort of like to imagine that she knows "You Really Got Me" was written for her and that she's out there still, an age-old diamond.

The Righteous Brothers—Bill Medley, left, and Bobby Hatfield—in 1965.

*GAB Archive/Getty Images*

# 8: You've Lost That Lovin' Feelin'

**THE RIGHTEOUS BROTHERS**

*Released: November 1964*

Many of the artists Phil Spector produced for his Philles label in the early 1960s had hit singles. The problem was that most of them, including the Ronettes, the Crystals, and the Blossoms, were girl groups. To diversify, Spector began looking for an all-male vocal group in 1964. His Wall of Sound approach—jamming Gold Star Recording Studios in Los Angeles with as many seasoned musicians as possible to create a dense instrumental backdrop he called "little symphonies for the kids"—was effective at creating drama and texture behind high-strung, soulful vocals. Spector's productions raised pop rock to operatic levels, with the Blossoms' "He's a Rebel," the Ronettes' "Be My Baby" and "Do I Love You," and the Crystals' "Then He Kissed Me." Spector wanted that same crowded sound behind a soulful male vocal group. Enter the Righteous Brothers.

In 1962, Bill Medley and Bobby Hatfield were singing in a vocal-harmony group in Southern California called the Paramours. When the band broke up later that year, Medley and Hatfield began singing as a duo at local clubs. According to Medley, one night when they finished a song, a Marine from a local base shouted out, "That was righteous, brother." Soon after, Medley and Hatfield were recording for Moonglow Records when they were asked to come up with a name. "The Righteous Brothers" sounded about right. Two years later, when the pair appeared at San Francisco's Cow Palace, Spector heard them and signed the duo to Philles.

When the Righteous Brothers recorded "You've Lost That Lovin' Feelin'" for Spector in October 1964, the song about lost love and a man's near-tears plea for its return ran 3:45. Fearful that the record's length would suppress airplay on AM radio, Spector simply changed the time listed on the label to 3:05 before the 45 was pressed. By February 1965, the single was No. 1 on *Billboard*'s pop chart, and it remains one of the finest examples of Spector's Wall of Sound technique. According to BMI, "You've Lost That Lovin' Feelin'" became the most-played radio song of all time in 2011, with 15 million airplays. It was inducted into the Grammy Hall of Fame in 1998.

## Interviews with BARRY MANN (cowriter), CYNTHIA WEIL (cowriter), and BILL MEDLEY (Righteous Brothers singer)

**BARRY MANN:** In 1964, Cynthia [Weil] and I were already married and working as songwriters at New York's Aldon Music, the publishing company in the Brill Building founded by Don Kirshner and Al Nevins. In the summer, Phil [Spector] called and asked us to come out to Los Angeles and write a song with him for two singers he had just signed—the Righteous Brothers. So we flew out and checked into the Chateau Marmont in Hollywood—the only hotel that let you roll a rented piano into your room. Later, up at Phil's house, he played us records by the Righteous Brothers. They were white, but sounded remarkably like the group Sam and Dave.

**CYNTHIA WEIL:** We all planned on writing together the next day, but back at the hotel, Barry and I started a draft. We loved the yearning and slow build of the Four Tops' "Baby I Need Your Loving," which had just come out in July. Then Barry came up with our opening line: "You never close your eyes anymore when I kiss your lips."

**MANN:** My heart had been broken a few times before I met Cynthia, so it wasn't a stretch to feel that lyric. I also might have been influenced by "I love how your eyes close, whenever you kiss me"—the opening line to "I Love How You Love Me," a song I had cowritten in 1961 with Larry Kolber, recorded by the Paris Sisters.

**WEIL:** About an hour later, Barry and I had two verses—the story part—and the chorus.

**MANN:** But we were stuck for a bridge and an ending. We called Phil and played him what we had over the phone. He said he had tears in his eyes when he heard Cynthia's line "It makes me just feel like crying/'Cause baby, something beautiful's dying."

**WEIL:** At Phil's the next day, Phil sang the "whoa-whoa-whoas." As a lyricist, I cringed. They sounded like filler.

**MANN:** For the bridge, Phil experimented on the piano with a "Hang on Sloopy" riff. It was brilliant. I built a melody on the riff while Cynthia shouted out lyrics: "Baby, baby, I get down on my knees for you" and so on. When we met the Righteous Brothers a few days later, we were nervous they might not like it.

**WEIL:** Bill [Medley] and Bobby [Hatfield] stood at the piano while Barry played and sang the melody and Phil sang harmony. At the end, there was dead silence. Bill said, "Sounds good—for the Everly Brothers." At first he didn't hear the soul. So Phil asked Bill and Bobby to try it.

**MANN:** But Phil wanted Bill to sing the verses alone, with Bobby joining only on the chorus. Bill had the deeper voice.

**WEIL:** They had always sung together, and Bobby wasn't happy. He said to Phil, "What am I supposed to do while the big guy is singing?" Phil snapped, "You can go to the bank."

**BILL MEDLEY:** Bobby and I went into the studio a few weeks later to record the vocals. Phil had already recorded and overdubbed a ton of instrumental tracks. When I put on the headphones, the music sounded as big as Montana, with a touch of New York. Phil had me sing the opening verse over and over until he had his take. Then we'd move on to the next part and repeat the process. This went on for two days—four hours each day. My emotion on there was real. Two years earlier, my wife at the time of the recording—Karen—was my girlfriend and had broken up with me for about six months. I really ate it. That's the ache you hear in my voice.

**MANN:** Several weeks after we returned to New York, Phil called and played us the finished record. But something was wrong, and I yelled over the phone to get his attention: "Phil, you've got it on the wrong speed." The song we had written had been about three ticks faster and a tone and a half higher. Phil came on and said, "No, no, Barry, that's the record."

**WEIL:** At first, we were surprised the song was a hit. It ran 3:45—which was an eternity on the radio back then. But Phil loved it.

**MANN:** One night in early '65, our phone rang at 3 a.m.

**WEIL:** It was Brian Wilson calling from L.A. He said, "Your song is the greatest record ever. I was ready to quit the music business, but this has inspired me to write again. I want to write with you guys." Half asleep, all I could say was, "Now?"

Smokey Robinson, left, backstage at Harlem's Apollo Theater in 1964 teaching David Ruffin (in glasses) and other Temptations "My Girl."

*Michael Ochs Archives/Getty Images*

# 9: My Girl
## THE TEMPTATIONS
*Released: December 1964*

Motown was at the start of a boom in 1964. The record label founded by Berry Gordy five years earlier had reached new levels of productivity and success, thanks largely to Gordy's factory-like business model, high standards of quality control, and pop sensibility. Artists were groomed for stardom by a team of image polishers and choreographers while house songwriting teams and session musicians gave songs drama and energy. In May 1964, Mary Wells's "My Guy" hit No. 1 on *Billboard*'s pop chart. Then the Supremes' "Where Did Our Love Go," "Baby Love," and "Come See About Me" all became No. 1 pop hits in the fall. Motown artists were fast becoming household names nationwide, resulting in stronger record sales, greater TV exposure, and more lucrative tours.

But from the vantage point of Gordy, the year's accomplishments were significant but not good enough. If his female artists could top the pop charts, there was no reason why one or more of his male vocal groups couldn't do the same. The key was to capture the hearts and imaginations of teenage girls. So Gordy asked Smokey Robinson to write a song for the Temptations. Rather than compose a hard-charging song with a pounding go-go rhythm, Robinson composed a mid-tempo ballad and had David Ruffin sing lead. Robinson figured that Ruffin's coarse tenor voice would be more tender and potent when ecstatic than the sweeter-sounding tenor of Eddie Kendricks.

In the recording studio, Motown's house musicians added a heartbeat bass line and exalted guitar riffs to frame Robinson's lyrics. Released in late December 1964, the single became the Temptations' first No. 1 pop hit, in March 1965. Over time, "My Girl," with its signature introduction and unrestrained expression of male joy, would become one of Motown's best-known and most successful singles. "My Girl" was inducted into the Grammy Hall of Fame in 1998.

### Interview with SMOKEY ROBINSON (songwriter)

**SMOKEY ROBINSON:** I've had so many surprises in my career as a songwriter, but "My Girl" is one of the biggest. It's my international anthem. Whenever I perform, I typically do a short medley of Motown songs that I wrote for the Temptations. The last one is always "My Girl." I can be in a foreign country where people don't speak English and the audience will start cheering before I even start singing "My Girl." They know what's coming as soon as they hear the opening bass line. [He sings the famous line created by bassist James Jamerson:] "Bah bum-bum, bah bum-bum, bah bum-bum." They all know the words, even if they don't know what they mean.

I didn't write "My Girl" in 1964 for the Miracles and me to record. My wife at the time wasn't the inspiration, either. And "My Girl" wasn't conceived as a response to "My Guy"—the No. 1 hit I had written for Mary Wells earlier that year. I wrote "My Girl" specifically for the Temptations, with hopes they would make it a hit.

Months earlier, I had written "The Way You Do the Things You Do" for them—with Eddie Kendricks singing lead. But after the song became the group's first big hit, all of Motown's staff writers and producers began trying to duplicate my success by writing songs for the Temptations, with Eddie singing lead. I had to come up with something different.

Fortunately, Eddie wasn't the only one in the group with a fine voice. I had heard David Ruffin sing lead while we were all on the same bill at a series of Detroit clubs. So while everyone else at

Motown focused on Eddie, I sat down at my piano in Detroit and composed a song for David.

Unlike Eddie, who was smooth, David had this gruff, tough, deep voice. You know, "Come here, girl, and let me love you"—that kind of thing. I figured if I had David sing something sweet and sincere, the contrast would connect with girls who listened to the radio and bought records. To bring that out, I imagined a pulsating, heartbeat tempo. I already had the key and chord changes in mind. The melody just came while I was working on a piano in Detroit.

A short time later, the Miracles were out on the road again with the Temptations. During a break in our rehearsal at New York's Apollo Theater, we went down to the stage and I played them "My Girl" for the first time on the piano. Then the Temptations gave it a shot. While David sang lead, the rest of the guys in the group began to add things. They made up their own background vocals, like "hey hey hey" and a series of "my girls" echoing David's vocal. The Temptations were the greatest background maker-uppers ever [laughs]. When we were finished, they said they loved the song. I think they loved that I was having David sing the lead. There was no complaining or infighting. They knew that both David and Paul [Williams] had great lead voices. I had Paul sing "Don't Look Back" on the same album.

In September '64, I went into the studio to produce the instrumental tracks. All of the Funk Brothers, Motown's studio band, were so great at adding little touches, provided you had the music's basics down. I came in with that pulse beat in mind. You just showed them what you wanted and they would come up with their own thing to enhance your music. We did two run-downs of "My Girl" to get comfortable.

At the start of the third run-down, Robert White stood up and started walking around the studio playing a guitar riff [sings the riff that comes right after the bass line starts and before the vocal]. But halfway in, Robert cut it off, saying, "No, no, no, no, no." He didn't think what he had was right. I said, "No, no, no, my butt.

That's going to be in the song." Now, of course, that line has become one of the most famous guitar riffs ever recorded.

The Temptations' vocal tracks were overdubbed in November. [Arranger] Paul Riser added the strings, which highlighted David's sweetness and the sincerity of the words. Then the single was released.

In February 1965, the Miracles and I were out touring. After we returned to Detroit, Berry called me into his office and handed me a $1,000 bonus check. He said, "You've got a No. 1 record coming." I thought he was talking about something the Miracles had recorded. When I asked which one, he said, "My Girl." I couldn't believe it. "My Girl" is still my dream come true.

The Four Tops in 1966, clockwise from top right—Abdul "Duke" Fakir, Lawrence Payton Jr., Renaldo "Obie" Benson, and Levi Stubbs.

*Pictorial Press Ltd / Alamy*

# 10: Reach Out I'll Be There

**THE FOUR TOPS**

*Released: August 1966*

In July 1965, Bob Dylan caused an uproar at the Newport Folk Festival when he came on stage and plugged a Fender Stratocaster electric guitar into an amp. Minutes into the first song, "Maggie's Farm," roughly a third of the 17,000 people in the audience began to boo. His hit "Like a Rolling Stone" followed, and didn't fare much better. In addition to the band's loud, electrified sound, the song's lyrics were unsettling, since they diverted from folk's traditional sing-along push-backs against injustice, exploitation, and inequality. Instead, the lyrics to "Like a Rolling Stone" wryly chastised the well-to-do for callously assuming they had nothing in common with the destitute and aimless.

As Dylan's "Like a Rolling Stone" climbed to No. 2 on *Billboard*'s pop chart in 1965, the hit's searing commentary on status and privilege was a wake-up call for many rock and folk songwriters and artists. Overnight, the song's judgmental message and snarling, dry delivery pushed rock and soul composers to channel their conscience and inner social critic. Songs that looked at hypocritical parents (the Rolling Stones' "Mother's Little Helper"), societal apathy (Simon & Garfunkel's "The Sound of Silence"), the vapid (the Beatles' "Nowhere Man"), and existential uncertainty (the Yardbirds' "Shapes of Things") soon followed.

Motown had avoided such songs, since they tended to be too heavy for its audience, and the label and its artists had too much to lose. Besides, why mess with a formula that worked? As a result, the label largely ignored shifting social and cultural trends until 1968, when the Supremes recorded "Love Child." But Motown's stance didn't stop songwriters Brian Holland, Lamont Dozier, and Eddie Holland from adapting Dylan's talk-sing, throw-down vocal delivery when they wrote "Reach Out I'll Be There" for the Four Tops. The song, which explored emotional despair and commiseration, was released in August 1966 and reached No. 1 for two weeks in late October. The single was inducted into the Grammy Hall of Fame in 1998.

**Interviews with LAMONT DOZIER (songwriter), ABDUL "DUKE" FAKIR (Four Tops singer), and PAUL RISER (arranger)**

**LAMONT DOZIER:** In the early summer of 1966, I walked into our small work space at Motown and heard Brian [Holland] at the piano. He liked composing in a ballad tempo—to feel and shape the melody. When I asked what he was playing, he said he wasn't sure and didn't know where it should go next. I suggested he pick up the tempo, and we played around with the song's introduction for about a half hour.

By then I had an idea, so I nudged Brian off the bench. This is how we worked—he'd often do the same to me on songs I started. In this case, I wanted to create a mind trip—a journey of emotions with sustained tension, like a bolero. To get this across, I alternated the keys—from a minor, Russian feel in the verse to a major, gospel feel in the chorus.

From the start, we knew "Reach Out" would be for Levi Stubbs and the Four Tops. But we had to work fast—they were due back in Detroit soon from a tour. During their time away, we had to create a catalog of new material for them that they could record for an album.

As soon as we had the song's melody down, I wrote lyrics for the chorus. [Singing:] "I'll be there, to always . . . see you . . .

through." I also wrote the story in the verses. In places where I didn't have the lyrics just right, I added a few words as placeholders. Then Eddie took my draft and turned it into a more polished story as I focused on production with Brian.

I wanted the song to explore the kinds of things women were going through and for Levi to come off as understanding and supportive. I also wanted the lyrics to be phrased in a special way—as though they were being thrown down vocally.

Back in '66, we were listening to a lot to Bob Dylan. He was *the* poet then, and we were inspired by his talk-singing style on "Like a Rolling Stone." Dylan was something else—a guy we looked up to. We loved the complexity of his lyrics and how he spoke the lines in some places and sang them in others. We wanted Levi to shout-sing the lyrics to "Reach Out"—as a shout-out to Dylan.

We went into the studio a few days later to record the basic rhythm track. Then Eddie recorded a demo for Levi—so he'd know how the melody went and where the action was. We also left little spots open where Levi could add his flavor.

**ABDUL "DUKE" FAKIR:** We [the Four Tops] first heard the song in the studio—just before we recorded it. We were making an album at the time, so there was a lot of material to cover and the key was a little higher than usual for us. I was the group's high tenor, so I had to hit the top notes without going into falsetto.

Levi was Jackie Wilson's cousin, and very talented with his voice. He was a baritone with a tenor range and wasn't afraid to attempt any note. For "Reach Out," Lamont purposefully put Levi at the top of his range, to make sure he'd have that cry and hunger and wailing in his voice.

The hardest part for Levi was the shout-singing. He had his notepad with him and wrote down things to help him get the right feel. But he laughed when he worked through it. The song was so different—he thought the Dylan approach Lamont wanted was a studio experiment, not the real thing.

**DOZIER:** After the Tops finished the vocal tracks, Paul Riser came in and we worked on overdubbing "the sweetness"— strings, chorus, and other instruments that enhanced the song's personality.

**PAUL RISER:** Lamont and I decided to add a piccolo and flute in the intro. The piccolo's piercing sound was essential. It's like a siren and gets your attention right away. It's also the sound of a heart crying. A flute alone would have been too warm and comforting. The hoofbeat drum pattern that follows was made using timpani mallets on the plastic head of a tambourine without its little metal cymbals. That sounded like a heartbeat speeding up and raised anticipation. All of these things were used to set the mood.

Then the Andantes [Motown's background vocalists] were added so there were female voices echoing Levi's lines. I also added strings to the song's chorus using classical chord inversions— different intervals between the bass notes—to widen the sound.

**DOZIER:** When we had everything on tape, we overdubbed a few last-minute touches—like hand-clapping and a tambourine, which emphasized a gospel feel. All of us sang the recording's shouted "Yah!" just before Levi came in. We did that to add a feeling of fire and to give the song a little shove forward.

**FAKIR:** Two or three weeks later, Berry Gordy called in the Tops. He said he was going to release our biggest hit. We said, "Great, when are we going to record it?" He said, "You already did." We said, "Which one?" He said, "Let me play you a little bit." When we heard the opening to "Reach Out," we begged him not to release it, to let us go down to the studio to record something else. For us, the song felt a little odd. Berry took it off and said, "I'm going to release it—and you're going to be surprised."

I first heard the song in September, in my car. By then it had all the sweetness in there and was already heading up the charts.

I drove to the office and asked to see Berry. His secretary said he was in a meeting. I walked in anyway. He looked up, surprised. I said, "Berry, please don't ever ask us again what we think of our records."

John Sebastian performing at Woodstock on the afternoon of August 16, 1969.

*Pictorial Parade/Getty Images*

# 11: Darling Be Home Soon

**JOHN SEBASTIAN**

*Released: February 1967*

Rock in the 1960s can be broadly divided into two styles that overlapped—pop rock, which was melodic and catchy and began early in the decade, and hard rock, which had a raw, aggressive attack and began roughly in 1967, with psychedelic influences. Pop rock in the 1960s was shaped largely by AM radio's need for singles that lasted only about three minutes. Stations felt the short duration wouldn't tax listeners' attention spans and would let them maximize the number of ads per hour between the records. Three minutes didn't give artists much time to captivate listeners, so proven musical formulas were used to improve the odds. Hit singles had a catchy opener, lyrics that told a compelling story, a chorus that listeners could sing, and instrumental riffs and hooks that aroused excitement.

But even with all these elements in place, pop-rock singles still needed a big sound. To ensure that a record had punch, top studio musicians were often brought in by producers to sight-read arrangements and add hooks and riffs. Using pros to provide the instrumental tracks instead of the less skilled members of the featured band was especially common in Los Angeles and New York. Professional studio musicians sped up the recording process, lowered the costs associated with retakes and overtime, and gave records a stronger, polished sound. Engineers and producers also were critical to the pop-rock hit process. Most singles were in mono and typically heard through small speakers in phonographs, jukeboxes, and radios. Sound-enhancing tricks were common and included reverb, overdubbing, and sped-up mastering to give the end result greater impact and urgency.

One pop-rock band that bucked the trend by playing on their recordings was the Lovin' Spoonful, led by singer-songwriter and multi-instrumentalist John Sebastian. The quartet had fourteen hits on the *Billboard* pop chart between 1965 and '69, including "Do You Believe in Magic," "Daydream," and "Summer in the City." Many of these hits were sweet, innocent love songs enriched by Sebastian's warm, woody vocals, but they were deceptively sophisticated in their construction. One of the group's most unusual hits was Sebastian's "Darling Be Home Soon," a ballad in which his protagonist sings about being parted from his lover and wishing she would return home soon. After the single was released in early 1967, it peaked at No. 15 on *Billboard*'s pop chart and was covered by artists as varied as Joe Cocker and Bobby Darin. One of Woodstock's most memorable moments was an unplanned solo performance of the song by Sebastian, who appeared on stage in between rain storms in white tie-dyed jeans and denim jacket.

### Interview with JOHN SEBASTIAN (Lovin' Spoonful singer-songwriter and guitarist)

**JOHN SEBASTIAN:** In early 1964, Zal Yanovsky and I formed a band in New York's Greenwich Village. We were still trying to come up with a name for the band when I ran into Fritz Richmond, a friend and musician. Fritz asked what we sounded like. I said a cross between Chuck Berry and Mississippi John Hurt. Fritz suggested we call ourselves the Lovin' Spoonful, a line from Hurt's song "Coffee Blues": "I got to have my lovin' spoonful." The name was perfect.

The following year, the Spoonful signed with Kama Sutra Records, and we had our first hit in August '65 with my song "Do You Believe in Magic." Around this time, our manager, Bob Cavallo, was approached by producers Jack Rollins and Charles Joffe, who wanted the Spoonful to record original music for Woody Allen's first feature film, *What's Up, Tiger Lily?*, due out in '66.

The band took the job, but we never had any contact with Woody, who I later learned wasn't that happy the studio had hired us, since he was a jazz fan. I wrote most of the songs and coarranged the music, which was recorded over a few days at a New York soundstage. When we finished, the Spoonful left on a tour of England, Ireland, and Sweden, returning to the States in the spring of '66. By then, we had three more hits—"You Didn't Have to Be So Nice," "Daydream," and "Did You Ever Have to Make Up Your Mind?"

That summer, after "Summer in the City" had become a No. 1 hit, Bob Cavallo told me that Francis Ford Coppola wanted us to record original music for his film *You're a Big Boy Now*. Francis was twenty-seven then and just starting out as a mainstream film director.

I first met Francis at his editing room in Midtown Manhattan in September '66. I liked him immediately. He didn't use fancy language and had a direct New York way of talking. I didn't ask many questions at that meeting. To me, Francis meant work, and work was money. I was a musician and I was supposed to be doing this. "Besides," I thought, "how often do you meet a guy who's making a film who is this with-it?"

Francis had an intensity behind his eyes and yet he was very easygoing. I think part of our simpatico was being Italian. Though my name is Sebastian, my father was a classical chromatic harmonica player born John Sebastian Pugliese. His parents had emigrated from Italy.

A few days later at his screening room, Francis ran the entire film for me, which was a dark comedy about a young awkward guy coming of age in New York. To be honest, I didn't care about the film, one way or the other. I felt I was on this adventure with a good guy at the helm and figured, "Hey, let's do this and see what comes of it."

At one point, Francis stopped the film during an extended no-dialogue love scene. It featured Bernard [Peter Kastner], the film's naïve and inexperienced male lead, being seduced by Barbara Darling [Elizabeth Hartman], a young woman who knew a lot more than he did. Francis had dropped music into the scene to illustrate the mood and tempo he wanted. The song was the Mamas and the Papas' "Monday, Monday," which had been released earlier that year.

After I left the screening room, I began composing. I knew that one of the most important songs was going to be the seduction scene with the "Monday, Monday" tempo. Like most songwriters who have the need to write songs frequently, I had bits and pieces of ideas in my head that I could flesh out when needed.

One of these ideas wasn't really a lyric or a melody but a concept that came in reaction to a lot of traditional pop songs I had heard on the radio then. Many of them were by West Coast artists singing things like, "Honey I love you so much and now my music is pulling me away and I'm on the road and it's so sad."

When I'd hear those songs, I'd think, "Gee, that's not how I'd feel about it. As a musician, I know I'm doing good when I'm out on the road making music and sending money home." Then I thought, "What would it be like if the roles were reversed, if the guy was the one waiting for his girlfriend to return from the road? I liked to flip convention when writing, since doing so often produced a more provocative outcome.

It took me a few days to write the song. From the singer's perspective, the verses are pleas for a partner to spend a few minutes talking before leaving. They resolve in a chorus yearning for the partner's return: "But darling be home soon/I couldn't bear to wait an extra minute if you dawdled." What made the song interesting is that you never knew if the other person was actually there listening or was already gone.

At the time, I was near the end of a romance but didn't want to admit it. I was too busy with my music, and the two of us didn't really fit. I saw myself as Bernard, who thinks it can work. I was trying to be Mr. Positive, and the song became a little adaptation of my life, a "Honey, it will all work out in the end" song. In effect, the song is about wishful thinking.

When I finished the music and lyrics, I sat Francis down and played him the song. He thought it was good. Next, I played it for the movie people, who felt it was too spare and wanted to add orchestration. We already knew Artie Schroeck, who had arranged for Laura Nyro and was highly respected, so we suggested him.

I first met Artie at our "Summer in the City" recording session in the spring of '66. After the twenty-fifth take of the song, when I was playing the keyboard, he stood up in the back of the studio and said, "Jesus Christ, John, it's so great when you play the guitar on this. Let me play the piano part." So he did, and in one take we had it.

The score for the film came down as a fait accompli—with the Lovin' Spoonful recording backed by Artie's arrangement for a studio orchestra. The arrangement had some unusual measures, so it was awkward for the band's drummer, Joe Butler, to play. Artie suggested studio drummer Billy LaVorgna. I played acoustic guitar and sang lead vocal, Zally [Zal Yanovsky] was on electric guitar, and Steve Boone was on bass.

The orchestra featured a roomful of serious musicians, including saxophonist [David] "Fathead" Newman and flügelhornist Clark Terry. It was a strange, exciting feeling. I never thought anything I composed would be of interest to people who wrote arrangements.

The Spoonful recorded "Darling Be Home Soon" in a day. When we finished, we all left, saying we'd see each other tomorrow. The second engineers stayed behind to clean up the tracks. The next day, when we returned, our producer, Erik Jacobsen, was pale. The guy cleaning up my vocal track had mistakenly erased it. I couldn't believe it. The track I had recorded was so heartfelt. It was the one.

Since all the tracks were recorded separately, they just needed me to rerecord my vocal. I did that right away, with the wound still fresh. What you hear on the record is me, a half hour after learning that my original vocal track had been erased. You can even hear my voice quiver a little at the end. That was me thinking about the vocal we lost and wanting to kill someone.

When the movie came out in early December '66, I went to see it. When I heard our music, I was happy with it. I felt like I had raised my game to be in Francis's league. But the film, with its hip, young soundtrack by the Spoonful, didn't get much traction. In some ways, *You're a Big Boy Now* became a lost Lovin' Spoonful album.

Erik, our producer, wasn't happy with it. We were hot in '67, and he thought we needed more time to add definition to the songs. Zally really hated "Darling Be Home Soon." He said, "What the fuck. You've lost your rock. It's too sincere." We were consistently upbeat, but we also felt we were always coming at songs from the insider's perspective. We wanted to be the band you wouldn't recognize from single to single. In "Darling Be Home Soon," we were being obvious and feelings were being expressed directly and intimately, which was different from our other hits. By early 1969, I wanted to go my own way, and the Spoonful broke up.

That summer, producer Paul Rothchild called. Before we got off the phone, he asked if I was going up to Woodstock in August, that there was going to be a big music festival there. I said, "Sure, why not." On Friday, August 15, I made it to the Albany, New York, airport and was looking for a flight to get me closer when I looked out the window and saw Walter Gundy, my old road manager, loading a helicopter with the Incredible String Band's equipment.

I gestured to him from the terminal and he waved for me to come out. So I opened the door and walked onto the tarmac. I had my ride. Twenty minutes later I was at the concert. Backstage, I knew everyone there. It was a small music business then. The Spoonful had dissolved, so I wasn't on the list of performers. I was just there to listen to the music. I had full access and would go up and down the plywood ramp to the stage. Along the way, someone there kept offering me tablets but I'd pass. I was a pot guy.

On Saturday, at around noon, it was pouring as I went up the ramp. The same guy was there offering me something, so I stopped and chipped off a bit with my thumbnail and took it. I wasn't performing and had three or four hours to relax and listen to bands. Backstage, I stood under one of the covered parts with concert producer Michael Lang and Chip Monck, the stage lighting director, and announcer.

Around 3:30 p.m., the rain stopped completely and Michael said he needed someone to go on with an acoustic guitar because they couldn't set up amps on stage for Santana until the water was swept off. Michael turned to me and asked if I'd do it. I ran backstage, and folk singer Tim Hardin loaned me his Harmony Sovereign guitar.

Chip announced me on the P.A. system, and I went out in what I was wearing—my tie-dyed white denim jacket and tie-dyed white jeans with the cuffs rolled up. I sang five songs, starting with "How Have You Been." I was gliding a little from whatever I had taken and that probably made me forget a lyric or two on the early songs. Seeing 400,000 people in the audience was transporting. Once I got going, I felt like I was working in front of an intimate club audience. It was strange. I wasn't one of those musicians in a wolverine coat being ferried in at the last minute by helicopter. I was one of the people who had come just to hear the music.

The fourth song I sang was "Darling Be Home Soon," which was easy to do as a solo. The audience didn't identify the song with the movie, since most probably hadn't seen it. Instead, they sort of quieted down and took it in as a love song. My job wasn't to incite but to mellow everyone out until the stage was swept. When I finished, the applause from so many people was loud and wide, and knocked the wind out of me. The feeling was delicious.

Today, when I perform, I almost always play "Darling Be Home Soon." It has a slightly different meaning now. I've been married for decades and always look forward to getting home soon. My Woodstock white tie-dyed jean jacket is at the Rock and Roll Hall of Fame. As for the tie-dyed white pants, they were stolen three weeks after Woodstock out of a laundromat on New York's Carmine Street.

The Doors in Los Angeles in 1969, from left—Jim Morrison, John Densmore, Ray Manzarek, and Robby Krieger.
*Estate of Edmund Teske/Getty Images*

# 12: Light My Fire

## THE DOORS
*Released: May 1967*

By early 1966, skilled rock bands that routinely performed at clubs and theaters in New York, Los Angeles, and San Francisco were growing frustrated with their record labels. Hamstrung by the short duration of 45s and under constant pressure to deliver hit singles, many of these artists wanted to record longer concert versions of their songs on albums. But record executives and producers dragged their feet. Studio time was expensive, and albums loaded down with extended solos and jams ran the risk of being long-winded and dull. The result could be poor album sales at stores and damage to the band's reputation. The other problem was that too few young record buyers owned personal stereo systems. Most played singles on portable phonographs, while albums were taken into living rooms and played on parents' large wooden phonograph consoles. If fingers weren't pinched trying to pry open the phonograph's heavy lid, teens could expect to hear parents' shrill demands to turn down the music.

Among the bands that viewed the single as stifling and the album as rock's expansive canvas of the future were the Doors. In 1966, the band signed with Elektra, an independent record label in Los Angeles. The Doors had been performing frequently at clubs on Los Angeles's Sunset Strip, where they had figured out how to extend songs to satisfy LSD-fueled crowds on dance floors. Those dancers wanted songs to last much longer than the short versions, and the result was psychedelic rock—music that mimicked and intensified the mind-bending effects of acid trips.

In August 1966, the Doors recorded a 7:06 rendition of "Light My Fire" for its eponymous debut album. After the album came out in January 1967, it reached No. 2 on the Billboard chart, and it was followed by the release of a 2:52 single version of "Light My Fire" in May. The single climbed to No. 1 and stirred interest in the longer album version, which became one of the first extended "album mixes" of a rock song. Perhaps most fascinating of all were the roles that John Coltrane's "My Favorite Things," Fats Domino's "Blueberry Hill," and even Stan Getz and João Gilberto's "The Girl From Ipanema" played in influencing the song's development. "Light My Fire" was inducted into the Grammy Hall of Fame in 1998.

**Interviews with RAY MANZAREK (Doors keyboardist), ROBBY KRIEGER (guitarist), and JOHN DENSMORE (drummer)**

**RAY MANZAREK:** In March 1966, the Doors were running out of songs. Up until then, I had been putting chord changes to whatever lyrics Jim [Morrison] would ad lib. At a band rehearsal, Jim said, "Everyone go home this weekend and write at least one song." But when we regrouped the following Tuesday, only Robby had written one. He called it "Light My Fire."

**ROBBY KRIEGER:** I was living at my parents' home in Pacific Palisades, California, at the time. In my bedroom, I came up with a melody inspired by the Leaves' "Hey Joe." I also liked the Rolling Stones' "Play With Fire." So I wrote lyrics that used the word "fire."

**MANZAREK:** We had been rehearsing in the downstairs sunroom of a beach house at the very end of North Star Street near Venice, California. The people who lived upstairs were at work during the day, so we could bang away without disturbing anyone. When

Robby played his song for us, it had a folk-rock sound, which was popular then. But John [Densmore] cringed. He said, "No, no, not folk rock." He wanted it to sound edgier, so he added a Latin thing.

**JOHN DENSMORE:** I've always been a jazz guy. I loved "The Girl From Ipanema" in 1964 and all the bossa nova albums that followed. So I went with a bossa beat during Jim's vocal verses, but kept it stiffer. I played the stick flat on the snare, tapping out a bossa beat on the rim. Then, on the chorus, where Jim sings, "Come on, baby, light my fire," I'd hit the stick in the middle of the drumhead, and kept it going through the extended instrumental.

**KRIEGER:** As Jim sang, he changed the melody line a little to give it a bluesy feel. Then he came up with a second verse right off the top of his head: "The time to hesitate is through/No time to wallow in the mire . . ."

**MANZAREK:** Once the lyrics and melody were set, we realized we could jam as long as we wanted on the song's middle two chords—A-minor and B minor—the way John Coltrane did on "My Favorite Things" and the album *Olé*. All of us dug Coltrane's long solos.

**DENSMORE:** It was the time of free-form psychedelic dancing. People were on the dance floor swaying, so we used the 1933 chords to extend songs when we performed to keep the scene going.

**MANZAREK:** But we needed some way to start the song. At the rehearsal, I started playing a cycle of fifths on my Vox Continental organ. Out came a motif from the Bach *Two- and Three-Part Inventions* piano book that I had used as a kid. It was like a psychedelic-rock minuet.

**DENSMORE:** The rest of us had taken a break and went outside to have chips and a beer while Ray worked out the intro. When we returned, Ray asked us what we thought. I liked it but said it seemed to come out of nowhere. My impulse was to start the song by hitting the snare as an introduction to Ray's Vox. It would be an attention-getter, letting people know that something big is starting here. Hello!

**MANZAREK:** We didn't use a bass player—I played the bass notes on a Fender Rhodes keyboard while my right hand played the Vox, which could be cranked up to a screaming-loud volume. My bass line for "Light My Fire" grew out of Fats Domino's "Blueberry Hill," which I loved growing up in Chicago.

**KRIEGER:** We started playing "Light My Fire" at the London Fog on the Sunset Strip in April and May 1966 and at the Whisky a Go-Go between May and July. On stage, the song became this rock-jazz jam. Audiences loved it.

**MANZAREK:** In August '66, when we went into Sunset Sound to record our first album, producer Paul Rothchild wanted us to record "Light My Fire" just as we had been playing it live. We recorded two takes—each one lasting over seven minutes. Nobody was recording extended solos on rock albums then.

**KRIEGER:** When we finished, Paul felt the song needed a little more drama at the end. Because Paul loved what Ray had done with the Vox at the beginning, he said, "Hell, let's put it at the end, too." So he spliced in a copy of Ray's minuet after Jim's vocal, as an outro.

**MANZAREK:** Paul brought in Larry Knechtel of the Wrecking Crew to overdub a stronger bass attack. Then the master was blasted into the studio's cement echo chamber and recorded, which gave the song reverb.

**KRIEGER:** A few months after *The Doors* album came out in January 1967, Elektra founder Jac Holzman called and said the label wanted a single of "Light My Fire" for AM radio. Dave Diamond, an FM disc jockey in the San Fernando Valley, had been playing the album version and was getting a ton of calls.

**MANZAREK:** But a single meant our 7:06-minute album version had to be cut down to just under three minutes so deejays would play it. Everyone groaned, but Paul said he'd take a crack at it. When we heard the result the next day, the organ and guitar solos were gone. Robby and I looked at each other and said to Paul, "Hey, you cut out the improvisation!" Paul said: "I know. But imagine you're seventeen years old in Minneapolis. You've never heard of the Doors and this is the version you hear on the radio. Would you have a problem with it?" Jim sat there and said, "Actually, I kind of dig it." We agreed.

**KRIEGER:** It was gut-wrenching to hear my guitar solo cut, but I actually liked the single better. I was never crazy about the album version. It had been mixed at a very low volume to capture everything. On the radio, it wasn't very loud or exciting. The single, though, snapped. The secret was that Paul had wrapped Scotch tape around the spindle holding the pickup reel, so the tape would turn a fraction faster. This made the pitch a little higher and brighter, and the song was more urgent.

**MANZAREK:** I first heard the AM single with my wife, Dorothy, in our VW Bug. Dorothy started bouncing up and down like a jumping jack. I was pounding on the wheel. What a feeling!

**KRIEGER:** At first, I didn't like José Feliciano's 1968 ballad version. It was so different and laid-back. But after a while, I came to love it. He made our song his own, which got others to record it. Thanks to José, the song is our biggest copyright by far.

The Young Rascals (c. 1965), from left—Eddie Brigati, Gene Cornish, Felix Cavaliere, and Dino Danelli.

*GAB Archive/Getty Images*

# 13: Groovin'
## THE YOUNG RASCALS
*Released: April 1967*

During San Francisco's cultural revolution of 1966 and '67, New York's music scene went through its own transformation. New York was still the country's corporate capital, and the music produced there—including pop rock and soul—often was under the tight grip of powerful record company executives. Yet emerging bands such as the Velvet Underground, with their close ties to New York's pop-art scene, were already thinking in terms of expressive albums, not formulaic singles. There also was a more raw, anti-social feel about the bands as songs took on a range of subculture subjects from androgyny to heroin use. But despite the rise of New York's cooler, more detached rock music scene, East Coast labels couldn't stop San Francisco's peace-and-love influences from infiltrating the music. In some cases, labels actively encouraged it, recognizing that the laid-back psychedelic movement had widespread commercial appeal.

San Francisco's communal values, earthy fashion sensibilities, and advocacy for dropping inhibitions weren't lost on New York's young musicians, artists, and art directors. In 1967, a paradigm shift began to take place. The album covers of San Francisco bands appeared with a new colorful, psychedelic aesthetic; underground comics by artists such as R. Crumb found their way to New York; "New Journalism" writers such as Tom Wolfe reported on the youth culture; and many young people who had visited San Francisco returned home with a looser outlook on music and life in general.

Formed in Garfield, New Jersey, in 1965, the Young Rascals recorded five top-five *Billboard* pop hits between 1966 and '68 with song titles that mirrored this new San Francisco aesthetic. Their hits included "Good Lovin'," "How Can I Be Sure," "A Beautiful Morning," "People Got to Be Free," and "Groovin'," which today remains one of the purest pop expressions of a stress-free lifestyle. When "Groovin'" was released in July 1967, the song's breezy lyrics, hypnotic Latin beat, and soulful vocal by Young Rascals leader Felix Cavaliere sent the song to No. 1 on *Billboard*'s pop chart for four weeks in May and June. The band even made a music video of the song in Central Park, with a San Francisco feel. "Groovin'" was inducted into the Grammy Hall of Fame in 1999.

**Interviews with FELIX CAVALIERE (Young Rascals lead singer and cowriter), CHRIS HUSTON (engineer), and GENE CORNISH (Young Rascals guitarist)**

**FELIX CAVALIERE:** Back in 1966, I was hopelessly in love with a girl I was dating named Adrienne. I had met her at a friend's house in Pelham Manor, New York, where I'm from, and she became my muse. Adrienne was my first serious girlfriend, and our relationship lasted about a year. Many of my best songs were written about her—or because of her—including "Lonely Too Long," "Girl Like You," and "How Can I Be Sure." Like most musicians, I always worked Friday and Saturday nights—which meant Adrienne and I only had Sundays together. "Groovin'" expressed the bliss I felt relaxing with her on Sunday afternoons, watching the world go by.

I wrote the music to "Groovin'" on an upright piano in the small apartment that [Young Rascal] Eddie Brigati and I shared on 79th Street near Park Avenue in Manhattan. Then we collaborated on the lyrics. Even though the song was about my relationship, Eddie did a beautiful job on the verses. We experimented with the song at the studios of our label—Atlantic Records. Our contract gave us unlimited studio time—but I wanted to record at Talent Masters on West 42nd Street, where many great R&B groups were making their singles.

**CHRIS HUSTON:** Visually, Talent Masters was a dump—it was an old fur-storage vault. But it sounded like a million dollars.

**CAVALIERE:** I decided we'd use a baión rhythm—to give the song a Latin groove. When I was in high school, I had led a house band at the Raleigh Hotel in the Catskill Mountains. Over those summers, I was exposed to Latin music and saw how many people loved dancing to it.

In the studio, we left out the drums and tried something different. For the basic track, I played piano, Dino Danelli played percussion, and Gene Cornish played tambourine. We overdubbed the background vocals later with Eddie and his brother David.

**GENE CORNISH:** Dino played the conga with a stick under his arm. At the bridge, he used the stick to strike a wood block taped to the drum. The ticking beats sounded like the clock you'd ignore on a beautiful Sunday afternoon.

**CAVALIERE:** Arif Mardin, who supervised the sessions, orchestrated a Carmen Cavallaro–style lounge-piano solo for me—to give the background a bit more texture. After we finished, I wanted a Latin bass line overdubbed on top of what we had recorded on the basic track.

**CORNISH:** I was going to record the bass part, but I couldn't quite get what Felix wanted. Chris suggested Chuck Rainey, who played bass in King Curtis's band. We booked him the next day for 8 a.m., but when we arrived he was already there and had recorded the track. He nailed it.

**CAVALIERE:** Adding the sound of birds was my idea. I had heard the Beatles' "Yellow Submarine" and flipped. These guys had created a sound environment for their single. Ringo sang about a sub—and there were sub sounds. Eddie and his brother David were experts at effects, and they whistled the bird sounds. When we were just about finished, Arif suggested adding a harmonica—to drive home the carefree, Sunday feel. But I can't remember who played it.

**CORNISH:** The harmonica on the single wasn't me. I played it several weeks later when we recorded the stereo album version.

**HUSTON:** When Arif wanted a harmonica, there was no time to make calls. That's when I remembered we had a guy at the studio who swept our floors, Michael Weinstein, who was in a band called the Gurus and could play. So we used him.

**CAVALIERE:** On the last day of recording, New York disc jockey Murray the K came in. He knew Sid Bernstein—our manager. After Murray the K heard a playback of the song, he went nuts. He said, "This is a smash, man." But Atlantic didn't think so. When the demo pressing landed on [executive] Jerry Wexler's desk, he called me into his office. He said, "What are you guys doing? You're a rock 'n' roll band. What's this conga stuff?" I said, "There's a whole world of Latin people out there who love to dance."

Jerry said, "Man, you're going to screw up everything. Put drums in there." Under our contract, the Young Rascals were the producers, so we had the final say—but Jerry had final say over whether a single would be released. We didn't want rock drums on there—just the conga—and I told Sid what had happened, that Jerry might not release it. A few days later Murray the K spoke with Jerry. He told him "Groovin'" was going to be a hit and that he was going to play it on the radio. Jerry backed off.

When "Groovin'" came out in April, a lot of people thought I was singing, "Life would be ecstasy, you and me and Leslie" as if I was with my girl and she brought along a girlfriend. The line, of course, is, "You and me, endlessly." The guys in the band used to make fun of how I slurred uneven words to squeeze them in to fit the beats. The problem was that there was a conga fill under "endlessly." Gear didn't exist then to separate the two—to make the three-syllable word clearer.

**CORNISH:** The song meant the same to me as it did to Felix and Eddie—our day off.

**CAVALIERE:** My girlfriend Adrienne knew "Groovin'" was written about her and us. When I played her the single, she smiled and said, "Wow, that's lovely." Adrienne was an angel who came into my life and left. We split up later that year, amicably, and eventually she married a dear friend of mine. Sadly, she died about ten years ago.

Grace Slick with a Nat Sherman cigarette in the San Francisco living room of the photographer in 1968.
*Courtesy of Herb Greene*

# 14: White Rabbit

**JEFFERSON AIRPLANE**

*Released: June 1967*

San Francisco in 1965 was fast becoming a counterculture refuge. Since the late 1940s, the city had been home to a thriving community of Bohemian poets, painters, musicians, and writers. But by the mid-1960s, thousands of young middle-class outcasts from around the country were migrating from suburbia to San Francisco to escape judgmental parents, boring jobs, traditional values, social conformity, and most adult responsibilities. Their goal was to embrace a more natural, whole-earth lifestyle and to eschew materialism, long-term planning, and hypocrisy. The city's Haight-Ashbury district quickly became an urban commune, offering low-cost living, free medical clinics, and comfortable winter temperatures that hovered in the fifties.

Music and the widespread availability of psychotropic drugs such as LSD were also part of San Francisco's appeal. Many long-form rock and blues-rock musicians were moving to the city in search of opportunities to perform at the expanding number of clubs, theaters, and coffeehouses. Acid Test parties held by author Ken Kesey found scores of participants, while Owsley Stanley, a soundman for the Grateful Dead, figured out how to produce mass quantities of LSD. Out of this turgid, experimental environment came powerful movements and catchphrases— including "flower power," hippies, gurus, "free love," progressive FM radio, psychedelic art, environmentalism, natural foods, serious rock journalism —and music that not only embraced the city's "drop-out, turn-on" culture but came to represent a generational mind-set and image.

Tired of working as a fashion model in San Francisco in 1965, Grace Slick quit her job to become a singer in the Great Society, a band she cofounded with her filmmaker husband, Jerry Slick, his brother Darby, David Miner, and Bard Dupont. Before long, Slick bought a piano and wrote "White Rabbit," a song inspired by Alice from *Alice's Adventures in Wonderland,* who, Slick says, had the courage to follow a rabbit down a hole alone and experiment with mind-altering drugs. After Slick quit the Great Society to join Jefferson Airplane in 1966, the band recorded "White Rabbit" on its second album, *Surrealistic Pillow,* which was released in February 1967. A single of the song followed in June, peaking at No. 8 on the *Billboard* pop chart. The song was inducted into the Grammy Hall of Fame in 1998.

## Interview with GRACE SLICK (Jefferson Airplane lead singer and songwriter)

**GRACE SLICK:** In the summer of 1965, I was living with my husband, Jerry Slick, in Larkspur, California, about a half hour north of San Francisco. I was twenty-five and working as a couture model at I. Magnin in San Francisco while Jerry was making short films. We didn't have much money. At I. Magnin, I had to change into expensive clothes every ten minutes and walk around as rich old ladies felt the fabric and asked what the dress cost. If a woman bought the dress, the store would make one up for her nine sizes larger than I was.

San Francisco was saturated with music then. Haight-Ashbury was a draw for kids, and bands were there from all over the country. In September '65, Jerry and I went off to the Matrix to hear a new band—Jefferson Airplane. Signe Anderson was the Airplane's lead singer, and as I watched from the seats, I decided that singing might be way more fun than modeling clothes for old bags.

So we started a band. Jerry had a set of drums and his brother Darby knew how to play guitar. Our friend David Miner could sing and play guitar, Bard Dupont played bass, and Peter van Gelder played sax and flute. We named the band the Great Society—sort of a snarky take on Lyndon Johnson's social program.

Our first gig was at North Beach's Coffee Gallery in October '65. I quit my modeling job and started writing music for the band. I didn't really play piano—I *used* a piano. I'd write lyrics and bang around until I came up with chord progressions. I was just a fuck-off who got lucky.

That fall, I found a small upright piano for $80 at a warehouse in San Francisco that sold old furniture. It was painted about ninety coats of bright, fire-engine red and was missing around ten keys in the upper register. I didn't play way up there anyway—the notes were too pingy—so I bought it. Jerry and I put the piano in our living room.

The more the band gigged, the more media coverage we got. In an interview with the *San Francisco Chronicle*, I argued in favor of marijuana and LSD, and somehow the article got back to my parents. It was painful for them, I'm sure, but I didn't care whether they minded or not. Parents were criticizing our generation's choices while sitting there with their glasses of scotch.

They also seemed unaware that many of the books they read to us as kids had drug use as a subtext. Peter Pan uses fairy dust and can fly, Dorothy and her friends in *The Wizard of Oz* cut through a poppy field and wind up stoned and fast asleep. I loved *Alice's Adventures in Wonderland* and *Through the Looking Glass*. The stuff Alice drank and ate made her high [tall] or brought her down [small]. There were all kinds of drug metaphors in there. The '60s were very much like that.

One afternoon in December or January, while Jerry was out, I started writing a song about Alice and all the drug metaphors going on in the story. I wrote the lyrics first. As I wrote, I'd read them out loud to be sure my voice could form a cadence. [Slick sings slowly to illustrate: "One pill makes you larger/And one pill makes you small/And the ones that mother gives you/Don't do anything at all."] I wasn't reworking the lyrics as much as I was making sure there was a beat in the words I had written. It was more like finessing than crossing things out and rearranging lines.

When the lyrics were done, I took the sheet of paper to the red piano and worked on the chords, writing the names of the ones I liked over the phrases. I wrote the song in F-sharp minor, a key that's ideal for my voice. Minor chords have a certain darkness and sadness. I've never written a love song with major chords—they're too cornball. The music was based on a slow Spanish march or bolero that builds in intensity. I've always had a thing for Spanish folk music. Back in 1963, Jerry and I were living with Darby and his girlfriend in San Francisco on Potrero Hill. One day we took acid and I put on Miles Davis's *Sketches of Spain*.

I loved that album and I listened to it over and over for hours, particularly "Concierto de Aranjuez," which takes up most of the first side. It's hypnotic. I've always been like this. Anything I love I'm going to cram into my ears, nose, and mouth until I use it up. *Sketches of Spain* was drilled into my head and came squirting out in various ways as I wrote "White Rabbit." It's like vitamins in food. They're in there but you don't realize it.

With the chorus—those are the Alice lines, like "Go ask Alice, when she's ten feet tall"—I shifted to major chords for a release and to celebrate Alice's courage for following the white rabbit down the hole. Once down there, she didn't have a prince charming. She had to save her own ass while going through all the insane hallucinogenic stuff.

I identified with Alice. I was a product of '50s America in Palo Alto, California, where women were housewives with short hair and everything was highly regulated. I went from the planned, bland '50s to the world of being in a rock band without looking back. It was my Alice moment, heading down the hole. "White Rabbit" seemed like an appropriate title.

When I finished the song, I made copies by hand of the lyrics and chord names for the band. I sat at the piano at someone's house and sang and played the song for the guys. Then they followed on acoustic instruments, to keep the noise down. "White

Rabbit" wasn't really that unusual. Writing weird stuff about Alice backed by a dark Spanish march was in step with what was going on in San Francisco then. We were all trying to get as far away from the expected as possible.

We first performed "White Rabbit" in early '66, at a dive bar on Broadway in San Francisco. Each night we'd play four thirty-minute sets for a handful of drunk sailors at the bar, or our friends would drop by to listen. We didn't cover other bands' stuff. That was a fast way to wind up playing at the Holiday Inn forever. The challenge was to write what you felt. At the dive bar, if the drunken sailors weren't aware we were playing, our original songs were probably in pretty good shape. Within a few months, we went from dive bars to opening for the Grateful Dead, Quicksilver Messenger Service, Janis [Joplin], and other artists at local auditoriums and theaters.

We performed "White Rabbit" at places like the Fillmore, Longshoreman's Hall, and the Matrix. At one point, we made a series of demos at Golden State Recorders for Autumn Records. [Label co-owner] Tom Donahue had Sly Stone come in to help us. We were so bad that Sly eventually played all the instruments so the demo would sound OK. Later I was in a record store and saw all of this material on an album that someone must have released without our knowing it. If I knew anyone would give a shit about any of this, I would have kept a diary.

By the summer of '66, some of the guys in the Great Society were talking about leaving the band to study the sitar in India. I figured the band's days were numbered. That October, Jack Casady, the Airplane's bassist, came up to me at the Carousel Ballroom, where we had opened for the band. Jack said Signe was leaving to raise her baby daughter and asked if I wanted to replace her.

Initially I was shocked, but it took me about two seconds to say yes. Down the rabbit hole I went, again. Jack, Marty Balin, Paul Kantner, Jorma Kaukonen, and Spencer Dryden were way ahead of the Great Society in terms of musicianship. Jerry was in film school by then, so he didn't mind.

When I joined the Airplane in October '66, I brought over "Somebody to Love," which Darby had written, and my "White Rabbit." Audiences liked the songs when the Great Society had performed them, and they were a good fit for the Airplane. For the next few weeks, I rehearsed the Airplane's material with the band and taught them the two songs I had brought along.

On "White Rabbit," the Airplane was better than the Great Society at designing an instrumental idea. The band could pull back or elaborate at will, adding flavor to the song. But on "White Rabbit," there was never a specific guitar solo. In concert, there might be a jam in the beginning but my vocal always ran about two and a half minutes. People in the audience thought I moved around on stage like a panther. I'm actually a klutz. The reason I moved so carefully was to avoid tripping and breaking my neck.

In November '66, we recorded the album *Surrealistic Pillow* at RCA in Los Angeles. After we recorded "White Rabbit," we all went into the control room to hear the playback on the monitor speakers. I was blown away. I wasn't aware I sounded like that, with all that vocal power. I was impressed. My mother had been a singer, but my voice was much louder and more powerful, and it was perfect for rock and roll.

I always felt like a good-looking schoolteacher singing "White Rabbit." I'd sing the words slowly and precisely, so the people who needed to hear them wouldn't miss the point. But they did. To this day, I don't think most people realize the song was aimed at parents who drank and told their kids not to do drugs. I felt they were full of shit, but to write a good song, you need a few more words than that.

Today, I'm still in favor of marijuana. Alcohol is a much more dangerous drug. Many people turn into assholes when they use it. I know, because I had to deal with it. I no longer drink and I don't use marijuana, because it makes me paranoid.

I never saw myself as a woman breaking the rock barrier. Women always sang. If I had been a Supreme Court lawyer, that would be different. What was new wasn't that I was singing rock but that the form was new—it was all electric and emotional. As a woman and a performer, your persona has to be in line with who you are and your true personality. You have to communicate with an audience with your body and eyes and face.

After the single of "White Rabbit" came out, RCA told us each week where the record stood on the charts. I didn't pay much attention. I didn't set out to write a single and I felt that radio only liked "White Rabbit" because it was short and they could get more ads in. Looking back, I think "White Rabbit" is a very good song. I'm not a genius, but I don't suck. My only complaint is that the lyrics could have been stronger. If I had done it right, more people would have been annoyed.

The Stone Poneys in 1967, from left—Bobby Kimmel, Linda Ronstadt, and Kenny Edwards.

*Michael Ochs Archives/Getty Images*

# 15: Different Drum

**THE STONE PONEYS**

*Released: September 1967*

After years spent working in the civil rights and antiwar movements, women began to mobilize on their own behalf in the late 1960s. While women played significant roles organizing against racial injustice and the Vietnam War, inside these movements they were often relegated to making coffee, not decisions. Fed up with second-class status, male sexual advances and harassment, and powerlessness, women began organizing to seek changes in laws governing their lives—from dating and pregnancy to marriage issues, spousal abuse, and workplace treatment and pay.

Women's anger over their treatment began to turn up in songs. By 1967, female artists were no longer singing solely about love itching in their hearts, white boots that were meant for walking, or being shot down by their baby. Socially-conscious female singers including Sandy Posey ("Born a Woman" in 1966), Aretha Franklin ("Respect" in 1967), Grace Slick ("Somebody to Love" in 1967), and others recorded songs about power, or the lack of it. Female singer-songwriters including Laura Nyro ("Goodbye Joe" in 1966), Janis Ian ("Society's Child" in 1966), and Janis Joplin ("Women Is Losers" in 1967) added their voices to the cause, recording pop songs that challenged the sexual status quo.

But few songs of this variety had the impact or visibility of "Different Drum." Written by a man (Michael Nesmith) in the early 1960s and first recorded by an all-male folk-roots band (the Greenbriar Boys), "Different Drum" was about a breakup over the male protagonist's need for independence and a more passionate partner—not an uncommon theme from the male perspective. But in 1967, Linda Ronstadt's evocative vocal on the Stone Poneys' version and the upbeat instrumental arrangement behind her gave the song a different urgency. When "Different Drum" was released in September 1967, the single reached No. 13 on *Billboard*'s pop chart, and it soon became identified with the feminist movement, though that wasn't Nesmith's or Ronstadt's original intent.

**Interviews with MICHAEL NESMITH (songwriter), LINDA RONSTADT (Stone Poneys lead singer), BOBBY KIMMEL (Stone Poneys guitarist), and DON RANDI (studio keyboardist)**

**MICHAEL NESMITH:** In 1964 I had been playing guitar in folk and bluegrass bands and wanted to sing solo. So I began writing songs. I wrote "Different Drum" early one morning on the back porch of my San Fernando Valley apartment. The lyrics, about a breakup, came fast—but they had nothing to do with my personal life. I was newly married with a pregnant wife.

Whenever I wrote, I liked creating little "movies of the mind." In the case of "Different Drum," I was thinking about two lovers— one of whom decides he loves different things in life: "It's just that I am not in the market/For a girl who wants to love only me." In later years, comedian A. Whitney Brown referred to "Different Drum" as the first "It's not you, it's me" breakup song.

In 1965 I met John Herald of the Greenbriar Boys trio. We sat down with our guitars and began sharing songs. John loved "Different Drum," and slowed it down when he recorded it the following year for Vanguard Records.

**LINDA RONSTADT:** I moved from Tucson, Arizona, to Los Angeles in 1965 to sing with Bobby Kimmel, a friend from Tucson. He was already working with Kenny Edwards, so the three of us performed together. There were plenty of gigs at folk clubs in L.A. then. Kenny played a Gibson mandolin, Bobby played a Martin guitar, and I sang harmonies.

Naming our folk trio the Stone Poneys was Kenny's idea. He got the name from Charley Patton's song "Stone Pony Blues." In those days, the word "stone" also meant "heavy, man." Bobby was writing most of the songs then—but songs that worked for his voice and range. At some point in late '66, I wanted a song that suited my voice so I could sing lead.

That's when I heard the Greenbriar Boys' single "Different Drum." I knew it could be a hit for us. In 1967, our producer at Capitol, Nick Venet, set up a recording session. It was at Capitol's Studio B, where Frank Sinatra had recorded. The plan was to record three songs in three hours that day.

I thought we were going to record an acoustic ballad version of "Different Drum" with Bobby and Kenny. But when I walked into the studio, Nick had brought in other musicians I didn't know. Bobby and Kenny played on two of the songs, but on "Different Drum," Nick asked them to sit out.

**BOBBY KIMMEL:** Kenny and I didn't mind. It was always going to be a solo vocal feature for Linda anyway, and Nick wanted more going on instrumentally behind her. Kenny and I stood in the engineer's booth and watched and listened.

**RONSTADT:** At first, I wasn't happy. I thought we'd have a better shot on the radio with an acoustic version, since groups like Peter, Paul and Mary were having hits. But Nick insisted. He said he had asked Jimmy Bond to write an arrangement and brought in Don Randi to play harpsichord, Al Viola on guitar, and Jimmy Gordon on drums. Bond played bass, and Sid Sharp arranged and conducted a string section. They were all there.

We didn't rehearse. I was just thrown into it. I was completely confused. I didn't have the lyrics in front of me—I sang them from memory. Since I can't read music, I didn't have a lead sheet, either. I knew I could remember the words, but I wasn't sure how to phrase them with the new arrangement and faster tempo.

Different instruments pull different textures out of my voice, which had been conditioned to sing with guitar and mandolin. The harpsichord and strings were going to be harder. We did a run-down take and then recorded the second take without any over-dubbing. That became the version you hear on the record.

**DON RANDI:** Jimmy Bond had me play a double-keyboard harpsi-chord, to give the song a psychedelic-pop feel. I only had the chord changes and made up the rest on the spot, including the solo. I had been trained as a classical pianist, so giving it a classical feel wasn't a problem.

By '67, I was recording as part of L.A.'s Wrecking Crew studio band on hundreds of rock recordings, including sessions with the Beach Boys and Phil Spector. This session with Linda was a nice change-up. Nick knew his stuff and went to bat for her with the guys in the studio before Linda arrived. Nick told me, "Wait until you hear this girl sing. You won't believe it." He was right. She had this innocence and humility that won me over. If she had been frightened, you'd never have known it. Linda was so down-to-earth and natural—she even recorded that song barefoot.

**RONSTADT:** I first heard the single on the radio when the band's car broke down in September '67. We pushed it into a gas station, where I heard the guitar-harpsichord intro faintly coming from a radio in back of the garage. The mechanics had it tuned to KRLA— L.A.'s Top-40 AM station. I was stunned.

**NESMITH:** I first heard Linda's record on the radio in Philadelphia while riding in a limo with the Monkees when I was in the band. No one in the car believed I had written the song. Linda did more for that song than the Greenbriar Boys' version. She infused it with a different level of passion and sensuality. Coming from the perspective of a woman instead of a guy, the song had a new context. You sensed Linda had personally experienced the lyrics—that she needed to be free.

**KIMMEL:** The irony, of course, is that I didn't get to sing or play on my group's biggest hit. But you know what? It wouldn't have mattered even if I had. It was Linda's time.

**RONSTADT:** I'll be honest—I was never happy with how I sounded. It took me ten years to learn how to sing before I had skill and craft. Today I will break my finger trying to get that record off when it's on. Art wasn't meant to be frozen in time like that. Everyone hears something in that song—a breakup, the antiwar movement, women's lib. I hear fear and a lack of confidence on my part. It all happened so fast that day.

Otis Redding performing backed by the Bar-Kays horn section in 1967.

*Michael Ochs Archives/Getty Images*

# 16: (Sittin' on) The Dock of the Bay

**OTIS REDDING**

*Released: January 1968*

Soul grew increasingly emotional and forceful in the late 1960s. Much of the music's expressive feel had originated in the black church, particularly where singers and congregations interacted with call-and-response exchanges. But while church music was at the heart of soul, the music was shaped by artists' experiences and regional flavors. Ray Charles brought the feeling of jazz and R&B to soul, Little Willie John and Little Jimmy Scott added the falsetto, Little Richard contributed the electrifying energy of Pentecostal churches, Sam Cooke brought a big-city vocal charm, Aretha Franklin added gospel power, and James Brown contributed the grind and emotive grunts of his Baptist church in Elko, South Carolina. And then there was Otis Redding.

Born in rural Georgia, Redding developed an approach that was earthy and combustible, and combined a crying-singing style with sweaty stagecraft. His honest and highly sensitive approach as a singer and songwriter would influence many rock, soul, and blues artists, including John Lennon, Janis Joplin, the Rolling Stones, Sly Stone, and Joe Cocker. In June 1967, producer Bill Graham added Redding to the Monterey Pop Festival lineup and exposed a largely white rock audience to Redding's passionate and growly vocals.

After the concert, Graham let Redding stay on his houseboat in Sausalito, California, about two hours north of Monterey. There, Redding began to write what would become his biggest hit—"(Sittin' on) the Dock of the Bay." The introspective song about pausing to watch boats pull into port and the bluesy thoughts that came to mind while doing so reached No. 1 in March 1968 and remained there for four consecutive weeks. But Redding never heard the single. On December 10, 1967—just eighteen days after the recording session—the twenty-six-year-old singer died in a plane crash in Wisconsin, which killed everyone on board except Ben Cauley, the trumpeter in his band. In the studio, guitarist Steve Cropper completed the song, which was inducted into the Grammy Hall of Fame in 1998.

**Interviews with STEVE CROPPER (cowriter and guitarist), BOOKER T. JONES (pianist), WAYNE JACKSON (trumpeter), and BEN CAULEY (trumpeter)**

**STEVE CROPPER:** In the fall of 1967, I was a producer at Stax Records in Memphis and guitarist in Booker T. & the MGs, the label's house band backing up Stax recording artists. In November, I was at the studio when Otis Redding called me from the Memphis airport. Usually when Otis came to town, he waited until he checked into the Holiday Inn before calling me to work with him on songs in his room. This time he couldn't wait. He said, "Crop, I've got a hit. I'm coming right over."

When Otis walked in, he said, "Crop, get your gut-tar," which is how he pronounced it. I always kept a Gibson B-29 around. He grabbed it, tuned it to an open E-chord, which made the guitar easier to play slide. Then Otis played and sang a verse he had written: "Sittin' in the mornin' sun/I'll be sittin' when the evenin' come/ Watching the ships roll in/And then I watch 'em roll away again."

I said, "Otis, hold on. If a ship rolls, it will take on water and sink." He said, "That's what I want, Crop." So we let it go and worked on the rest of the song. Otis told me he had started writing the song while playing in San Francisco. Producer Bill Graham must have let him stay on his houseboat in Sausalito. Neil Young later told me he had stayed on the boat right after Otis left to come back east.

When Otis and I finished writing the rest of the song's music and lyrics, I arranged the song and we scheduled studio time. On the date, I was on acoustic guitar, [Donald] Duck Dunn was on bass, Al Jackson was on drums, Booker was on piano, and Wayne Jackson was on trumpet and there were two other horns.

**BOOKER T. JONES:** I played piano instead of organ on most of Otis's songs. The piano supported his voice without getting in his way. "Dock of the Bay" was beautifully simplistic—all major chords. For some reason, the piano had been moved across the studio, so that the horns were on my right instead of across from me and Otis was to my left. Usually I saw him behind a partition but on this date I was next to him, which made it easier for him to hear me.

**WAYNE JACKSON:** We rehearsed the horns with Booker. We always played a chord, with each of us taking a different note. What we put across behind Otis was simple and funky, like a call-and-response in church.

**CROPPER:** Otis always liked to ad-lib at the end of songs, so I added in about ten measures of instrumental background for him to do so. But when the time came, Otis couldn't think of anything and started whistling, which, of course, made the song.

**JONES:** Otis's lyrics touched me—about leaving home and watching the bay, trying to figure things out as everyone's pulling at you. My notes on the piano fed into that. I wanted to capture a maritime feel—the sound of a boat on the Mississippi River, and the sounds of gospel and New Orleans. I put those flourishes around Otis's voice.

**CROPPER:** On Friday, December 8, Otis stuck his head in the studio before leaving to play a series of regional concerts and said, "See ya on Monday." After he left, I overdubbed the electric guitar fills on a Telecaster with two pickups and a little Fender Harvard amp. I was trying to imitate the sound of gulls. Otis had been fooling around in the studio before the session by cawing like the seabirds up in Sausalito.

The next day, me, Booker, Duck [Dunn], Al [Jackson], and our singer, Dave Porter, flew up to Indiana State to play a concert. On Sunday, we flew on a puddle jumper to Indianapolis to catch our connecting flight to Memphis. The whole north was icy, and we arrived in Indianapolis late, missing our connection. David went to call his wife, to tell her we were going to be late. When he came back, he looked like he had seen a ghost. His wife had told him Otis had died in a plane crash. We couldn't believe it.

**BEN CAULEY:** I was sitting behind Otis on the plane—back to back, next to the door. I fell asleep and the next thing I knew the pilot was telling us he was having trouble. The plane hit the water and I managed to get out and hold on to a seat cushion. I didn't know how to swim and one of my shoes had come off. It was so cold. About twenty minutes later a boat came and pulled me out. I was in shock. Everyone else was gone.

**CROPPER:** Back at Stax on Monday, Atlantic Records producer Jerry Wexler called. Atlantic handled Stax's distribution. Jerry said we had to get an Otis single out right away. I said, "Jerry, we just lost Otis. We don't have anything mixed yet, and I can't even think about it." Jerry insisted. So early on Tuesday morning I began mixing "Dock of the Bay" alone. I wanted to enhance the bay image, sort of like a secret message to Otis. I called a local friend for sound effects of the sea and the gulls and added them lightly in places.

When I finished the mix the next morning, I took the master tape to the Memphis airport and handed the box to an attendant flying up to New York. She was met in New York by an Atlantic rep,

and the label made a test pressing for Jerry. But Jerry had a problem with it. He wanted Otis's vocal to be louder and wanted me to
remix the tape. I felt it was perfect and didn't want to touch it.

Then I had an idea. The tape Jerry had was a stereo mix—with
the bass and guitar coming out of the left speaker and the drums
and vocal track on the right. By turning the stereo mix into a mono
mix—having the same audio information coming out of both
speakers—the vocal would come up two decibels. So that's what
I did, but I never thought I'd fool Jerry. Well, I did. He loved what
I sent, and that's what you hear on the single.

Years later, I was in Sausalito on tour and found myself at a place
by the bay having a hamburger. I was watching the water when my
eye caught something. The ferries crossing from San Francisco
turned a little as they came in to slow themselves down. The move
created a rolling wave to cushion their arrival at the pier. That's
when it hit me. Otis had been watching the ferries roll in.

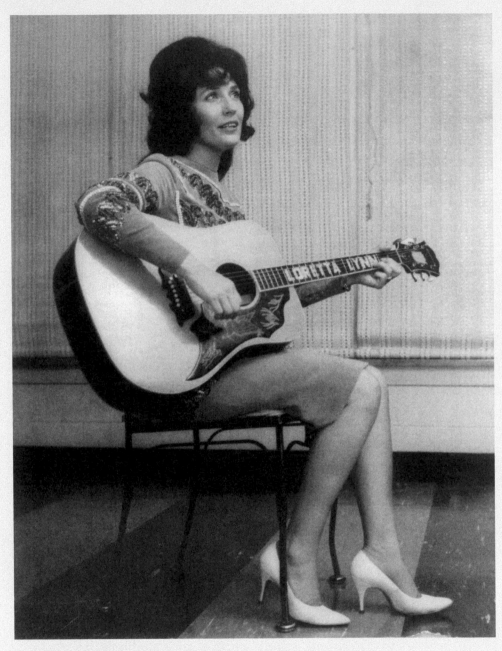

Loretta Lynn, c. 1965, with her iconic customized Epiphone Excellente flattop guitar.

*Michael Ochs Archives/Getty Images*

# 17: Fist City
## LORETTA LYNN
### *Released: February 1968*

In the years after World War I, radio's popularity spread rapidly nationwide. As the number of stations surged in the 1920s and networks emerged in the early '30s to provide coast-to-coast programming, music broadcasts were the next natural step. By the mid-1930s, with the arrival of the Swing Era, dance bands were routinely featured on the radio and most major stations employed their own orchestras. Despite network radio's national reach, many parts of the country retained their regional taste in music—particularly in the South and West. Rural music in the 1930s and '40s was racially divided between African-American blues and jazz and white string-band and cowboy music. Record companies and music publishers came up with a series of names for the white music of Appalachia, including "Hill Country Songs and Ballads," which music trade publications began calling "Hillbilly" for short. In 1949, during an overhaul of its chart names, *Billboard* began referring to rural white music as "Country and Western." "Country" stood for the unpretentious, rural folk music that reflected everyday life in the mountains of the South and included jug-band music and bluegrass. "Western" stood for the cowboy ballads and Western swing popular in Texas that often featured the steel guitar. But by the late 1950s, with the advent of better phonographs, improved fidelity, and stereo sound, Nashville began adding a slick, pop backdrop to country music with polished studio musicians.

As Nashville's pop-country sound developed, songs by many male vocalists cast women as heartbreakers or troublemakers. Top female singers such as Kitty Wells, Patsy Cline, Jean Shepard, and

Brenda Lee added a more emotional feel, focusing on lost love and falling to pieces. In 1966, with the Nashville sound well established, Loretta Lynn began writing and recording autobiographical songs about a cheating husband, female rivals, spousal alcoholism, and other sensitive marital issues that weren't typically discussed, let alone addressed on recordings.

In 1967, when Lynn caught wind of her husband's indiscretions, she wrote a song—not about what she was going to do to him but how she would handle the home-wrecker. Recorded almost tongue in cheek, "Fist City" didn't hold the husband of the song's protagonist accountable for his philandering. Instead, she playfully threatened the woman who was tempting him by warning her to steer clear of town unless she wanted a beating. Initially, there were concerns that radio stations wouldn't play a song about two women going at it, since such behavior was viewed as unbecoming. But "Fist City" climbed to No. 1 on *Billboard*'s country singles chart anyway, thanks in part, Lynn says, to the many women who connected with the message and bought the record. "I think my story sounded a little familiar," she said, laughing. The album also reached No. 1 on the country chart.

### Interview with LORETTA LYNN (singer-songwriter and guitarist)

**LORETTA LYNN:** I married early and started singing late. "Doo" [Oliver "Doolittle" Lynn] and I were wed in 1948 when I was just fifteen and he was twenty-one. A year later, we left Butcher Hollow, Kentucky, so he could take a logging job in Custer, Washington. I was pregnant then, and there would be three more babies before I was twenty.

Doo loved my singing voice and encouraged me to perform at local clubs in Custer in the late 1950s. I cut my first record in 1960 when I was twenty-eight, and I signed with Decca later that year. We moved to Nashville soon after, and my career took off.

In 1966, me and Doo were out drivin' around looking at houses. We had owned a little farm in Goodlettsville, Tennessee, but I gave it to one of my close friends. In the car, we passed this big old Colonial. I said, "I want that house right there."

Doo went to the local bank and found out nobody had lived there for some time. When we decided to buy the house, we discovered from the bank that a little town—Hurricane Mills—came with it.

After we moved in, I began touring regionally for weeks at a stretch. Doo wouldn't come with me. He preferred staying home and farming the 350 acres out back. Unfortunately, there were plenty of girls in the area trying to get his attention, and succeeding.

I first found out what was going on when I returned from the road. Cissie, one of my children, came home from school one day and said, "Momma, the bus driver told me she went out with Daddy." I said, "Your daddy didn't do that." I suspected there was some truth to it, but I didn't want our kids to know.

I waited until I found the bus driver alone. She was on the bus, without any kids on board. I confronted her, and she admitted what had been going on. I went right into action. You don't wait for someone to go first. As a woman, I went for the hair. She was bigger than me, but I held my own.

The inspiration for "Fist City," however, was a different girl who had moved close to Hurricane Mills so she could make a play for Doo. I could see what was going on between them when I saw them together. I couldn't confront her like I did the school-bus driver. That would have been too messy.

The last straw was hearing rumors about them while I was in Nashville recording for Decca. Driving home to Hurricane Mills that afternoon in my Cadillac, I was real mad and wrote "Fist City" in my head during the seventy-five-mile trip. All I could think about was what she was doing to my family and what I wanted to say to her.

The words started to hit me just outside of Nashville. The further I drove, the madder I got. As with any song, after I had the first two or three lines, the melody just followed. By the time I got home, the song was done, and I was pretty angry.

When I walked in the door, Doo said, "What the hell are you so mad about?" I went straight into my home office, sat down at my desk, and wrote what I had come up with on the highway. The lyrics covered three pages in my writing tablet.

Then I let the words sit overnight, so I could look at them fresh. The next day, I changed a few things so they'd be able to play the record on the radio [laughs]. Sometimes I write songs in a way where they can't play 'em.

The lyrics were a warning to that woman to steer clear of Hurricane Mills and my husband and what would happen if she didn't. [She sings softly:] "Now you've been makin' your brags around town that you've been lovin' my man/But the man I love, when he picks up trash/he puts it in a garbage can/And that's what you look like to me, and what I see is a pity/You better close your face and stay outta my way/If you don't wanna go to Fist City."

I didn't have to simplify anything in the lyrics. I write songs plain enough from the start. I didn't have education enough to put too big of a word in there. I just wrote it all plain. Once the lyrics were set, I took out my guitar and played and sang along to what I had written.

I didn't jot down the notes or chords. I don't know music. I just sing and play on my guitar. I couldn't tell you one note from another. When I was done, I didn't play the song for Doo. I did confront him, though, and we had it out. Eventually, he came to his senses, since I had told him it was either her or me.

As I recall, I played the song first for Owen Bradley, my producer. Whenever I'd arrive at his studio in Mount Juliet, Tennessee, he'd say, "How many songs have you written so far?" He didn't want me bringing in songs that didn't belong to me. He liked my songs best.

From the start, Owen was fine with me writing songs like this. Most songwriters tended to write about falling in love, breakin' up, and being alone—things like that. The female view I wrote about was new. I suppose Owen felt that's what made me different. I just wrote about what I knew, and what I knew usually involved something that somebody did to me.

On a song like "Fist City," Owen didn't worry about the trouble we might get into with disc jockeys. He sensed the song would be a hit and that he'd just have to work harder to get the DJs to play it. He said, "If they listen to it, they'll play it." And they did.

We recorded "Fist City" in early January 1968 at Bradley's Barn, Owen's recording studio. He was in the control room and let me alone to do what I wanted. "Just go in there and sing your song, just like you wrote it," he said.

He always hired terrific musicians. On "Fist City," we had Grady Martin on lead guitar, Pete Drake on pedal steel guitar, Floyd Cramer on piano, Owen's brother Harold Bradley on bass, and Buddy Harman on drums. The background singers were added later.

Grady, bless his heart, would set a quart of whiskey next to his chair. When I first met him, I said to Owen, "We don't want him playin' on my record if he's drunk, do we?" Owen said, "He'll do better drunk than sober, so let's leave him alone."

I recorded my vocal in the booth, which isolated my sound. But we were all in the studio together. While I sang, I listened to the guys and could hear them trying to outplay each other. I knew that as long as they were doing that, I was gonna have a good record.

When the record came out, it was banned from the radio. I couldn't understand that. Apparently, a woman singing about fighting another woman was too much for 'em [laughs]. But then one DJ played it, followed by others all over the country.

Men went out and bought the record. So did women. In fact, the more I'd sing about fightin', the more women would buy the record and play it for their husbands—"This is what you're gonna get," they'd tell them [laughs].

The first time Doo heard "Fist City" was when I sang it at the Grand Ole Opry. Instead of coming inside, he preferred listening to me on the radio in the car parked out in the alley. When I finished, I walked outside and got in the car.

Doo said, "That record will never go." I said, "Why not?" He said, "Because you're telling guys to lay off my man." I said, "I didn't say 'guy.' I said 'I'm here to tell you gals to lay off my man.'" "Well," Doo said, "it will never make it." Well, it did.

We never did talk about the song and the meaning of all the words, but I sensed he knew exactly what it was about. Nearly every song I wrote back then was about one of his indiscretions. My old man was sleeping out on me, and he wound up making me a lot of songwriting and recording money doing it [laughs].

Despite his ways, though, I loved him. Doo's been gone now since 1996, and I still miss seeing him out in the field on his tractor. What I miss most, though, is his smartness. If I needed to know anything, I used to go to him. I would always listen, and usually he was right. If he wasn't, I'd tell him right there.

I'm sure the woman I had in mind knew the song was about her. After the record came out, she stayed away for a good long time. Then, in 1996, when Doo was on his deathbed and I was taking care of him, the bell rang. When I opened the front door, this woman walked right past me.

I didn't know who she was at first, but then I realized it was her. She found Doo in his bed and was talking to him. Can you imagine? Honestly, I felt like killing her. As you probably can tell, I still don't like her to this day.

Doolittle and Loretta Lynn with twins Patsy and Peggy around 1968.

*Loretta Lynn Enterprises Inc.*

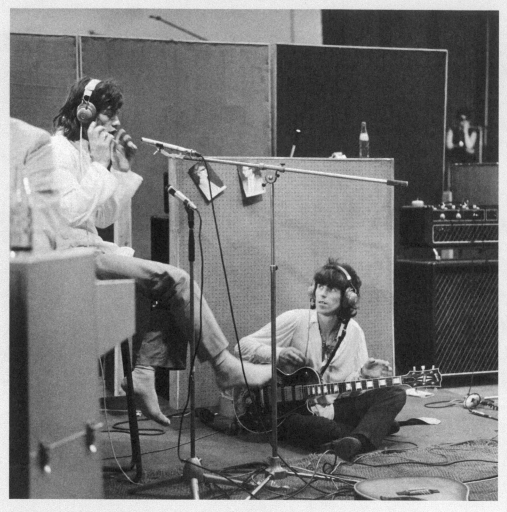

Guitarist Keith Richards and Mick Jagger in the spring of 1968 rehearsing at London's Olympic Studios during the Rolling Stones' recording of *Beggars Banquet*, which included "Street Fighting Man."

*Keystone Features/Getty Images*

# 18: Street Fighting Man
## THE ROLLING STONES
### *Released: August 1968*

The history of the guitar's "power chord" dates back to blues recordings of the early 1950s, when cheap portable amps first came on the market. The power chord—marked by distortion and played hard for emphasis—was first used by guitarists Willie Johnson, on Howlin' Wolf's "How Many More Years" in 1951, and Pat Hare, on James Cotton's "Cotton Crop Blues" in 1954. Then in 1955, Bo Diddley popularized the power chord on "Bo Diddley," his No. 1 R&B single. Before long, British teens in the 1950s began to discover the blues and the power chord.

Throughout the 1950s and into the '60s, U.K. teens were unable to hear R&B and rock on British radio which was controlled by the BBC and generally limited in its fare to classical and adult pop. Teens could pick up Radio Luxembourg and pirate radio stations broadcasting from ships off the coast in international waters. But for the most part, if you wanted to hear American rock 'n' roll, R&B, and blues in Britain, you had to head off to your local record store. As a result, many of Britain's aspiring rock musicians in the late 1950s became careful students of American blues records, which featured a gritty sound and lyrics bemoaning a bleak life not unlike their own working-class existence.

The Kinks' Dave Davies was among the first British rock guitarist to make effective use of the power chord, in the band's 1964 hit "You Really Got Me" [see Chapter 7]. Other British guitarists soon followed his lead, including the Rolling Stones' Keith Richards. His fuzzy chords that kick off "(I Can't Get No) Satisfaction" marked the start of the band's use of such chords on openers. The

Stones later extended the sound to "Jumpin' Jack Flash," "Gimme Shelter," "Midnight Rambler," and "Brown Sugar," among other songs. But perhaps Richards's most textured power chords appeared at the start of "Street Fighting Man." The chords combined the electronic distortion of Bo Diddley and the jangly and metallic sound of guitarist Robert Johnson, with psychedelic elements added for color. When "Street Fighting Man" was released in August 1968, the song only reached No. 48 on *Billboard*'s pop chart. Richards told me that's part of the song's charm: "I doubt most people at the time knew what it was all about, you know?"

### Interview with KEITH RICHARDS (Rolling Stones lead guitarist and cowriter)

**KEITH RICHARDS:** "Street Fighting Man" is one of my favorite Rolling Stones songs—probably because the music came together through a series of accidents and experimentation. We recorded it in a totally different way than anything we had done up until that point, and the results were pretty exciting and unexpected.

The music came first—before Mick [Jagger] wrote the lyrics. I had written most of the melody to "Street Fighting Man" sometime in late 1966 or early '67—before "Jumpin' Jack Flash"—but I couldn't figure out how to get the sound I wanted. It's hard to explain. If you think of a melody as a song's shape, then the sound is its texture. The two were inseparable in my mind. I tried recording the melody in the studio in '67, but nothing happened. So I took the concept home to my Redlands farmhouse in Sussex, England, to work on it.

Around this time, I became fascinated by one of the early cassette tape recorders made by Philips. The machine was compact, so it was portable, and it had this little stick microphone, which would allow me to capture song ideas on the fly. So I bought one, but as I watched the small tape-cartridge reels turn, I began to think of the machine not as a dictation device but as a mini recording studio. The problem is I couldn't use an electric guitar to record on it. The sound just overwhelmed the mike and speaker. Then I tried an acoustic guitar instead and got this dry, crisp sound on the tape—the exact sound I had been looking for on the song.

At the time, I was experimenting with open tunings on the guitar—you know, tuning the strings to form specific chords so I could bang out the broadest possible sound. That's how I came up with the opening riff on "Street Fighting Man"—even before I bought the Philips. I based the rest of the song's melody on the seesaw tone pattern of those odd sirens French police cars used [sings the siren and lyrics to illustrate].

Sometime in early '68, I took the Philips recorder into London's Olympic Sound Studios and had Charlie [Watts] meet me there. Charlie had this snap drum kit that was made in the 1930s. Jazz drummers used to carry them around to practice when they were on a bus or train. It had this little spring-up hi-hat and a tambourine for a snare. It was perfect because, like the acoustic guitar, it wouldn't overpower the recorder's mike. I had Charlie sit right next to the mike with his little kit and I kneeled on the floor next to him with my acoustic Gibson Hummingbird. There we were in front of this little box hammering away [laughs]. After we listened to the playback, the sound was perfect.

On that opening riff, I used enormous force on the strings. I always did that and still do. I'm looking at my hands now, and they look like Mike Tyson's. They're pretty beat up. I'm not a hard hitter on the strings—more of a striker. It's not the force as much as it is a whip action. I'm almost releasing the power before my fingers actually meet the strings. I'm a big string-breaker, since I like to whip them pretty hard.

Once Charlie and I had the basic track down, we played back what we had recorded through an extension speaker with a recording mike in front of it. We put that track onto an eight-track recorder, which gave us seven additional tracks for overdubbing. That damn little Philips recorder: I realize now I was using it as a pickup for the acoustic guitar—only it wasn't attached to the instrument.

Then Charlie added a bigger bass drum on one of the seven remaining tracks and I added another acoustic guitar to widen the sound. In fact, the only electric instrument on the entire recording is the bass. Bill [Wyman] wasn't around and things were moving fast, so I just recorded the bass line I had in my head. Everything happened so quickly. Dave Mason [of the band Traffic] came in later to add a bass drum and a *shehnai* [a South Asian oboe] at the end of the song. Brian [Jones] played sitar and tambura, and Nicky Hopkins added the piano part.

Early on, I had played the tape of my melody for Mick, and his lyrics were about brutal adults. We recorded them and called the song, "Did Everyone Pay Their Dues?" But we weren't that crazy about the results, and the lyrics underwent several rewrites once we saw what was going on in the streets in London and Paris in 1968. While we were in the studio, Mick had been at a huge demonstration against the Vietnam War in London's Grosvenor Square in March. And we were both in Paris in May during the violent protests by students demanding reforms. The French cops were pretty nasty about it.

As we traveled around, Mick and I would look at each other and realize something big was happening in two major capitals of the world and that our generation was bursting at the seams. Mick knew that "Dues" needed a lyric overhaul that better matched what was going on. I came up with the line "What can a poor boy do" and threw it out to Mick. He completed the thought with "'Cept to sing for a rock 'n' roll band." He wrote the rest of the new lyrics in the studio. That's often how we worked. One of us would have a piece of a lyric that sounded interesting, then hand it off to the other to get things going.

I love the songwriting process, but I really don't like writing by myself. I love the bounce of one person's ideas off the other. Mick wrote down a ton of lines. Then we tore the lines into strips and moved them around. Reams of pages were flying around—and some of them wound up burned [laughs]. Eventually they took shape and we laid down the vocal tracks.

Like any of our songs, "Street Fighting Man" not only had to hold together musically and tell a story but also had to work for a certain bunch of guys who played in a very specific way. We had to make sure that what we came up with was something the other guys in the band could get behind. For instance, if Charlie had turned up his nose at what we came up with, I knew the song wouldn't have worked. But he loved it.

Actually, I think "Street Fighting Man" is Charlie's most important record. Listen to him on there—he has this Wall of Sound thing going the way he's hitting that snap kit and the bigger drum. When you experiment the way we did as a band, the smallest little things can happen that turn out to be a big deal. You just need the determination to go there. It's also amazing what can happen when you have the right instruments—and the right amount of echo [laughs].

To his credit, our producer, [the late] Jimmy Miller, brought incredible enthusiasm to what we were doing on "Street Fighting Man." He was one of the warmest guys and an incredible friend. We made our best records with him. He always knew when to engage and when to stay out of the picture. He knew I was going for something special on the song and interjected only when he thought we were losing it and needed a break.

"Street Fighting Man" was the first time I had a sound in my head that was bugging me. That would happen again many times, of course, but after that song I knew how to deal with it. Only in the studio could I put the two things together—the minimalist sound and the overdubbing. That's where the vision met reality. When we finished recording "Street Fighting Man" and played back the master, I just smiled. It's the kind of record you love to make—and they don't come that often.

Tammy Wynette at a Nashville recording studio with producer Billy Sherrill (c. 1970).

*Courtesy of Cathy Sherrill Lale*

# 19: Stand By Your Man
**TAMMY WYNETTE**
*Released: September 1968*

The modern female country singer can be traced back to Kitty Wells. Born in Nashville, Wells had her first hit—"It Wasn't God Who Made Honky Tonk Angels"—in 1952. The song was a proto-feminist response to Hank Thompson's hit "The Wild Side of Life," in which the song's protagonist blamed the woman he picked up at a bar for wrecking his marriage. What set Wells apart from the female country singers who preceded her was a low-twang approach, leaning more heavily on a warm folk sound in her voice than the more typical country and western inflection. Wells's dignified image and string of hits encouraged Nashville labels to sign more female country singers.

Female vocalists who followed Wells in the 1950s included Jean Shepard, Skeeter Davis, Betty Foley, Patsy Cline, and Connie Smith, whose 1964 hit "Once a Day," about grieving for a lost love, reached No. 1 on the country chart and remained there for eight weeks. Smith became the first female country artist to top the chart with a debut single, and the song was the longest-running No. 1 hit on the *Billboard* chart by a female country artist up until then.

Smith's rapid success wasn't lost on Tammy Wynette, a hairdresser from Mississippi who came to Nashville in 1966. After winning over top producer Billy Sherrill, she had a series of hits about women struggling to make their relationships work. In 1968, Wynette recorded "Stand By Your Man," a song that urged women to overlook the flaws of their boyfriend or husband and to instead focus on the good he provides. In 1968, the song became a No. 1 country hit for three weeks, and then crossed over to the pop chart, where it reached No. 19. The song was inducted into the Grammy Hall of Fame in 1999.

## Interviews with BILLY SHERRILL (cowriter and producer), HARGUS "PIG" ROBBINS (pianist), and JERRY KENNEDY (guitarist)

**BILLY SHERRILL:** In 1966, I had just started working as a producer at Epic Records in Nashville. One day in August, the office receptionist buzzed and said there was a woman there named Virginia Pugh who wanted to talk to me about writing songs. I was busy, so the woman sat outside my office and waited. Finally, she got up and just walked in. She didn't have any tapes, so I gave her my guitar to play. She had a fine voice, but I didn't have anything going on at the moment for her. I asked her to leave me her number and I'd give her a call. The poor girl just wilted. She left and wound up going to see a producer friend of mine at another label. He later called me and sort of bragged about not being very nice to her. I felt bad.

By then I had heard a single by Bobby Austin called "Apartment #9." I called Virginia in and played it for her. I said, "If you learn this song, we'll record it." A week later she came to the Quonset Hut—a now famous recording studio in Nashville owned by Owen Bradley. When I put on Bobby's single of "Apartment #9" so the guys could learn the chords, Virginia listened. Then we recorded. After she finished, the guys just looked around. They were amazed. Guitarist Jerry Kennedy came up to me after and said, "Do you realize what you've got here?"

I signed Virginia right away, but I asked her to change her name. I said, "Look, don't get mad, but 'Pugh' is a horrible name." She said, "What do you want to call me?" I had just seen this old movie called *Tammy and the Bachelor* with Debbie Reynolds. "Tammy" sounded friendly. I said, "Let's take your middle name—Wynette—and make it your last, and let's put 'Tammy' in front of it." She said, "Sounds good to me."

I began producing Tammy exclusively, and we had a hit in '66, two No. 1s in '67, and another No. 1—"D-I-V-O-R-C-E"—in early '68. The goal was to keep the streak going. For some time, I had been carrying around a folded sheet of paper in my wallet with chords and lyrics to a song I wrote. My title was, "I'll Stand By You"—but it didn't sound right for Tammy. She needed a twist. I reworked the lyrics so the story came from the perspective of a woman singing to another woman—as if she were giving advice to a friend who was a little unsure about how to hold on to her man.

In August 1968, when Tammy was in the studio for a recording session, she and I went up to my office on a break. I had an old upright piano in there, and Tammy sat on the bench next to me while I played and sang. She liked the song and changed a few lines. I said, "Do you want to hear it again?" She said, "No, why don't we go downstairs and record this thing?" Back in the studio, I played and sang the song a few more times for the band—Pete Drake on pedal steel guitar, Ray Edenton on guitar, "Pig" Robbins on piano, Bob Moore on bass, and Buddy Harman on drums.

**HARGUS "PIG" ROBBINS:** I've been blind since I was a kid. A teacher gave me my nickname after I became dirty playing on the fire-escape slide at my blind school. The name sort of stuck. At the Quonset Hut, I played a Steinway Grand Model B. They put Tammy right behind me and the choir a little more distant—so her voice and theirs would wrap around me. The bass and drums were to my left and the guitar was on my right, with the pedal steel guitar a little farther away.

I had been recording with Tammy for a couple of years by then, but I had no idea what she looked like. What came out through her lungs was enough to tell me what kind of soul she had—especially on that song's chorus.

**SHERRILL:** When we recorded, the guys didn't use a formal arrangement, just numbers—like 1-1-1-5 and 5-5-5-1 and so on. The numbers stood for chords. If we played in the key of C, then No. 1 would be C. This allowed us to change keys if we had to without transposing the music. When the song ended, it was like a graveyard. Everyone just sat there and looked at each other. Someone finally broke the ice by saying, "Damn." Tammy started laughing when she realized that everyone was as much in love with the song as she was.

When we listened to the playback, I was awestruck by her voice. But in the days of singles and radio, the opening was critical. Pete [Drake] had kicked it off with his wonderful pedal steel guitar, but to me the sound gave away too much. Tammy said, "Let's try something else," and she was right.

**JERRY KENNEDY:** I wasn't on the original session. Billy called me to do it but I was in Chicago that day. When I came back to town two days later, Billy played me the tape. He wanted something less obvious at the start—the simpler the better, so Tammy could grab the song away from the musicians. Billy had me overdub the opening, and I came up with a simple riff. I used my 1961 Gibson ES-335, which had a real big, manly sound. Billy also had me overdub lines here and there to support Tammy's vocal and add flavor.

**SHERRILL:** How a record sounded on the radio meant everything back then. The radio did strange things to music, and I didn't want the single to sound too twangy or too flat. Before I approved the final mix, I sent an acetate disc to a disc-jockey friend at WKDA in Nashville and asked him to play it. He agreed to do that for me, and when the time came for it to air, I went out and sat in my black 1953 Buick to listen on the radio. When I heard the song, I loved its snap.

A few weeks ahead of the single's release, I called a friend at Epic in New York and told him the song was going to be big. He played the single up there at their weekly promo meeting, and they loved it. After the record came out, Epic took out a full-page trade-magazine ad. All it said was, "Tammy Wynette's Answer to Women's Lib" and the name of the record. But that was just media and marketing hype.

Women's lib never entered my mind. Or Tammy's. Tammy was already liberated. Even in '68, with her early hits, she continued to drive back and forth to Iuka, Mississippi, where she lived and was a hairdresser. Throughout her career, up until her death in 1998, she always kept up her hairdressing license, in case things went sour. "You never know," she'd say.

Steppenwolf lead singer John Kay appearing on a television show in 1969.

*Jan Persson/Getty Images*

# 20: Magic Carpet Ride
**STEPPENWOLF**
*Released: September 1968*

The Beatles were one of the first rock bands to deliberately use feedback during the opening of a studio recording. The feedback appears at the start of "I Feel Fine," which was recorded on October 18, 1964, during a nine-hour studio session. The effect was created when Paul McCartney played an open bass string and John Lennon leaned into his amplifier with a semi-acoustic guitar. As George Harrison notes in *The Beatles Anthology*, "John got a bit of feedback unintentionally and liked the sound and thought that it would be good at the start of the song. From then on he started to hold the guitar [near the amp] to create the feedback for every take that we recorded."

Actually, the sound Lennon was trying to emulate with distortion was the two chords played by horns at the start of Bobby Parker's "Watch Your Step" (1961), a single that Lennon later said was one of his favorite records. Lennon then followed with a lick adapted from the same Parker recording. As Lennon noted in *The Beatles Anthology*, purposefully using feedback was common by bands during live performances but not in studio sessions. Jimi Hendrix used slightly longer distortion to open "Foxey Lady" during the December 1966 recording of his album *Are You Experienced?* There, too, it was used to create contrast between the disorienting sound of distortion and the churning electric guitar chords that follow.

In 1968, Steppenwolf took distortion to the next level, using it for a twenty-second passage to open "Magic Carpet Ride." Guitarist Michael Monarch created the feedback and distortion, but unlike the Beatles and Hendrix, Monarch's electronic sounds weren't originally planned for the song's opening. Instead, the passage was spliced in when the band realized it didn't have a suitable introduction. The electronic effects, John Kay's gruff blues-rock vocal, and the strength of the strong guitar riff by Mars Bonfire became a prototype for heavy metal, which would follow in the early 1970s. When "Magic Carpet Ride" was released in September 1968, the song reached No. 3 on the *Billboard* pop chart.

### Interviews with JOHN KAY (Steppenwolf lead singer and cowriter) and MICHAEL MONARCH (guitarist)

**JOHN KAY:** In 1948, when I was four, my mother and I escaped from East Germany to West Germany, and then moved to Toronto, Canada, in 1958. There, I listened relentlessly to rock 'n' roll on the radio and began playing guitar. When I was twenty, I moved to Los Angeles, and from 1964 to '65 I played folk-blues guitar at coffeehouses. I played my way back to Toronto in 1965 and joined a rock group called the Sparrows.

In early 1966, the Sparrows left for New York. We had attracted a young, well-off Canadian businessman who offered to be our manager who had connections in New York. Our demos helped us land a deal with Columbia Records, but it never amounted to anything more than a misunderstanding. We wanted to record an album and Columbia wanted us to cut radio-friendly singles. Our only release was "Tomorrow's Ship," which someone sarcastically referred to as "No. 49 with an anchor." But we were still signed to the label.

We spent the spring of '66 in N.Y. playing at places like Arthur, the Jet Set; the Barge in Westhampton, New York, where the Young Rascals had been discovered a year earlier; and the Downtown Club, where we alternated weeks with the Chambers Brothers. Bette Midler was the coat-check girl there.

We got our chops together in New York, since we could stretch out on much of the bluesier stuff we were playing. But none of it was really going anywhere. Eventually, I told the guys we should be in Los Angeles, not New York. By the summer of '66, we moved out there, checking into the Tropicana Motel on Santa Monica Boulevard. All of the bands stayed there, and it had a cool diner that was a musician's hang.

We played the Whisky a Go Go, the Galaxy, and It's Boss. Everything was going well until the Sunset Strip riots in November '66, when local merchants called the police to clear nightly crowds of loitering kids. After the riots, most clubs in West Hollywood admitted only people who were twenty-one or older. We were effectively starving for work.

So we moved up to San Francisco, and for the next eight months we played the Avalon and Fillmore ballrooms and clubs like the Matrix and the Ark. One day, Columbia producer David Rubinson came up to hear us. He was sent by the label to determine if they should drop us or record us again. He brought us down to L.A. to record a few blues-rock tracks, but it didn't work out, and Columbia released us from our contract. I told the guys we should move back to L.A., where I was far more connected.

We did, but work was slow. One night, after an argument with the owner of a club, the Sparrows broke up. Our bass player went off in a huff and the guitar player, Dennis Edmonton, the brother of our drummer, changed his name to Mars Bonfire and got a solo writer deal with Uni Records. Organist Goldy McJohn and drummer Jerry Edmonton sat tight.

At this point, my Toronto girlfriend, Jutta, had gotten her U.S. immigration visa and joined me in L.A. We moved into a tiny apartment above a garage at 7408 Fountain Avenue. Goldy and Jerry also had girlfriends and moved into a place a few minutes away from me. The three of us were basically twiddling our thumbs trying to figure out our next move.

Then a girlfriend of Jutta's from Toronto moved in next door with her new husband, Gabriel Mekler, who happened to be a producer at ABC/Dunhill Records. Gabriel played me some things he had produced at Dunhill and I played him reels of our live shows.

I told him how the Sparrows had broken up and that two of the guys lived down the road.

Gabriel urged me to contact Goldy and Jerry and to get a bass player and lead guitarist from local sources. He said if I did, he probably could get Duhhill to spend a few hundred bucks for some demos once we had rehearsed. Goldy and Jerry were all for re-forming. I called Michael Monarch, the seventeen-year-old guitarist who had sat in with us at clubs on the Sunset Strip. He came aboard.

For the bassist, we posted a notice on a bulletin board at a record store. A guy named Rushton Moreve responded. He looked like a hippie, but he was a natural-born bass player. He understood instinctively the concept of grooves and melodic content, not just droning away on the root note of a chord.

We started rehearsing in the garage below my apartment, utilizing songs from the Sparrows repertoire and a few I had written using arrangements with a much raunchier guitar sound and more inventive bass lines. Every so often, Gabriel would stick his head in to give us input. At some point, Gabriel said we were ready to cut demos. So we went into the studio and cut everything on a two-track recorder.

At the end, a guy in the booth asked us the band's name. Gabriel told me he had just read Herman Hesse's *Steppenwolf,* which was popular on college campuses. Gabriel said he liked the sound of the word and how it looked in print. He said, "You guys have this aggressive, primal sound. I think this could work." We agreed and Gabriel wrote it on the tape box.

After Gabriel submitted the demos to ABC/Dunhill, I went with him to see the label president—Jay Lasker. I liked Jay, but he was old-school—a burly former New Yorker with a big cigar. He said, "John, I played your demos and I don't get it. But my sixteen-year-old daughter, she loves it. Steve Barri, who produced the Grass Roots, he thinks it can work. So we'll sign you."

Jay pulled out a contract and showed me where to sign. First I asked him for two contingencies: a $1,500 advance to get the rest of our gear out of hock, and a written guarantee that the label would not only let us record an entire album, but would release and promote it. Jay added both terms to the contract.

In the late summer of '67, we went into the studio that Gabriel used then—United Western, on Sunset. The moment we started playing, an engineer said, "Look, you're driving the needles into the red in here. You turn down out there and I'll turn you up in here." So we wound up with a tape of music by a small-sounding band played back loudly.

After ten days at United Western, we weren't getting anywhere. The engineers couldn't capture our sound. Then Morgan Cavett, who had cowritten songs with me, played a demo of a female singer who had been in a group called the Womenfolk. After listening, I said, "Your demo sounds fuller and better than what we've been able to cobble together in ten days on four tracks at United Western. Where did you record this?" Morgan told me about American Recording Company in Studio City. It was a converted restaurant owned by two musicians—Richie Podolor and Bill Cooper. So Gabriel and I went to see them. We paid $9,000 for four days and cut Steppenwolf's first album there.

Singles from the album, including "Born to Be Wild," were released, and they climbed the charts. We went out on a cross-country tour, and when we returned in mid-'68, the label told us they wanted two albums a year, which was an archaic model. On top of this, we were supposed to write our own songs, rehearse and record them, promote them on the road, do television, tour internationally, and have some kind of private life. Two albums a year was insane.

We went into the studio to record our second album. But we didn't have a complete album's worth of stuff. In the studio, Rushton Moreve, our bass player, liked to goof around with this bouncy riff he had come up with. One day, Mars, Jerry Edmonton's brother, came in to show us a new song he had written called "Faster Than the Speed of Life." At some point, as Rushton started with his riff, Mars heard it and started playing chords to it on his Fender Jazzmaster guitar.

Mars had an incredibly good subtle right wrist and was one of the tightest rhythm guitar players I'd ever heard. Goldy hears Mars and starts adding organ chords and Jerry jumped in, too. The guys in the booth went nuts. They came on the speaker and said, "Hey, keep doing that. That's really good."

So we kept at it, but eventually we started to wonder where it was going. All we had was this cool riff. Mars suggested we add an instrumental interlude—a breakdown. He played these chords that led into the jam, for which I later write the lyrics, "Close your eyes, girl/Look inside, girl/Let the sound take you away."

When we had been in New York, during the Sparrows' session for Columbia, we recorded "Isn't It Strange," an experimental song that included me using a bottleneck on my guitar with tons of echo. I played these creeping, high-pitched melodic little things that sat on top of a slow, pulsating track. It sounded like a good idea here.

Michael, our lead guitarist, loved thick distorted guitar notes and had a Fuzz Face guitar effects pedal. I said to him, "Let's go back into the studio—you do your feedback routine, the really nasty, growly animal, monster sounds. Whenever I hear something approaching a note, I'll contrast that with a high-pitched single note slide on my guitar. They will be these slow-moving pinging sounds that are the opposite of what you'll be doing."

We did that for two cycles. The guys in the booth were excited. Meanwhile, Bill had hit the "record" button. When we went into the booth to hear what we had, it sounded really good. Then the music went back to the riff. Except all we had was the riff and a breakdown. We didn't have a real introduction or anything on top to hold the ear. So Michael went back into the studio to create one.

**MICHAEL MONARCH:** I cranked up the Fender Concert amp full open. Then I took my Fender Esquire and leaned into the amp, to overload it and create midrange-to-bottom feedback. I was being real physical with the instrument, bending notes and hitting the strings hard with the bottom of my fist so the strings would touch the pickup underneath. Normally, they never touch, so when they did the way I hit them, it sounded sort of like a spaceship landing.

I gave the guys in the booth about thirty seconds of that. Then they asked me to do it all again. I did but it came out different, of course. What you hear on the record are the two takes I recorded overlapping. The first part is my distortion and bending the guitar strings while playing. The second part is me hitting the strings rapidly against the pickup to get that chugging sound before John's vocal comes in and the riff starts.

**KAY:** Bill loved it and spliced Michael's experimental electronic sounds onto the start of the tape so the song would open with this electronic overdub. Now we had a track, but we didn't have a song. We still needed lyrics. Bill made me a cassette tape and I took it home to Fountain Avenue. As royalties from the success of our first album had started to come in, Jutta and I replaced our lousy stereo with a top-notch system from a high-end audio store in Beverly Hills. Our living room was tight, so we set up the two Aztec Gauguin speakers on either side of a sofa that doubled as a daybed. When you listened to music, it sounded as if you were wearing head-phones. When I came home from the studio that night, I grabbed a pad and put the cassette in.

As soon as I heard the electronic sound effects in the opening, the song's lyrics popped into my head: "I like to dream/Yes-yes, right between my sound machine/On a cloud of sound I drift in the night/Any place it goes is right/Goes far, flies near, to the stars away from here." The lyrics were about how great our new stereo system sounded.

The opening verse was done, but I had a problem. If I drift in the night on a sound cloud, I had to go someplace. I came up with "Last night I held Aladdin's lamp" and all the imagery of making a wish. The "little girl" in the song wasn't supposed to be anyone specific. It was open-ended and could have been universally applied to anyone. For me, it was Jutta.

The next day, I went into the studio and cut the vocal track. Gabriel thought the lines "You don't know what we can see/Why don't you tell your dreams to me/Fantasy will set you free" needed a harmony. So I overdubbed a falsetto to give it some thickness. But we didn't want to fade the psychedelic free fall to close out the song. "Magic Carpet Ride" needed to be a single, but we didn't want to hurt the album version.

Bill copied one of the finished vocal choruses onto a second machine and spliced that extra chorus at the end, right after the jam section. He spliced it in after my slide does a little lick, which tells the ear the soloing section is ending. We faded out the added chorus.

The song actually had a movie cameo. Many people think *Easy Rider* in 1969 was the first film we were involved in with "Born to Be Wild." Actually, it was *Candy,* in 1968, a dark comic film adaptation of Terry Southern's novel. The film was sort of a surreal sex farce about a naïve girl named Candy. At one point, "Magic Carpet Ride" comes out of the radio on a nightstand. I guess it worked because of my lyric "Why don't you come with me, little girl/On a magic carpet ride."

I didn't drop acid before writing the lyrics, as many people later assumed. And the lyrics weren't about an acid trip. I may have smoked a joint that night, but that was it. Since birth, I've had achromatopsia—complete color blindness. If I had dropped acid, I would have been hallucinating in vivid black-and-white. I doubt that would have helped me or the song much.

Valid Friday only    $3.00

Valid Saturday only    $3.00

Singer-songwriter John Fogerty of Creedence Clearwater Revival recording in San Francisco in 1970.

*Ed Caraeff/Morgan Media/Getty Images*

# 21: Proud Mary
## CREEDENCE CLEARWATER REVIVAL
*Released: January 1969*

Acoustic instruments were becoming scarce in rock bands by the mid-1960s. The British Invasion of 1964 and '65 had created a strong audience appetite for the electric guitar, bass, and keyboards. The amplified instruments not only allowed groups to crank up the music in concert, but also gave bands a cooler, more sexually charged image with fans. But some bands, including the Byrds, Simon & Garfunkel, Buffalo Springfield, and the Beau Brummels, retained an acoustic presence. By the late 1960s, with the pop charts dominated by electric rock bands, several major artists began adding acoustic elements of the rural South to push back against the electric incursion.

Bob Dylan was at the forefront of this early roots rock movement, hiring a group of acoustic musicians in 1965 and '66 as his touring band before recording with them extensively in upstate New York. By 1968, this group began to appear as the Band, going on to record ten albums on their own. Dylan also embraced the South on *Blonde on Blonde*, recording the album in Nashville in 1966. On his 1967 album *John Wesley Harding*, Dylan shifted to a traditional, acoustic framework. Overall, the Americana movement of the late 1960s was an attempt to reestablish authenticity and musicianship in rock, free from electric gimmickry, pop trappings, or psychedelic effects.

Chief among the early roots rock bands was Creedence Clearwater Revival. Founded in San Francisco in 1967, the band incorporated rural elements and Americana imagery. When Creedence

Clearwater Revival's "Proud Mary" was released in January 1969, the song reached No. 2 in March on *Billboard*'s pop chart, and remained there for three straight weeks. The song about a Mississippi riverboat was so potent that it was covered twice in 1969— once by soul singer Solomon Burke and again by the Checkmates Ltd., an R&B band produced by Phil Spector. In 1971, Ike and Tina Turner released their cover version as a sexually unhinged opus that starts "nice and easy" as a ballad and then lurches into a rip-roaring, "rough" grinder halfway through. Their version went to No. 4 on the *Billboard* pop chart and was inducted into the Grammy Hall of Fame in 2003. The Creedence Clearwater Revival original was inducted in 1998.

**Interviews with JOHN FOGERTY (Creedence Clearwater Revival singer-songwriter and lead guitarist), SONNY CHARLES (Checkmates Ltd. lead singer), TAMIKO JONES (producer), PERRY BOTKIN JR. (arranger), and BRENT MAHER (engineer)**

**JOHN FOGERTY:** Back in the fall of 1967—before the release of our first Creedence album—I bought a small notebook and began keeping a list of song-title ideas. My first entry was "Proud Mary." I didn't really know what those two words meant, but I liked how they sounded together.

I was living in an apartment in Albany, California, near San Francisco, with my wife at the time and our newborn son. I was still in the Army Reserve and was concerned about being sent to Vietnam. One day, in the early summer of 1968, I saw an oversize envelope on the steps of our apartment building. It was my honorable discharge. In the blink of an eye, I was a civilian again. I did a handstand and flipped a few times on the small lawn out front.

Then I went inside, picked up my Rickenbacker guitar, and began playing a song intro I had been working on. The chord riff was based on the opening to Beethoven's Fifth Symphony, which I had first heard on TV growing up. I didn't like how Beethoven had composed it. I preferred hitting the first chord hard for emphasis, not the fourth.

When I added rhythm to the chords, the song had the motion of a boat. I had always loved Mark Twain's writing and the music of Stephen Foster, so I wrote lyrics about a riverboat. The line "rollin' on the river" was influenced by a movie I once saw about two riverboats racing. I finished most of the song in two hours. Then I opened my notebook for a song title. There was "Proud Mary."

A few weeks later, I played the song for Creedence. We had been rehearsing in my brother Tom's garage in nearby El Cerrito. I showed them how the song went, but for a period of days it didn't sound right. So I wrote out music parts for everyone.

When we recorded the tracks at RCA Studios in Hollywood in October '68, I channeled Wilson Pickett and Howlin' Wolf with my lead vocal. Just as we were extending the final chorus at the end of the last and best take, the tape reel ran out. Luckily we had enough on there to create a fade-out in the final mix.

Listening to the playback, I wasn't happy. The band's background vocals sounded harsh—like punk rock, not harmonious. I had wanted a gospel feel. When I told the guys I was going to overdub the vocal harmony tracks myself, we had a big fight. Bruce Young, our road manager, took them to dinner.

I stayed behind and overdubbed all the background vocal parts. I also overdubbed a guitar solo using a Gibson ES-175—a big jazz guitar that I had bought for the recording session. I recorded my solo line twice so it would sound fuller.

When I went over to the restaurant, the guys were still angry, and threatened to quit. I convinced them to hear the results. Back at the studio, I played them the song with my vocals. Nobody said anything. Then Bruce said, "Wow." The single came out in January '69 and topped out at No. 2 on *Billboard*'s pop chart. The band eventually broke up in '72.

**SONNY CHARLES:** In '69, I was lead singer of an R&B band called the Checkmates Ltd. Solomon Burke had just had a hit with a "Proud Mary" cover in May. It was medium-tempo and opened with him talking about the riverboat.

**TAMIKO JONES:** I coproduced Solomon's single at the Muscle Shoals Sound Studio in Alabama. Solomon and I talked before he recorded. I told him to do his own thing, to start the record by telling people how he felt about the riverboat. When Ike and Tina's version came out a year later, Solomon and I laughed. We could hear they had borrowed his talking-intro approach.

**CHARLES:** When I went into the studio to record my vocal tracks for our Checkmates album, our producer, Phil Spector, told me that he and Perry Botkin Jr. had written an up-tempo gospel arrangement of "Proud Mary." It was terrific, and Phil had already recorded the instrumentals in that Wall of Sound style of his. When our A&M album came out, Phil released "Black Pearl" as a single, and it became a hit. "Proud Mary" was supposed to be next, but Phil sat on it, releasing it only in the U.K. in late '69. Soon I heard that Ike and Tina Turner were performing a version similar to ours. Maybe Phil played it for them. Who knows.

**PERRY BOTKIN JR.:** Phil Spector told me how he wanted the Checkmates' arrangement to go. The decision to speed up the original was all Phil. I hadn't heard Ike and Tina Turner's version yet—if there even was one at that point. And I have no idea how they heard the Checkmates' version. Their "River Deep—Mountain High" had been produced by Phil in '66 and was reissued in late '69—by A&M—but it didn't do well. Maybe Phil let them hear our "Proud Mary" for inspiration and to make it up to them.

**BRENT MAHER:** When I engineered and mixed Ike and Tina Turner's "Proud Mary" in '70, they were already performing it on the road. Before recording at United in Las Vegas, Ike asked me to see their show at the Hilton. So I went. I had never seen or felt intensity like that on stage.

In the studio the next day, I set up the band and mikes the way they had been arranged on stage. I also put three mikes on the drums—one overhead, one on the snare, and one on the bass drum. I had Tina record in the studio with everyone else, not in an isolation booth. I didn't worry about instruments leaking into each other's mikes. I wanted to create a larger-than-life ambience. When the band listened to the playback later in the control booth, it was like a party going on. Ike always watched Tina, and when she was into it, he knew they had a master take.

FOGERTY: In the fall of '68, just before our "Proud Mary" came out, I went down to Memphis to see the Mississippi River. I had never seen it before. I was taken to a place where a riverboat was dry-docked. Tourists didn't know about it, only local kids. It was very emotional for me. It's funny—the dry-docked boat looked exactly as I had imagined it.

Edwin Hawkins (at the piano) with Dorothy Morrison (right) and the Edwin Hawkins Singers in 1970.

*Michael Ochs Archives/Getty Images*

# 22: Oh Happy Day
## THE EDWIN HAWKINS SINGERS
*Released: April 1969*

Gospel played a significant role in the development of R&B. Sister Rosetta Tharpe's spiritual recordings of the 1940s were profoundly influential on electric guitarists of the '50s. The a cappella approach of church gospel groups also turned up in R&B's vocal harmony groups, including the Ravens and the Flamingos. And the childhood church experiences of many R&B and soul stars of the 1950s and '60s can be found in their later recordings. Yet up until 1967, pure gospel recordings never managed to cross over to the R&B or pop charts. The closest that spiritual vocal groups came to secular success were as background singers. These groups included the Jordanaires with Elvis Presley and the Soul Stirrers behind Sam Cooke.

The gospel sound first found its way into the mainstream through folk. "We Shall Overcome," adapted from the hymn "If My Jesus Wills" and popularized by Pete Seeger after he heard it in 1947, became the civil rights movement's unofficial anthem in 1959. Joan Baez had a pop hit with the song in 1963. Throughout the 1960s, many gospel-flavored R&B songs were hits, including Marvin Gaye's "Can I Get a Witness" (1963), Gaye and Tammi Terrell's "Ain't No Mountain High Enough" (1967), Aretha Franklin's "Chain of Fools" (1967), and Laura Nyro's "Eli's Coming" (1967). Nevertheless, gospel groups were unable to land secular hits, largely because black churches strongly discouraged them from recording for secular labels.

But in early 1969, a series of events led to the release of "Oh Happy Day," a song recorded in 1967 by the Edwin Hawkins Singers, featuring Dorothy Morrison on lead vocal. When the single was released in April 1969, it became the first pure gospel recording to reach *Billboard*'s secular charts, climbing to No. 4 on the pop chart and No. 2 on the soul chart. Immediately following the success of "Oh Happy Day," pop artists began releasing church-flavored singles, including Simon & Garfunkel's "Bridge Over Troubled Water" (1970); George Harrison's "My Sweet Lord" (1970); Melanie's "Lay Down (Candles in the Rain)," featuring the Edwin Hawkins Singers (1970); and Broadway's *Godspell* soundtrack (1971), which yielded the 1972 gospel-flavored hit "Day by Day." The Edwin Hawkins Singers' single was inducted into the Grammy Hall of Fame in 1999.

## Interviews with EDWIN HAWKINS (songwriter and pianist) and DOROTHY MORRISON (lead singer)

**EDWIN HAWKINS:** Growing up in Oakland, California, my family belonged to the Good Samaritan Church of God in Christ. Each year, the church attended a national Pentecostal church conference but never sent a choir. So in May of 1967, when I was twenty-three, I formed the Northern California State Youth Choir with Betty Watson, a friend. More than forty young people joined from nearby Pentecostal churches. When we performed at the conference that year, we finished in second place. Returning home, we began regular rehearsals.

**DOROTHY MORRISON:** When I joined Edwin's choir, I had been singing at my Pentecostal church in Richmond, California, and at local R&B clubs—secretly, because the church would have frowned on that. Edwin knew I could sing from our Monday night church union meetings at the Ephesian Church of God in Christ in Berkeley, so I didn't have to audition.

**HAWKINS:** In 1968, I hired Century Records, a local vanity label, to record an album of songs by the choir. My plan was to order five hundred copies and have members sell them for about $5 each to raise money for our church. One of the eight songs I wrote and arranged for the album was "Oh Happy Day," based on "O Happy Day, That Fixed My Choice"—a formal eighteenth-century hymn with a lovely, simple message. A year earlier, I had updated the hymn with new chord voicings and a gospel feel.

One of my influences at the time was pianist Sergio Mendes. I liked how he alternated between major and minor keys and created rhythmic patterns on the keyboard. My piano intro was along those lines. Our recording was made at the Ephesian Church during the summer of 1968. I chose Dorothy Morrison, one of our most experienced vocalists, to sing the lead.

**MORRISON:** Edwin asked me to have the lyrics memorized by the recording date. But it wasn't until the drive over with my husband that I began to commit them to memory. The lyrics were simple and they rhymed, but they were a lot to remember. At the church, I wrote two sections on my palms with a pen. The third section I memorized. During the recording, I put up my hands, with my palms facing me. Everyone thought I was feeling the spirit. I was—but I also was reading the lyrics. I ad-libbed on "When Jesus washed, oh, when he washed, my sins away" And I threw in a James Brown "good God" toward the end, which made the song feel even more current.

**HAWKINS:** Our album—*Let Us Go Into the House of the Lord*—was ready a few weeks later. I gave ten copies to each choir member to sell for the church. I was sure that "Joy, Joy!" or "To My Father's House" was going to be the song that would sell the album.

**MORRISON:** One Sunday morning in early 1969, I was listening to a gospel radio show on KSAN-FM in San Francisco when our recording of "Oh Happy Day" came on. I froze. I said to myself, "Oh my God, that's us—that's me."

**HAWKINS:** When the song caught on in San Francisco in March 1969, I began receiving calls from major record companies. They all wanted to buy the rights to release the recording nationwide on their labels. I asked Mel Reid of Reid's Records, a gospel music store, in Berkeley, for advice. He said to go with Buddah Records. A company representative flew out from New York to talk with me. Then I flew to New York to sign the deal. Meanwhile, the church thought what we were doing was sacrilegious and insisted we remove the choir's name from the record. So Buddah renamed the choir the Edwin Hawkins Singers.

In early April 1969, Buddah released "Oh Happy Day" as a single on Pavilion—a label it had set up for gospel music. By the end of May, it was No. 4 on *Billboard*'s pop chart. In June, we appeared with the Isley Brothers at Yankee Stadium. That's when I realized the song's magnitude.

**MORRISON:** I wasn't paid for the record, but that doesn't matter. I was singing in the church, singing for the Lord. Soon after, I was hired to sing backup on Simon & Garfunkel's "Bridge Over Troubled Water," which led to work with Van Morrison, Boz Scaggs, and so many other artists. Edwin performs the song today with his singers, and I do, too, with the Blues Broads. Audience reactions are always strong. People want to have a happy day, and that song helps them do it. My delivery is still innocent and real, but sometimes I get so caught up I have to stop and cry. Hey, the song gets to me, too.

Elvis Presley and producer Chips Moman at American Sound Studio in Memphis in early 1969.

# 23: Suspicious Minds
## ELVIS PRESLEY
*Released: August 1969*

In 1968, Memphis was to soul what Nashville was to country. The city had fast become a recording center for regional African-American soul and gospel musicians and singers who recorded singles on local labels such as Stax, Hi, Goldwax, and Designer. When these labels recorded artists, they often used local studios that staffed top songwriters and house bands. Among the best operations in town was Chips Moman's American Sound Studio. Although Elvis Presley owned a sizable home in Memphis, his music in the 1960s had steered clear of soul influences, weaving instead through a range of genres that included rockabilly, spirituals, and movie soundtracks. But by 1968, Presley had lost his touch. His last No. 1 pop hit had been released in 1962 ("Good Luck Charm") and his previous seventeen pop hits weren't even in the top 20.

In an attempt to revive his image, Elvis taped an NBC broadcast in June 1968 called *Elvis,* which aired on Dec. 3. Much of the TV show featured predictable material—old favorites and some new songs—but it was the show's closer that generated the most heat. Dressed in a tapered white suit and burgundy kerchief, Presley sang "If I Can Dream," an impassioned gospel-flavored ballad meant to honor the legacy of Dr. Martin Luther King Jr., who had been assassinated earlier that year in Memphis. When the single was released in November 1968, just before the TV special aired, it soared up the *Billboard* pop chart, reaching No. 12 in early 1969.

Based on sales of "If I Can Dream," Presley's road back to the top of the charts would clearly require earthier material that better connected with social themes of the day. In late 1968, Presley booked time at American Sound Studio, and in January 1969 he began recording the album *From Elvis in Memphis*. The first single, "In the Ghetto," was released in April and went to No. 3 on *Billboard*'s pop chart. The second single, "Suspicious Minds" was released in August and climbed to No. 1. The song was inducted into the Grammy Hall of Fame in 1999.

## Interviews with MARK JAMES (songwriter) and CHIPS MOMAN (producer)

**MARK JAMES:** In early 1968, Chips Moman called and asked me to come to Memphis to write songs for his music publishing company. I was living in Houston at the time and had written three hits that reached No. 1 in the South. Chips's American Sound Studio in Memphis was just starting to get hot—the Box Tops had just recorded "The Letter" there—so I relocated.

Late one night, while fooling around on my Fender guitar and using my Hammond organ pedals for a bass line, I came up with a catchy melody. I was married then to my first wife but still had feelings for my childhood sweetheart, who was married back in Houston. My wife suspected I had those feelings, so it was a confusing time for me. I felt as though all three of us were caught in this trap that we couldn't walk out of.

As soon as I had finished writing the song—"Suspicious Minds"—I went into American Sound to record it, with Chips producing. I sang the lead vocal and the house band there backed me. The strings, horns, and Holladay Sisters vocal chorus were overdubbed later. After the tape was mixed, Chips and I flew to Scepter Records in New York, where my manager had contacts. They loved the song and put it out, but the label didn't have the dollars to promote new talent, so the song didn't chart.

Later that year, Don Cruise, Chips's partner, told me Elvis had booked American Sound to record what would become his *From*

*Elvis in Memphis* album. Don kept asking if I had any songs that would be a good fit for him. Tom Jones was hot at the time, and I knew Elvis needed a mature rock 'n' roll song to bring him back. Don and I thought of "Suspicious Minds," and I began urging everyone to get Elvis to hear it.

**CHIPS MOMAN:** When Elvis arrived at my studio in January 1969, he was looking for new material. I played him Mark's record of "Suspicious Minds" for Scepter Records. Elvis was crazy about it. He wanted to hear the record over and over again, and he learned it on the spot.

**JAMES:** I wasn't at Elvis's recording session for the song. Days earlier I had walked into the control room and sensed he was uncomfortable with me being there. He was like, "Who is this guy? I met him twice, why is he here?" I didn't want to jinx the song, so I stayed away.

**MOMAN:** We finally got around to recording Elvis on "Suspicious Minds" after midnight [early on January 23, 1969]. I had a Ping-Pong table, and Elvis was pretty good at it [laughs]. He wanted to use the same arrangement Mark had on his single and most of the same American Sound studio musicians.

When we finished, Elvis's crowd of businesspeople standing around said they wanted half my publishing rights. I told them they were barking up the wrong tree. I accused them of stealing, they got angry, and I threatened to halt the entire session. Fortunately, RCA's Harry Jenkins said, "This boy is right, and we're going to finish the session just the way he wants to." Jenkins sensed "Suspicious Minds" was going to be big and knew there would be plenty to go around.

**JAMES:** The next day I heard the track at the studio. At first I thought it sounded too slow. But when I heard how it was embellished later, I was blown away.

**MOMAN:** Felton Jarvis [Elvis's longtime producer] was never happy that Elvis recorded at American. It was a control thing. So when Jarvis took the tape of "Suspicious Minds," he added this crazy fifteen-second fade toward the end, like the song was wrapping up, but then brought it back by overdubbing to extend it. I have no idea why he did that—maybe so there was a short version and a long version for disc jockeys so they had choice. Whatever the reason, he messed it up. It was like a scar. None of which mattered, though. Soon after the song was released, Elvis was back on top of the charts with it.

**JAMES:** In the years that followed, whenever I saw Elvis, he'd cross the room just to say hello to me—no matter who was with him. After he died, I heard that after recording "Suspicious Minds," he'd always ask the guys in the studio, "Did Mark send me any more songs?" Golly, I wish I had known that.

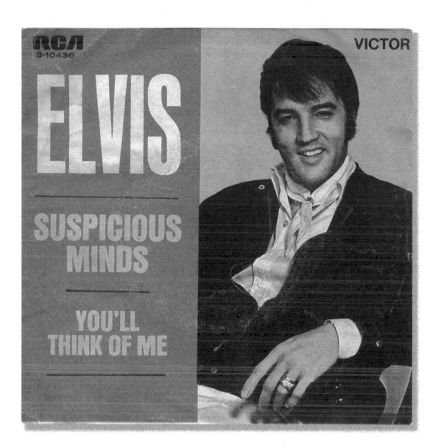

RCA
3-10436

ELVIS

VICTOR

SUSPICIOUS
MINDS

YOU'LL
THINK OF ME

Led Zeppelin in London in December 1968, from left—John Paul Jones, Jimmy Page, Robert Plant, and John Bonham.
*Dick Barnatt/Redferns/Getty Images*

# 24: Whole Lotta Love
## LED ZEPPELIN
### *Released: November 1969*

In 1968, record companies were becoming more comfortable letting unproven rock bands experiment on albums. In prior years, only seasoned musicians and proven moneymakers like the Beatles, the Beach Boys, the Rolling Stones, and Bob Dylan had that opportunity. The rest had to focus on tightly controlled singles, with albums functioning merely as collections of those short records. Starting in 1968, the album began to be viewed by a growing number of labels as a separate creative platform for rock bands, particularly those with electric guitarists who could wail on longer solos. There were two reasons for the abrupt shift. First, the rising sales of stereo systems were creating an appetite for rock albums. Second, a growing number of stereo FM radio stations were promoting rock albums as a more sophisticated and better-sounding format than pop singles.

Unveiled in the early 1930s, FM radio didn't catch on until the early 1960s. Up till then, most U.S. radio manufacturers didn't bother adding the FM band on their units, since consumers were perfectly content with AM radio. But when car companies began offering the FM band on the radios of new models in the early 1960s, AM stations started investing in FM operations. As FM activity picked up, the Federal Communications Commission insisted in 1964 that FM stations be devoted to original programming, not the duplication of AM broadcasts. The turning point for FM radio came in the late 1960s, when Japan began exporting inexpensive stereo components to the U.S. Among the electronics arriving in stores were solid-state integrated stereo receivers that featured both AM and FM radio bands. The availability of FM radio on many new stereo systems led to the rise of stereo stores and the proliferation of FM radio stations, particularly near college campuses. But since FM radio was so new in 1968, stations had trouble attracting advertisers, leaving a glut of airtime to fill. Many stations allowed program hosts to play whatever they wished, including long album tracks and even entire sides.

By 1969, with the consumer market for rock and soul albums expanding rapidly, record companies invested in bands that could fill the longer format imaginatively. One group that benefited from the shift was Led Zeppelin. After signing a major deal with Atlantic Records, the British band toured the U.S. in late 1968 and early '69 before releasing *Led Zeppelin*, its first album. The band then embarked on two more arduous North American tours in 1969, releasing *Led Zeppelin II* in October. The album opened with "Whole Lotta Love," a song that revolutionized the sound of the rock vocal and electric guitar. The album went to No. 1 on the *Billboard* pop chart for seven weeks. After "Whole Lotta Love" was released as a single in November 1969, it reached No. 4 on *Billboard*'s pop chart, and in 2007 it was inducted into the Grammy Hall of Fame.

**Interviews with JIMMY PAGE (Led Zeppelin guitarist and cowriter), GEORGE CHKIANTZ (recording engineer), and EDDIE KRAMER (final-mix engineer)**

**JIMMY PAGE:** I came up with the guitar riff for "Whole Lotta Love" in the summer of 1968, on my houseboat along the Thames in Pangbourne, England. I suppose my early love for big intros by rockabilly guitarists was an inspiration, but as soon as I developed the riff, I knew it was strong enough to drive the entire song, not just open it. When I played the riff for the band in my living room several weeks later during rehearsals for our first album, the excitement was immediate and collective. We felt the riff was addictive, like a forbidden thing.

By January 1969, we cracked America wide open with the release of our first album and our first U.S. tour. I had this avant-garde master plan for "Whole Lotta Love" and could hear the construction coming together in my head. From the start, I didn't want "Whole Lotta Love"—or any of our songs—to be a single. I had been a session musician since the early 1960s, as had [bassist] John Paul Jones. We had recorded on hundreds of singles and hated the abbreviated, canned format. I also knew that stereo FM radio was emerging in America and playing albums. I wanted to develop our songs emotionally, beyond just lengthy solos.

Our label, Atlantic Records, got it, but there was really very little risk on their end. John Paul and I knew our way around a recording studio, so we weren't going to waste studio time or produce something that wasn't cohesive. More important, I wanted to expand our approach to ensure that our album wouldn't be chopped up into singles for AM radio. To make sure that didn't happen, I produced "Whole Lotta Love"—and our entire second album—as an uneditable expression, a work that had to be aired on stereo FM to make sense.

During the band's rehearsals in early '69 for our second album, "Whole Lotta Love" sounded strong enough to open it, so I wanted to record the song first. In April, we went into London's Olympic Studios and cut "Whole Lotta Love" with engineer George Chkiantz, who had recorded Jimi Hendrix there.

**GEORGE CHKIANTZ:** There were two studios at Olympic—one large and one small. Management had installed our sixteen-track recorder in the small one with hopes of luring rock bands in there and away from the larger sixty-by-forty-foot space with twenty-eight-foot ceilings, where we recorded mostly classical works and film scores. But Jimmy chose the larger one—even though it had only an eight-track recorder. He wanted the extra space so the drums could be miked properly for stereo.

I was a relative novice then, and what Jimmy wanted was a stretch, given Olympic's traditional way of miking drums. So I invented a new way. I didn't mike the snare, since that would have reduced the size and space of the drum sound. Instead, I used a stereo mike on an eight-foot boom above the drums, along with two distant side mikes to give the tom-toms edge, and a huge AKG D30 mike positioned about two feet from the bass drum. Jimmy knew that high-end mikes didn't have to be up against an instrument to maximize the sound.

**PAGE:** For the song to work as this panoramic audio experience, I needed Bonzo [drummer John Bonham] to really stand out, so that every stick stroke sounded clear and you could really feel them. If the drums were recorded just right, we could lay in everything else.

**CHKIANTZ:** To make the drums sound impressive, I placed them on a platform about one and a half feet off the floor. The floor at Olympic was made of wood, not cement, which meant I needed to keep any drum movement from transmitting rumble across the wood floor to other microphones. When we began taping, [lead singer] Robert Plant sang in the studio, but eventually he moved to the vocal booth to better isolate his voice. At one point, Jimmy began fooling around with a theremin [an electronic instrument] that he brought to the studio. We worked it in when the song shifted into a weird, free form.

**PAGE:** The theremin's eerie sound begged for more experimentation. To get my guitar to sound surreal, I detuned it and pulled on the strings for a far-out effect. I was playing a Sunburst 1958 Les Paul Standard guitar I had bought from [James Gang guitarist] Joe Walsh in San Francisco when we were out there on tour. The Standard had this tonal versatility, allowing me to get a blistering high pitch. Robert's vocal was just as extreme. He kept gaining confidence during the session and gave it everything he had. His vocals, like my solos, were about performance. He was pushing to see what he could get out of himself. We were performing for each other, almost competitively.

When we toured the U.S. again in May and June, we took the rough-mix tapes along with us in a large trunk. In Los Angeles, we'd work at studios like Mirror, Mystic, and A&M to overdub material. In New York, we worked at Mayfair, Groove, and Juggy studios. Today, digital files are e-mailed all over the place, but back then you actually had to take your tapes if you wanted to work on the road.

When we were ready to mix all the songs for the album, I wanted Eddie Kramer to do it. Eddie had engineered several of the album's songs from scratch in London, and he had worked with us in the American studios. He also had engineered Jimi Hendrix's albums. But by the summer Eddie had relocated to the States, so when we were in New York in August, we called him. "Whole Lotta Love" was all there on tape, but it needed a big, polished mix for the album.

**EDDIE KRAMER:** The first time I heard "Whole Lotta Love" was in August '69, when Jimmy and I started working on the album's final mix at New York's A&R Recording. Jimmy and I had first met in 1964, when he was playing on the Kinks' first album [*Kinks*] at Pye Studios and I was the assistant engineer. I also had heard Led Zeppelin early on in '68, when John Paul Jones played me an acetate of Led Zeppelin's first album, before it was released. I was blown away—it sounded so hard and heavy.

In New York, the recording console at A&R was fairly primitive. It had only twelve channels, with old-fashioned rotary dials to control track levels instead of sliding faders, and there were just two pan pots [control knobs] to send the sound from left to right channels. But as Jimmy and I listened to the mix, something unexpected came up.

At the point where the song breaks and Robert slowly wails, "Way down inside . . . woman . . . you need . . . love," Jimmy and

I heard this faint voice singing the lyric before Robert did on the master vocal track. Apparently Robert had done two different vocals, recording them on two different tracks. Even when I turned the volume down all the way on the track that we didn't want, his powerful voice was bleeding through the console and onto the master.

Some people today still think the faint voice was a pre-echo, that we added it on purpose for effect. It wasn't—it was an accident. Once Jimmy and I realized we had to live with it on the master, I looked at Jimmy, he looked at me, and we both reached for the reverb knob at the same time and cracked up laughing. Our instincts were the same—to douse the faint, intruding voice in reverb so it sounded part of the master plan.

**PAGE:** I hadn't heard anything like that before, and loved it. I was always looking for things like that when I recorded. That's the beauty of old recording equipment. Robert's faraway voice sounded otherworldly, like a spirit anticipating the vocal he was about to deliver.

**KRAMER:** By adding reverb, we made his faint voice more dynamic, and it became part of rock history. I also used the pan pots on Jimmy's guitar solo to fling it from side to side, so it would move from one speaker to another. I loved the sonic imagery, and I like to think of my mixes as stereophonic paintings.

On the break after the first chorus, where the song gets quiet and we hear Bonzo's cymbals and percussion and Jimmy's distortion, Jimmy and I went nuts on the knobs. We had eight dials controlling the levels on eight individual tracks, so we rehearsed the choreography of what we were going to do to create the far-out sounds. Then we did it and printed the result onto the master stereo reel. Because Jimmy was a studio brat, he really understood how we could push the limits. When you have limitations in the studio, you go for it and stretch your imagination.

**PAGE:** Some people said later that "Whole Lotta Love" was based on Willie Dixon's "You Need Love" [recorded by Muddy Waters and released in 1962] and the Small Faces' "You Need Loving" [released in 1966]. My riff—the basis for the entire song—sounds nothing like either of them. Robert had referenced the Dixon lyrics because with my riff, they felt right. This eventually forced us to give Dixon a cocredit on our song. But if you take Robert's vocal out, there's no musical reference to either song.

When we were done, "Whole Lotta Love" ran 5:33, which was great since at the time it was too long to edit for a single. So Atlantic released the album version as a single. We loved that. But soon after, Atlantic cut the single down to 3:12 to satisfy AM radio. Weeks before its release, they sent me an acetate of the edit. I played it once, hated it, and never listened to the short version again.

Janis Joplin on the roof of New York's Chelsea Hotel in June 1970.
*The Estate of David Gahr/Getty Images*

# 25: Mercedes Benz

**JANIS JOPLIN**

*Released: January 1971*

Once record companies granted rock artists their wish to record albums in the late 1960s, the pressure ramped up. From the start, record labels demanded that artists deliver at least two albums a year, an industry standard then that gave fans six months to digest what they had bought before another album by the artist landed in record stores. The two-album annual minimum also made artists worthy of investment and profitable to produce. But from the artist's perspective, a six-month turnaround was enormous pressure. New material had to be written and rehearsed, often on tour, and working in the studio wasn't an easy process. What's more, many bands found it hard to hold on to key members over long stretches. After the first or second album, many artists felt the pressure of label demands, concerts, and stardom, and they burned out. Relentless work schedules compromised personal lives, sleep habits, diets, and health. Drug and alcohol abuse increased as artists sought ways to energize before concerts, loosen up during studio recording sessions, wind down at odd hours, and offset the emotional stress of isolation and the physical demands of performing.

In 1970, Janis Joplin was just barely coping. She had resumed her heroin use after returning from a cleansing trip to Brazil early that year. Then came the end of a serious romantic relationship. In May, she began touring with her new group, the Full Tilt Boogie Band, and her performing schedule filled up through the fall. Though she had halted her heroin use that summer and seemed full of energy and enthusiasm, Joplin felt cornered by creative

demands and resumed her heroin habit in the early fall, according
to a biography by older sister Laura Joplin. For Janis Joplin, alcohol wasn't efficient, since it prevented her from working.

In August 1970, Joplin was in Port Chester, New York, to perform at the Capitol Theatre. Before the concert, Joplin, songwriter-
friend Bob Neuwirth, and actors Rip Torn and Geraldine Page hit
a local bar. After a few drinks, Joplin began riffing on a line from
a Michael McClure poem about asking God for a Mercedes-Benz.
Joplin improvised lyrics as she sang, and Neuwirth jotted them
down on bar napkins, throwing in a verse of his own. A half hour
later Joplin performed the new song on stage. She also sang it
again in October while recording her album *Pearl*. Three days
later, Joplin was dead of a heroin overdose, and "Mercedes Benz"
would be the last song she recorded. *Pearl* was released in January
1971, just three months after her death, and the album went to
No. 1 on *Billboard*'s chart for nine weeks. It was inducted into the
Grammy Hall of Fame in 2010. "Mercedes Benz" was issued as a
single in April on the B-side of "Cry Baby," which only reached
No. 42.

**Interviews with JOHN BYRNE COOKE (Janis Joplin's
road manager), BOB NEUWIRTH (cowriter),
MICHAEL MCCLURE (cowriter and poet),
CLARK PIERSON (drummer in Joplin's Full Tilt Boogie Band),
and BRAD CAMPBELL (bassist in the Full Tilt Boogie Band)**

**JOHN BYRNE COOKE:** Back in the summer of 1970, Janis and the
Full Tilt Boogie Band were on tour, arriving in New York at the
start of August. On Saturday, August 8, Janis and the band performed at the Capitol Theatre in Port Chester, New York, and
then appeared at Harvard Stadium on August 12. Three days later,
she attended her high school reunion in Port Arthur, Texas,
before traveling to Los Angeles in September to record what
would be her final studio album, *Pearl,* at Sunset Sound. She was

happy in L.A. and knew she was hitting a new level in her singing career.

**BOB NEUWIRTH (COWRITER):** I first met Janis before she was famous. We both played the same small clubs in San Francisco in 1965. In early August 1970, I was living in New York when Janis came to town for a series of performances. She was staying at the Chelsea Hotel. On August 8, she wasn't exactly thrilled about having to travel an hour north to perform in Port Chester. She felt the opening acts—Seatrain and Runt—would attract a crowd that didn't understand her music.

Janis had spoken often about how much she admired actress Geraldine Page. I knew Geraldine's husband, Rip Torn, and since they both were in town, I invited them to travel up to Port Chester with us late that afternoon in the limo. While Janis was still upstairs getting ready, Rip and Geraldine came over for a drink at El Quijote, a Spanish restaurant in the hotel. I didn't tell Janis they were coming. I wanted it to be a surprise. When Janis came down and saw Geraldine, she lit up. A few margaritas later, they were old pals, and we were ready to go. We rode up in one car and the band traveled in another.

Around 7 p.m., after the Capitol sound check, we had a couple of hours to kill before Seatrain and Runt finished their sets. So the four of us walked to a bar about three minutes away called Vahsen's [at 30 Broad Street]. At the table, Janis and Geraldine bonded again, and all of us were getting into it. At some point, Janis sang out, "Oh Lord, won't you buy me a Mercedes-Benz." Earlier, in San Francisco, Janis had heard Michael McClure's song that opened with a line like that and it had stuck with her. But she couldn't remember the rest of it.

**MICHAEL McCLURE:** Allen Ginsberg introduced me to Bob Dylan when Bob was in San Francisco in December 1965. After we met and hung out, Bob gave me an autoharp—a stringed Appalachian folk instrument. Bob knew I wanted to write songs. I kept the instrument on my mantel for three months before learning to play it. In 1966, while I was writing "Freewheelin' Frank" with Hells Angel Frank Reynolds, [musician] George Montana came over in the evenings with strange instruments, and we'd add music to the songs I was writing and singing.

One of my songs started, "Come on, God, and buy me a Mercedes-Benz." The song would get longer and shorter each time I sang it. One day I got a call from [actor-singer] Emmett Grogan. He had heard me sing the song at my house and began singing it with his friends at a local pool hall. On the phone, he said he was shooting pool with Janis and that now she was singing it, too. I told him I had nothing against that.

**NEUWIRTH:** At the Port Chester bar, Janis sang the line a few times. Then Rip and Geraldine began banging their beer glasses on the table to keep time. It was like a sea shanty. Janis came up with words for the first verse. I was in charge of writing them down on bar napkins with a ballpoint pen. She came up with the second verse, too, about a color TV. I suggested words here and there, and came up with the third verse—about asking the Lord to buy us a night on the town and another round.

Janis and I were giggling and showing off a bit in front of Rip and Geraldine. The alcohol wasn't meant to do anything except keep us laughing in that bar, but it assumed control, and what followed was "Mercedes Benz." I figured that what we were doing there was just an exercise to impress Rip and Geraldine and pass the time, nothing more.

While we were lost in all this blather and laughter, John Cooke, her road manager, came blasting in close to 9 p.m. to tell Janis she was on in fifteen minutes. The next thing I knew we were back up the block at the Capitol. Janis came on stage, and after opening with "Tell Mama" and "Half Moon," she surprised everyone by announcing she wanted to sing a new song.

On the bootleg recording from the concert, she says from the stage: "I'd like to do a song of some significance now. I just wrote it at the bar on the corner, so I don't know all the words yet. I'm going to do it Acapulco," which had been my funny way of saying "a cappella." I think she decided to sing it to further impress Geraldine and Rip.

Janis stomped off the beat and began belting out the lyrics, the way she had done at the bar. The band tried to fit in as best they could, and then they reprised the last verse. What's interesting is that the second verse doesn't include the "Dialing for Dollars" line. She must have added it later before recording in the studio in L.A., since it's not on the Harvard Stadium bootleg either.

When Janis finished at the Capitol in Port Chester, she seemed proud of herself and eager to explain the song and its origins. She said to the audience: "Thank you, thank you, thank you. That's not even a song, you know. They turned the jukebox up [at the bar], but we kept singing it anyway. They turned up 'Hey Jude' so loud we had to order another drink."

**CLARK PIERSON:** The band was pretty surprised she sang "Mercedes Benz" that night. We didn't have a key for the song and didn't realize she was going to sing it alone. We just all looked at each other and tried to follow along. Janis could remember lyrics stone-cold flawlessly, so that wasn't a surprise to me. The audience was just staring at first, like, what's going on? Then they had smiles and were clapping along in time. Several nights later she sang it again at Harvard Stadium, which turned out to be her last concert.

**BRAD CAMPBELL:** On "Mercedes Benz" at the Capitol, Janis wanted to accompany herself on guitar. She took out her Gibson Sunburst and whispered to us, "Watch me boys." But instead of playing it, she just sang. We eventually played a few notes here and there and sang where we could, figuring she wanted us to follow her.

**MCCLURE:** At some point in August 1970, Janis called. She said she was performing the "Mercedes Benz" song but that hers was different than mine. She sang it over the phone. When she was done, I said it was OK. Then I went for my autoharp and sat on the stairs and sang her mine over the phone. Janis's version was sweet and wry and had the grace of a riddle. Mine was much more outspoken, funny, and ironic. Janis laughed and said she liked hers better. I said, "That's OK, you can sing yours." And that's the last I heard of it until *Pearl* came out in January '71 and I saw my name with Janis's on the song credit. [Neuwirth's name was added later.]

**PIERSON:** On October 1, 1970, the Full Tilt Boogie Band and Janis were at Sunset Sound in L.A. recording *Pearl* when something happened to the tape recorder. Everything came to a halt. As producer Paul Rothchild tried to fix it, we started getting antsy, especially Janis, who didn't like sitting around. She was still in the vocal booth and could see through the glass that our energy was fading. To kill time and keep us amused, she started to sing "Mercedes Benz" in there.

**CAMPBELL:** I could see Janis in the booth. She beat off time by stomping her foot on the floor with her sandals. The bracelets jangling on her arm and the stomping of her feet provided the rhythmic sound you hear on the record. Her eyes were open as she sang, but they seemed closed, as if she were far away. When the song was done, she said, "That's it," followed by her famous cackle. She always surprised herself.

**NEUWIRTH:** Paul Rothchild told me later the problem was with his two-inch tape recorder. The heads had shifted or something and needed to be readjusted. Paul always had a quarter-inch safety reel going as a backup in case there was an artist idea he missed in between takes when the two-inch main recorder was off. While Paul worked to fix the two-inch tape recorder, Janis sang "Mercedes Benz" on a whim. Fortunately, the safety tape caught it.

COOKE: "Mercedes Benz" was the last song Janis recorded. Three days later I found her body in her room at the Landmark Motor Hotel. She had overdosed on heroin that was way stronger than street heroin had any right to be. For the next few days, everyone was in shock. That Thursday, Paul Rothchild played for us everything he had on tape. It was almost an album. Paul and the band worked for another ten days to create the best instrumental tracks to go with the existing vocals. Although she had sung "Mercedes Benz" a cappella, Paul knew we had to use it as is, without overdubs or embellishment.

NEUWIRTH: About twenty years ago, I had a guitar case overflowing with stuff. It was so full I couldn't close the lid with the instrument inside. I went through all the junk in there and found four bar napkins on which I had jotted down the "Mercedes Benz" lyrics in 1970. I have no idea where those napkins are today. I'd love to find them. I put them someplace in my house, but I can't remember where.

Mick Jagger on tour in Los Angeles with the Rolling Stones in early June 1972.

*Photograph by Norman Seeff*

# 26: Moonlight Mile
**THE ROLLING STONES**
*Released: April 1971*

Meeting the new album production schedules of record labels in the late 1960s and early '70s was demanding work, even for top rock musicians, but touring posed another set of hardships. Out on the road, there was little in the way of security for major acts at increasingly larger performance spaces. Concert dates often were added to schedules at the last minute, and there were long periods of downtime between performances, which led to drug and alcohol abuse and encounters with groupies to pass the time. Band managers who were eager to hold down costs often chose the least expensive lodging and transportation, while some siphoned off the gate revenue. While early rock tours in the 1950s and '60s had been relatively short and were staged in ballrooms and auditoriums or outdoors at fairs, farm shows, and amusement parks, by the late 1960s concert spaces were mostly theaters, stadiums, and newly built indoor sports arenas. Larger venues meant growing stacks of on-stage speaker systems, damaged eardrums, and higher stress levels. Meanwhile, stoned audiences raised the risk that fans would charge the stage.

In Europe, where top American and British bands toured, travel between concert sites was often done at night. It was more cost-efficient for a manager to have a band jump on a bus or train after a performance than to pay for another night at a hotel, especially since the overnight trip meant the band could catch some rest before arriving at the next destination. In addition, traveling during off-hours provided the shroud of darkness, minimizing the number of fans who might mob bands at stations and aboard trains. For some bands, European audiences could be particularly problematic. Many fans who were high or drunk became rowdy, or simply wanted to mimic the unruly behavior of fans at previous concert sites written about in local papers.

The summer and fall of 1970 were particularly rough for the Rolling Stones during their tour of Continental Europe. During the band's eighteen-city, two-month tour, Mick Jagger was particularly down, coping with a growing feeling of isolation and a series of stage confrontations with concert audiences. Fans were rough in Hamburg, Germany, and in Milan, Italy, engaging in police battles and halting performances. In response, Jagger wrote a song between engagements aboard a night train while looking out the window at the moonlit landscape flying by. The ballad expressed his weariness with touring—the relentless travel, the madness of fans, the crush of clutching strangers. Back home in England just after the tour, Jagger, along with guitarist Mick Taylor and drummer Charlie Watts, recorded the basic track for "Moonlight Mile." Jagger sang it with the melancholy feel of a Delta blues. The song appeared on the Rolling Stones' *Sticky Fingers* album, which hit No. 1 for four consecutive weeks in 1971 on the *Billboard* chart and was inducted into the Grammy Hall of Fame in 1999.

### Interview with MICK JAGGER (Rolling Stones lead singer and songwriter)

**MICK JAGGER:** I wrote some of the early lyrics to "Moonlight Mile" in a songbook I carried around when we were on tour in the summer of 1970. I was growing road-weary and homesick then. I'm sure the idea for the song first came to me one night while we were on a train and the moon was out. I don't recall. I know I didn't want to literalize how I was feeling. That's not really a very good thing to do when you're writing lyrics, you know? The feeling I had at that moment was how difficult it was to be touring and how I wasn't looking forward to going out and doing it again. It's a very lonely thing, and my lyrics reflected that.

I came up with an Oriental-Indian riff on my acoustic guitar on the train. At some point during the tour I played it for Mick Taylor, because I thought he would like it. At that point, I really hadn't intended on recording the song. Sometimes you don't want to record what you're writing. You think, "This isn't worth recording, this is just my doodling."

When we finished our European tour in October 1970, we were at Stargroves, my country house in England. We were sitting around one night and I started working on what I had initially written. I felt great. I was in my house again and it was very relaxing. So the song became about that—looking forward to returning from a foreign place while looking out the window of a train and the images of the railway line going by in the moonlight.

But the lyrics I wrote didn't come across like that, because they weren't so on-the-nose. They were more imaginative and wistful than if I had written them straight, like, "I'm tired of the road," you know? The feeling I wanted was the image of elongated space that you're traveling through to get home: "Oh I am sleeping under strange, strange skies/Just another mad, mad day on the road/My dreams is fading down the railway line/I'm just about a moonlight mile down the road." It was about the difficulty I was going through of being away.

In most cases now, I try to analyze what I'm writing and try to make sense of it and re-jig the grammar and everything. I try not to cross between first person and third person and all that. Back then, I didn't really do that, and in this song, I don't really think it mattered. I think it's good that I just did what I was feeling. There are a lot of different images jumbled in there that come across as one. But it's definitely not about cocaine. There's no hidden meaning in there about that. It's feeling I'm finally home and thinking about the times when I was lonely on the road.

Sometimes you write songs on your own and you do the demo and then you go into the studio and change it around. But sometimes you just write songs and record them at the same time. This was one of those songs, though I did add a bit more to it later. So at Stargroves, I was just doodling the song and I worked out a couple of different parts to it.

At some point during the evening, I think Keith [Richards] left to go home, and Bill [Wyman] for some reason wasn't there. After Keith left, just Charlie, myself, and Mick [Taylor] were in the room. I finished doodling pretty late, probably around midnight, and we started playing the song to see how it sounded.

I'd already come up with the guitar riff, so I started playing it and singing. I was playing my guitar when Mick added something, and then Charlie started playing. That's when I realized it was more than doodling, that this was a real song we could record as we fooled around with it. The instrumentation was really interesting and created this really interesting mood.

Several hours later, we decided to record. At the house, there was a big living room when you walked in, sort of a big double-height imitation-Gothic hall. It had a nice high ceiling, so we recorded most everything in there. Mick and I were both familiar with the song's melody lines. But then you get someone like Charlie playing the drums and you find you're building an atmosphere.

Honestly, I wasn't really thinking about whether the song's opening would be Japanese or Indian. Obviously, the tones or scales I used gave it an Oriental flavor, which is echoed later in the string writing. Most of the song is more Indian to me. I listened to a lot of Indian music then, and little bits rubbed off on me. These things were hinted at when the song goes into the B section, where the beat comes in [sings]: "Oh I'm sleeping under strange, strange skies"—when it goes into that. Then it's kind of left behind and it goes into something else. The verses are also slightly Indian in their inception.

Charlie's use of the mallets was remarkable and let him dispense with the big offbeat. So you get this rhythmic subtlety that goes along with the guitar lines. It's so moody. But nothing was planned. It was all spur-of-the-moment, which is the beauty of the song. Of course, some of the things we added later were there to enhance the mood we had come up with—like overdubbed guitars by Keith and Mick, Bill's bass, Jimmy Price's piano, and Paul Buckmaster's strings. It was a question of building the song and then bringing down the dynamic and how you use the instrumentation to do that.

What makes "Moonlight Mile" special is that it's a song and a recording at once. All these things —the strange plinking piano, the tom-tommy mallets on the drums, the different guitars—they all came together to produce a feeling of vulnerability and loneliness, you know what I mean? I think the three of us finished recording the basic track around 6 a.m. The sun was coming up.

Later, I added a bit of double-tracking to fill out my vocal, but not much. I actually do that quite a lot on recordings. Sometimes you don't hear it or you're not even aware of it. On "Moonlight Mile," I double-tracked the odd lines just for emphasis. On some records I'll double-track the lead vocals and then do harmonies up and harmonies down to give them a stronger feel. In this case, we mixed the song so the double-track sound was just marginally there.

It was my idea to use Paul [Buckmaster] to arrange the strings. I had used him before, on the end of "Sway" [on *Sticky Fingers*]. For this piece, we thought it would be nice to build the song with strings and have those hinted quarter tones that Paul's so good at. His orchestration echoes what I'm singing and builds into the coda, so it amplifies all the stuff you heard before in a rather subtle way. Then he has a really nice edit that mellows when I sing, "Yeah, I'm coming home."

The other day I was listening to the original "Moonlight Mile" before we rehearsed it in Los Angeles for the Zip Code tour. I was with Bernard Fowler, who has been my background vocalist since '85. He does my double-track voices on stage in concert. Unfortunately, I can't do them live [laughs]. Anyway, it was quite a process. We went through the lines on the original recording to analyze which ones I had done alone and which ones I had doubled. In performance, the doubling effect is even bigger than on the album, because there are more people singing on it.

On our 2015 tour, I played electric guitar on "Moonlight Mile" instead of acoustic guitar, which I played on the original. I played the electric guitar open-tuned, the same way I did on *Sticky Fingers*. I don't really like how acoustic guitar sounds live. It sounds all banjo-y to me. The amplification of an acoustic guitar isn't really brilliant, you know? To be honest, it's much easier playing electric on stage, because it's more controllable—the sound and effects and everything. So I sounded slightly different, but the arrangement had the same mood. We also had a really nice string sample that sounded close to the original strings. That helped the ending build.

Keith played an open-tuned guitar with me on stage. He kind of did a bit of what my part is and did other things, too. There was a lot going on with the live version, so it was tricky to make sure it wasn't too cluttered. The way we do it now live is much more confident than on the album, and I'm a lot more confident with it. When you get the song out in a very big place, it still seems quite intimate. Yet it's still hard to do in a large arena, you know? It's hard to get it right. I more or less do the vocal in a similar style, and it's pretty personal and honest.

When I hear "Moonlight Mile" now, I really like it. I think it's a good piece of music. It's unusual, and it's still accessible and delicate and has a climax and comes back down and ends quite well. I suppose I've also grown a little more accustomed to touring [laughs].

Rod Stewart in a London office in mid-August 1973.

*John McKenzie, London*

# 27: Maggie May
## ROD STEWART
*Released: August 1971*

The mandolin has always been a bit player in rock. Developed in Italy in the early eighteenth century, the instrument was compact and lightweight, making it ideal for itinerant musicians to tote around Europe. When waves of European immigrants arrived in the U.S. in the late 1800s, they brought along the instrument. There was enough of a demand in the U.S. that Gibson began producing mandolins in 1894, and the instrument soon found its way down South, becoming a mainstay of early blues artists and string bands in the 1920s. In the 1940s, mandolinist Bill Monroe formed the Original Bluegrass Band and became the instrument's first pop virtuoso.

Over the decades, the mandolin has kept a relatively low profile in American pop music, turning up most often in roots, folk, and Celtic music, or in the soundtracks of movies such as *The Godfather* to add Old World flavor. In the late 1960s, some folk and rock artists began including the mandolin to add an Americana touch to their music. But even then, the instrument was used sparingly, given its nervous energy and high-pitched twang. Prior to 1971, the mandolin was mixed in sparingly on songs by bands including the Rolling Stones ("Love in Vain"), the Band ("Rag Mama Rag"), and the Grateful Dead ("Friend of the Devil").

In 1971, as Rod Stewart planned his third solo album, *Every Picture Tells a Story*, he wanted to feature the mandolin prominently on several of the album's songs to provide a more quaint, Gaelic feel. Ray Jackson, from the folk-rock group Lindisfarne, was brought in to add the mandolin, and the instrument's rustic sound provided depth and character behind Stewart's distinctive voice on *Maggie May*. After the song about a deflowered protagonist was released as a single in August 1971, it hit No. 1 on *Billboard*'s pop chart for five weeks, while the album was No. 1 for four weeks.

**Interview with ROD STEWART (singer-songwriter)**

**ROD STEWART:** In July 1961, a few of my mates and I went off to the south of England to camp out at the Beaulieu Jazz Festival. The concert was held on the lawns of an estate owned by Lord Montagu, who was a big jazz fan. I was sixteen and just coming out of my beatnik phase, wondering whether I should become a Mod. It was a transitional period for me, with days of much confusion.

At the time, I was into mainstream jazz—not Dixieland or modern but guys like [saxophonists] Tubby Hayes and Johnny Dankworth. A year earlier, there had been a riot at the jazz festival, so going there in '61 came with a bit of intrigue.

That afternoon, we snuck into the festival through a large runoff pipe and eventually made our way to a beer tent. There, I met an older woman who was something of a sexual predator. One thing led to the next, and we ended up nearby on a secluded patch of lawn. I was a virgin, and all I could think is, "This is it, Rod Stewart, you'd better put on a good performance here or else your reputation will be ruined all over North London." But it was all over in a few seconds. Her name wasn't Maggie May, but the experience I had with her would influence the writing of the song ten years later.

In 1971, I was both the lead singer in the Faces and I was signed to Mercury as a solo artist. I was planning to record my third solo album, *Every Picture Tells a Story*, when I met Martin Quittenton, a guitarist and songwriter who had been in a blues-rock band called Steamhammer.

Martin seemed like a very sophisticated, educated guy, and I was looking for good acoustic musicians for my upcoming album.

I invited Martin over to my house in Muswell Hill, which had a beautiful view of North London. As we sat and talked in my sitting room, Martin took out his guitar and started running through an old Bob Dylan song. It may have been Dylan's "It's All Over Now, Baby Blue," but I can't recall.

Then Martin began playing chords to a song he had written. I rather liked them. I told him, "You strum and I'll sing." I still write like this today. I'll work with a guitarist, and when I hear a lovely set of chords, I'll start humming and adding words to see what comes of it.

As Martin played, I started singing "Maggie Mae," an old Liverpudlian folk song about a prostitute. The Beatles had included it on *Let It Be* a year earlier. As I sang, the idea of a hooker popped into my head, then the jazz festival when I was sixteen, and then losing my virginity. It all flooded back as Martin and I got into it and I started coming up with words.

But I didn't write anything down. I merely created a vocal sketch in my mind of the song by humming along and improvising lines here and there to match Martin's melody. Lyrics weren't important at that point, only the feel. As with any song I eventually record, I first wanted to develop an emotional connection.

Martin and I kept at it until we were both satisfied with what we had. When we finished, I said, "Right, we have enough of a line here to bring it into the studio. Let me book drums and bass and we'll produce it all there."

We recorded a rough instrumental track at Morgan Sound Studios in Willesden, London. I sang abstract lines on top of the music to remind me later of the feel I wanted. [He hums the melody to "Maggie May," singing words here and there, such as "Since you've been away it's been so long" and "Just because of you, all my nights are blue."] When we were done, I took the tape home to write the lyrics.

Even today, I always want the melody line first. Then I put the words and music together later like a jigsaw puzzle. With "Maggie May," I listened back a few times to the demo tape we had made and paused, saying to myself, "Right, what have I got here?" It's sort of like sizing up the music to help determine the story I want to tell. I began thinking back on that day at the jazz festival and I came up with a song about a young guy who has been with an older woman and the aftermath going through his head.

I still have the black notebook with red binding down the back that I used to write all the lyrics. My scribbling for "Maggie May" filled about twenty pages. What was unusual about the words is that they turned out to be more of a story than a traditional song that circles back to a sing-along chorus. That was my fault, really. Telling stories is what I'm best at. I also didn't use the name "Maggie May" in the lyrics—just the name "Maggie." "May" popped onto the end of "Maggie" in the title at some point.

When it was time to record, we didn't rehearse. That's the beauty of what we did back then. I just got together with the five musicians on the session (guitarist/bassist Ronnie Wood, guitarist Martin Quittenton, organist Ian McLagan, mandolinist Ray Jackson, and drummer Micky Waller) and told them what I wanted to do with the music and where in the song I wanted things to happen. Both Ronnie and Mac [Ian McLagan] were in the Faces with me. I didn't have a clue about the technical aspects of music, but I could feel it. If you can feel it, you can speak it. That's the innocent beauty of what we did. But we had a problem.

Micky, who was a studio drummer then, showed up without a full drum kit. Somehow he had forgotten his cymbals, so all he had were his drums. I was relatively unknown then and couldn't really afford to cancel the session, pay the musicians, and pay them again for another session just so Micky could grab all his gear.

Fortunately, Micky was superb. Like [Rolling Stones drummer] Charlie Watts, Micky had come up in Britain's jazz world. That's why on the record, the drums sound pronounced. We overdubbed the cymbals later, which is why you hear them faintly. Micky forgetting to bring his cymbals actually gave "Maggie May" a sharper beat.

I knew I wanted Ronnie to play eight bars on the electric guitar for the intro and then play guitar and bass behind Martin's acoustic guitar. I also wanted Ronnie to overdub bluesy guitar solos in the middle and toward the end, to break up the song, which meant we had to leave room on the song for those.

I had Ian hold his organ chords for full measures, so the song would have a density behind the guitar work. Ray was in the folk-rock band Lindisfarne at the time, and I asked him if he could give me sort of a joyous mandolin solo at the end, which I knew would add the traditional folk feel I was looking for.

Once all of the music was recorded, my vocal was last to go on. The falsetto "whoo hoo-hoo" I added at the end had first popped out when we were making the demo, so I added it again on the recording.

At first, "Maggie May" wasn't going to be on the album. It was too unusual. The song ran longer than five minutes and it didn't have a catchy chorus. But as we finished up the album, we found we were a song short. So we added "Maggie May," since it was already produced.

For the album version, we added a short, thirty two-second intro called "Henry" that Martin wrote and, as I recall, handled on mandolin. Since there would be a gap between his intro and "Maggie May," Martin would get paid separately for "Henry." I wanted to give him an extra bonus. No matter how long a stand-alone song is, you still get credit and royalties for it. But I have no idea why Martin called it "Henry."

When the single was released, Mercury for some reason put "Maggie May" on the B-side, with "Reason to Believe" on the A-side. It wasn't until a radio disc jockey in the States flipped over the 45 and began playing "Maggie May" that the song began to catch on.

At first, I didn't think much of "Maggie May." I guess that's because the record company didn't believe in the song. I didn't have much confidence then. I figured it was best to listen to the guys who knew better. What I learned is that sometimes they do and sometimes they don't.

Joni Mitchell in Big Sur, California, in 1970 with her Princess mountain dulcimer, which she played on her album *Blue* in early 1971.

*GAB Archive/Getty Images*

# 28: Carey
## JONI MITCHELL
*Released: August 1971*

In the summer of 2014, I pitched Joni Mitchell on an interview about the writing and recording of her song "Carey," which appears on her acclaimed album *Blue* (1971). Mitchell liked the idea and suggested we do the interview at her home in Los Angeles rather than talk by phone. I flew out in October, and after I arrived at her 1920s Spanish Revival house and parked on the steep decline of the driveway, I was ushered out to a covered tile patio bordering a courtyard. As I looked down at a swimming pool one level below on her wooded Bel Air property, a husky voice came up behind me, "Hey, New Yorker." Mitchell had arrived barefoot, her hair down, wearing a flowing white top and long skirt. For the next two hours, she chain-smoked American Spirit cigarettes and talked about her months in Matala, Crete, in 1970 and her relationship with Cary Raditz, the song's namesake.

When Mitchell recorded "Carey" in early 1971, the female singer-songwriter era was just unfolding. Mary Travers, Jackie DeShannon, and Laura Nyro, among others, had started the ball rolling in the early 1960s. Then Judy Collins had a hit with Mitchell's "Both Sides Now" in 1967. In February 1971, Carole King released the album *Tapestry*, and in April Carly Simon released her eponymous album featuring "That's the Way I've Always Heard It Should Be." Mitchell's *Blue* arrived in June and it was clearly a personal, long-form work, an anxiety-driven concept album that connected with women on an almost secretive, metaphysical level. Though "Carey" charted at No. 93 when it was released as a pop single in August, *Blue* reached No. 15 on *Billboard*'s album chart and is among Mitchell's most critically acclaimed recordings. *Blue* was inducted into the Grammy Hall of Fame in 1999.

What I remember most about my two hours with Mitchell are her eyes. She had a way of making a point and then fixing on you with a locked gaze as she took a drag from her cigarette. The gaze tended to linger longer than it should have and seemed to be sizing up whether a point she had made resonated. Even though her articulation was clear and immediately understood, her eyes seemed to have their doubts or were seeking more animated confirmation, perhaps out of habit. Eventually, Mitchell let go and moved on. To this day, her gaze reminds me of an overly cautious mother watching her kids board a school bus and following them with her eyes until they are seated.

### Interview with JONI MITCHELL (singer-songwriter)

**JONI MITCHELL:** Everyone said I broke Graham Nash's heart when our relationship ended in late 1969. But that's not quite accurate. We both knew it was over, and it wasn't an ugly ending. Reasons for the break are complicated, but Graham and David Crosby were becoming inseparable, which was increasingly tough on me. In late January of 1970, David asked me to sail with him on his boat, the *Mayan*. But when I came aboard in Jamaica in early February, no one told me Graham would be there. It was an awkward thing to do, to put us in that position. When we reached Panama, I left, flying to San Francisco to meet my friend Penelope and start a preplanned trip to Greece.

The truth is after Graham and I separated, I was really depressed. I believed in that relationship, and suddenly it was over. I had a hard time believing in my own word. I also lost most of my Los Angeles friends, who had been my constant community. When I left him, they took his side. All of this was very painful.

In Greece, Penelope and I spent the first few days in Athens. I didn't think I looked like a hippie, but I definitely didn't look Greek.

My fair hair made me stand out. During the day, I'd pile it up on my head. It was a conservative look, like a schoolteacher. Still, my hair seemed to offend people, mostly men, who called out with a big grin on their faces, "Sheepy, sheepy, Matala, Matala." I asked around about the phrase and was told it meant, "Hippie, hippie, go to Matala in Crete. That's where your kind are."

A few days later, Penelope and I were on a ferry to see what Matala was all about. We arrived in Heraklion on Crete's north coast and stayed in a hotel the first night. The next day, I rented a VW Bug and we drove forty-five miles to Matala, a fishing village on the south coast. There weren't any homes in Matala, just two grocery stores, a bakery where the owner made fresh yogurt and bread, a general store with the only phone in town, two cafes, and a few rental huts. Most of the "hippies" who had traveled there slept in small caves carved into the cliff on one side of the beach.

After we arrived, Penelope and I rented a cinder-block hut in a nearby poppy field and walked down to the beach. As we stood staring out, an explosion went off behind us. I turned around just in time to see this guy with a red beard blowing through the door of a cafe. He was wearing a white turban, white Nehru shirt, and white cotton pants. I said to Penelope, "What an entrance—I have to meet this guy." He wasn't hurt, but all the hair on his arms and legs were singed from the blast. He was American and a cook at one of the cafes. Apparently, when he had lit the stove, it blew him out the door. That's how Cary [Raditz] entered my life—ka-boom!

The next night, Penelope and I went to the Mermaid Cafe for a drink with Cary. Several hippies were there, along with some soldiers. Someone recommended this clear Turkish liquor called Raki. I wasn't a big drinker, and after three glasses I woke up the next morning alone in Cary's cave. The stacked leather heels of my city boots had broken off, apparently from climbing a mountain the night before. I had no recollection of the climb. Later, when I returned to my hut, Penelope was gone. I was told she went off with one of the soldiers from the Mermaid the night before. That was the last I saw of her for many years.

With Penelope gone, I was alone—and vulnerable. You have to understand the fragile emotional state I was in. I was still in pain, and had no one to talk to. Also, I had a bit of fame by then, and wherever I'd go, hippies would follow. I latched on to Cary because he seemed fierce and kept the crowd off my back. Soon I moved into one of the caves.

Originally the Minoans had lived in the caves, and then the Romans came and improved them by carving sleeping crypts and niches for statuary. But sleeping up there was tough. To soften the surface, beach pebbles were placed on the stone slab and covered with beach grass. I borrowed a scratchy afghan blanket and placed it on top. But there was no real comfort. When the waves were high and crashed on the beach, they shook the caves.

I enjoyed Cary's company, and his audacity. He had steely-cold blue eyes and a menacing grin, and he was a bit of a scoundrel. We were constantly in each other's company, and spent our days talking, taking long walks, going swimming, cooking, and doing the laundry. We just lived. One time we were in a park in Heraklion, where we sometimes went for the day. We were sitting on a bench when one of the tourist photographers came up to us and asked if we wanted our picture taken. He had a colorful box camera on a wooden tripod, so we said, "Yes." The pictures developed in minutes.

I also had my dulcimer with me from the States. It was lighter and less bulky than a guitar, and I took it with me everywhere. I used it to write "Carey" over a period of weeks in different locations in and around Matala as a birthday present for Cary. When hippies didn't follow me on hikes, I'd find solitary places to write. My lyric, "Oh Carey get out your cane" referred to a cane Cary carried with him all the time. He was a bit of a scene-stealer, and the cane was a theatrical prop for him. Sometimes he'd twirl it or balance it on his nose.

When I played the song for Cary on his birthday, I don't recall his reaction. He was always detached and sometimes even disrespectful—either trying to belittle me or make me feel afraid. I think at the time he felt greatly superior to women, which is why I refer to him in the lyrics as "a mean old Daddy." As for the extra *e* in his name in the song's title and lyric, that was a misspelling on my part.

In April, theater people in Matala cast hippies for a Greek production of *Hair*. Weeks later, Cary and I traveled to Athens to see them in the musical. The lead actor was Greek and had shorter than Beatle-length hair parted on the side and a Frank Sinatra-style beige raincoat over his shoulder as he sang, "I'm a hairy guy." We cracked up. It was so funny.

Athens was a turning point for me. I had had enough of Matala and, as I wrote in the lyrics to "Carey," I missed "my clean white linen and fancy French cologne." My hair was matted from washing it in seawater for months, I had beach tar on my feet, and I was flea-bitten this was very rugged living. I also realized I was still heartbroken about my split with Graham.

Instead of returning to Crete with Cary, I flew to Paris. There, I wrote "California" and referenced Cary in the lyrics as "the red, red rogue who cooked good omelets and stews." "Carey" and "California" are really part of the same musical novella, so Cary is in two scenes.

Back in the States, I wrote additional songs, and in early '71, I went into A&M Studios in Hollywood to record *Blue*. "Carey," like the rest of the album, is pretty sparse, instrumentally, and we recorded it behind locked doors. If someone came in, I'd burst into tears. I was in great psychological pain while recording all of *Blue*. It took several years for me to get over how I felt. On "Carey," I played the dulcimer and Stephen [Stills] played bass.

For me, recording songs like "Carey"—about deeply personal experiences—presented an artistic challenge. Songs I wrote were already a day, a week, a month or ten years old when I went into the studio. To rekindle my emotions, I used sense memory—which is like method acting. It happens naturally with me and helps me recall my feelings—the joy, anxiety, and vulnerability I felt when composing the song. I was emotionally wide open when recording *Blue,* and incapable of guile.

I haven't spoken to Cary in years. We remained friends, then he married and we lost contact. But every so often Matala comes back into my life. A couple of years ago, a friend sent me a newspaper article about Matala. It has been built up a bit, and there's an annual musical festival held there now. The article said that in Matala I'm more popular than Zeus. I thought that was funny, you know?

## Tracking Down the Real "Carey"
### Interview with CARY RADITZ (financial executive and the subject of Joni Mitchell's "Carey")

After interviewing Joni Mitchell about her song "Carey," I realized I needed to find the real Cary Raditz, to capture his side of the story. It took a little doing, but five calls later, I reached him, and we had a warm conversation about his time with Mitchell in Matala, Crete, in 1970. Over the phone, I could hear in Raditz's voice the intensity that Mitchell had talked about during our conversation at her home in Los Angeles. But I also heard someone who was still deeply moved by Mitchell and treasured the time they had spent together— free of responsibilities and most modern conveniences. For both Mitchell and Raditz, their Matala months would be a once-in-a-lifetime experience, immortalized in the lyrics of Mitchell's song. Cary wasn't such a "mean old Daddy" after all.

### How did you wind up in Matala?

In July 1969, I quit my job as a copywriter at an ad agency in Winston-Salem, North Carolina, flew to Luxembourg, and hitch-hiked to Munich to visit my girlfriend, who was interning for a chemical company. By October, the weather was getting colder and we decided to head to a warmer place, leaving the destination to fate. We stood in the fork of a southbound road in Munich and stuck out our thumbs. If our ride went right, we'd go to Spain. If the ride went left, we'd go to Greece, and that's how we wound up in Matala on Halloween of 1969. Two months later, I went to Afghanistan in a VW bus to buy jewels for a leather-sandal business I had started with a friend. When I returned to Matala in February, my girlfriend had gone home to the States.

## When did you meet Joni Mitchell?

I think Joni arrived in Matala in late February. We met either while I was watching a sunset or when I was blown through the door of Delfini's, a taverna where I cooked. I knew Joni was in Matala—there was buzz among the fifty or so hippies who lived in the thirty-odd caves in the cliff about a famous singer who had arrived in the fishing village. I hadn't followed her career closely, so I wasn't sure who she was.

One night soon after she arrived, I was cooking at Delfini's when she came to have lunch, surrounded by fans. I resented how her fame had turned my friends into adoring sycophants. After she finished eating, she politely cleaned her table and brought the trash to me. She was just being a good person. In this taverna, we were used to drinking and dancing there until all hours and breaking plates and glasses on the floor in celebration. So I shrugged and threw her trash on the floor, I guess as an intended slight to her fame. Not long after, I was outside on a break when Joni came over and started talking.

Or we may have met on the afternoon I was in the kitchen of Delfini's. One of the owners was fiddling with the stove. There was a propane tank in there that had been on. The guy had an unlit cigarette dangling out of his mouth. At one point, he reflexively took out his lighter. I didn't have time to stop him. He lit it and there was a big explosion. It blew me out the door and gave him second-degree burns.

**Why did she refer to you in the song as a "mean old Daddy"?**

Looking back, I wasn't as nice to her as I should have been—or to anybody, I guess. I was a little hard on people around me. One day we were walking around at these ancient Roman baths outside of town with friends. She showed me a piece of driftwood and said it looked like a mermaid, asking me what I thought. I said it looked like a piece of driftwood. Not very nice, I know. I suppose I was taking a swipe at her poetic fantasies.

**Why were you so mean?**

I had a nasty, aggressive character then, and I was feisty. I was always getting into fights at the taverna—probably losing more of them than I won. I suppose she hung around me after her friend left because she knew people wouldn't dare come up to my cave without permission, so it was a haven for her of sorts, even though the cave was small—around eight by sixteen feet.

**In the song, she sings about your cane.**
**Where did you get it?**

It was a broken shepherd's crook that only came up to my waist. I guess a shepherd had discarded it in a field. It was useful for climbing the rocky hills around Matala. The "silver" Joni sings about refers to her Navajo jewelry that she usually wore when she went out at night.

**Did you hear her composing music?**

All the time. It was a fascinating process. She was clearly a great musician with a great ear. She liked to try out these chords on her dulcimer—playing them over and over again like a mantra until she figured out where she wanted to go with them. She'd go into a kind of trance, and things would come out of that. I'm not a musician, but what sounded to the average ear like monotony eventually flowered. She's also a technician who likes to mess with the tuning of her instrument.

**When did you first hear "Carey"?**

On April 19, 1970—my twenty-fourth birthday—in my cave. Joni played it for me as a present. She also gave me ten Mickey Mouse chocolate bars. They came with these Disney character cards that the cave people traded. When she sang the song, I was surprised by it, since I'm the subject. But I wasn't blown away. It sounded like a ditty, something she had tossed off. I believe the song went on longer than the final version on *Blue*. I think she changed some of the lines, too. As I recall, she sang something like, "Last night I couldn't sleep, the sea was full of sheep." One of the local expressions was that when the sea was choppy, the whitecaps looked like sheep.

**Did the song sound like a farewell letter to you?**

Yes—but Joni was leaving all the time. She was always saying she was going to take off soon, so her intentions were clear. Months earlier she was an elegant lady living in Laurel Canyon, and Matala was as foreign to her world as you could get. Life was very simple and raw in Matala, and eventually she wanted to return to her home and career. I liked Joni a lot and didn't like losing her company. But on the road, you already know that the friendships you develop are short-lived. That's built into the experience.

**Where did you two take that photo together?**

On Easter morning in a park in Heraklion on the north coast of Crete. We often went to Heraklion to visit or so I could buy leather there for my sandal shop. We drove there in the VW Joni had rented weeks earlier. While we sat in the park, an old photographer came up to us and asked if we wanted our picture taken. It was a tourist thing. He had an old wooden box camera on a tripod, and we agreed. After he took the picture, he went into a makeshift darkroom to develop the image. Fifteen minutes later he emerged with the photo, and we bought it.

**How did you feel when she left for Paris?**

It was painful, but I understood. I liked Matala and was preoccupied with my business. After she left, I traveled around Crete early that summer and returned to the States in July of '70 to visit her.

**When did you first hear "Carey" on *Blue*?**

When I visited Joni again in Los Angeles in 1971. She invited me to A&M Studios in Hollywood. [Engineer] Henry Lewy grabbed me and put me in a room with headphones. He played a tape of the album, which they just had finished. I thought it was fantastic. "Carey" didn't surprise me, since I had heard it in Matala. "California," however, was a shocker. I was taken aback that she referred to me as a "redneck on a Grecian isle." I was from North Carolina, so my accent was strong, but I was hardly that. But look, she was just writing songs. You can't really take these things all that seriously. And I did take her camera, as the song says, but I didn't sell it. I gave it back to her later.

**Did you tell her she had misspelled your name?**

I pointed that out later and Joni apologized and said it was a spelling mistake.

## So you really didn't care when she left Matala?

The truth is I was in love with Joni and missed her. We had spent virtually every day together for nearly two months. But I knew I was in way over my head. I couldn't earn a living then, and she was way too talented for me. I tried for some time after not to become too caught up in the whole thing.

Joni Mitchell with Cary Raditz and her dulcimer in a park in Heraklion, Crete, in the spring of 1970.
*Courtesy of Cary Raditz*

The Staple Singers in 1970, from left—Cleotha, Roebuck ("Pops"), Mavis, and Yvonne.

*Michael Ochs Archives/Getty Images*

# 29: Respect Yourself

**THE STAPLE SINGERS**

*Released: September 1971*

Otis Redding's death in a plane crash in December 1967 came as an emotional and financial blow to Stax Records, the Memphis label that produced Redding and so many other regional soul artists. Redding had been Stax's best-selling artist, and when he died, Stax was stuck. Stax had signed a contract with Atlantic Records in 1965 that gave Atlantic the rights to all of the records it distributed for Stax between 1960 and 1967. When Atlantic was purchased by Warner Bros.–Seven Arts two months before Redding's death in '67, all of Stax's masters wound up in Warner's vaults. Redding was Stax's biggest source of revenue, and when he died, Al Bell, the company's executive vice president and co-owner, had to not only rebuild Stax's music catalog from scratch but also develop new artists to replace Redding's lost revenue. Bell urged artists and songwriters to write and record what they felt, no matter how far-out or funky, and a new sound began to emerge at the label that was groove-driven and socially in tune with the times.

One of the first groups Bell signed, in 1968, was the Staple Singers, a family gospel group he had known and admired since the 1950s. During their first two years at Stax, the Staple Singers recorded songs that were church-themed, including "The Gardener" and "All I Have to Do Is Dream." But by 1970, singing about a brighter day seemed out of touch with the culture of protest that had grown up around the civil rights movement and the Vietnam War. The black power movement, with its strong sense of pride and self-determination, had also become a cultural force, motivating Stax artists to take risks when writing and recording message songs about injustice, street life, pollution, drugs, and other social issues.

At first, the Staple Singers weren't sure they could make the transition comfortably. Roebuck "Pops" Staples, the family's guitarist and patriarch, and his daughters—Mavis, Cleotha, and Yvonne—wanted to stick with their brand of uplifting music. But in 1971, they were open to funkier music if they could retain their positive outlook. The Staples' first single using this new approach was "Respect Yourself," a message song by Mack Rice and Luther Ingram that was produced by Al Bell. The lyrics were a sermon of sorts, urging listeners to respect themselves and others. Released in September 1971, "Respect Yourself" became the Staple Singers' biggest hit to date, reaching No. 12 on *Billboard*'s pop chart and No. 2 on the soul chart. Bigger hits would follow for the Staples, but none would be as gripping a reminder that for change to be effective, it had to be accompanied by dignity. "Respect Yourself" was inducted into the Grammy Hall of Fame in 2002.

## Interviews with AL BELL (producer) and MAVIS STAPLES (singer)

**AL BELL:** One afternoon in early 1971, Mack Rice came by my office. I was co-owner and executive vice president of Stax Records in Memphis then, and creative people like Mack always had easy access to me. He was one of our top house songwriters.

Mack said, "Doc, I have a song I think will work on the Staple Singers." He sat down with that guitar of his with three strings and began singing and playing a song he had written called "Respect Yourself."

When he finished, I was knocked out and asked what inspired him. Mack said he was talking with songwriter Luther Ingram about all the things going on with our people. At one point, Luther said, "Black folks need to learn to respect themselves."

Mack said he loved that phrase and had used it to write the words and music, giving Luther cocredit for the inspiration. Mack also said he was moved by "I Am Somebody," the poem Reverend William Holmes Borders had written that Reverend Jesse Jackson recited on an album for our Respect label.

I told Mack to go put a demo tape on his song. So he went into Stax's Studio C with his guitar and recorded exactly what he sang for me. When he was done, I began living the song by listening to the demo over and over.

Like me, Mack loved Pops Staples and his family—the music they were singing and the uplifting message they were putting out. Mack thought the song was a natural for them, and he was right.

**MAVIS STAPLES:** We were in a studio at Stax singing when Mack Rice came in. He listened to us and when we finished, he said to my father, "Pops, I got this song for you   it's called 'Respect Yourself.'" Pops liked the title and its positive message. He said, "Let's hear it, Mack."

When Mack gave you a song, he didn't just sing it for you. He sang all the parts—the bass, horns, and everything he had in mind. You couldn't help but listen. [She sings softly:] "If you disrespect anybody that you run in to/How in the world do you think anybody's s'posed to respect you."

Then Mack ad-libbed between the verses halfway through [She illustrates:] "Deep, dee-diddy, dee, dee/deep, dee-diddy, dee, dee." Pops cut him off. "Wait a minute, Mack. That's not us. We're church people." Mack said, "Pops, you got to do that part, man. You'll get all the kids singing it." Yvonne, Cleo, and I liked it. It was fun and made us feel joyful. When the three of us tried the song, Pops liked how we sang that part, so it stayed.

**BELL:** I had known Mavis and her family from the late '50s and knew she could turn Mack's song into a powerful message. When

I was in radio in Little Rock in 1957 and '58, I booked the Staple Singers, Aretha Franklin, Reverend C. L. Franklin, and other groups into huge gospel concerts. The last one I produced was in Pine Bluff [Arkansas], at the high school. I loved the Staples so much. I always made sure I was out in the audience when they sang. That night, Mavis sang a song by herself—"On My Way to Heaven." I listened to her, with that contralto voice. All of a sudden I saw she was crying, and at the same time I was crying.

Years later, I asked Mavis if she remembered singing that song in Pine Bluff. I said, "Mavis, why did you start crying?" She said they had been out on the road a long time and was thinking about her mother. "I was on my way home to see her, and I was over-joyed," she said.

Mavis started listening to Mack's demo tape over and over. Once I knew she loved "Respect Yourself," I set up a recording session—but not in Memphis. The house musicians at Stax were tremendous, but they could be intimidating for me. As someone who wasn't a musician, I needed to feel free to talk to musicians about what I was feeling in nonmusical terms. This was my inse-curity, but it was what it was.

Around this time, I had been talking to Marvell Thomas, son of recording artist Rufus Thomas and a Stax keyboardist. I told him I was going to produce an album on the Staples but I needed musicians who could hear me out. Marvell said there were these four young white guys at Muscle Shoals Sound Studio in Sheffield, Alabama, who were sharp. He said he had recorded with them and that they knew all about me, which gave me confidence.

Before I went down there, I did some research. These musicians were known as the Swampers, but they had played on some incred-ible recordings and could play rock, country, R&B, soul—all of that, with enormous feel. All of this was perfect, since I wanted to create a folk sound for the Staples, to inch them out of gospel but not compromise their integrity as gospel performers.

Soon after we spoke, Marvell and I flew down in a small plane to introduce me to the guys. As soon as I met Barry Beckett [keyboards], Roger Hawkins [drums], Jimmy Johnson [guitar], and David Hood [bass], I felt there was something special in their spirit and in that room. Before I left, I set up a recording date. My goal was to have the guys record the song's rhythm track. Though the master vocals would come later in Memphis, I wanted Mavis and the Staples to be there, to give the guys their feel on the song.

At the studio, I played Mack's demo but told the guys it wasn't how I wanted the Staples' record to go. Mack's rhythm feel on the tape was faster, and it didn't have the right color. It was straight-ahead, with a funky groove, which was good for what he was doing, but Mavis and I agreed it wouldn't fit the Staples' more intimate, conversational approach.

Then I told Barry and Jimmy what I had in mind for the feel. I illustrated by playing a couple of records, and they got it. Barry was behind the electric piano and began playing what I had described while Roger picked up on it and was feeling me on the drums.

In addition, Jimmy had brought in Eddie Hinton from Nashville to play lead guitar. He had the country thing in him, but he also had the rock feel. He'd sit back and listen to what was being built and then add his thing. Mavis moved around the studio and sang as the guys played.

**STAPLES:** At Muscle Shoals, Al had told Barry, Roger, Little David, and Jimmy what we wanted, and they just started playing. Muscle Shoals was the best place to work things out. Nobody could come in and nobody knew we were there. Those guys were so good and flexible, and the sound of the room just hugged the notes. The electric piano intro was Barry's idea. Beautiful, isn't it? These guys were the greatest. They'd come up with lines and hooks you wouldn't believe. Barry was the arranger and gave each of them a page of music. They all knew what to do.

As great as those musicians were, I wanted to sing right in front of each one of them, to get them into my space and make them familiar with my flavor. I also needed to feel what they were doing and incorporate that into my vocal. I like moving around when developing a vocal approach. I need to feel the vibe physically, not just in my head.

**BELL:** As soon as the guys heard Mavis sing a line from the song, they jumped in and you didn't think about Mack Rice's demo anymore [laughs]. When we left, we took copies of the tape so the Staples could live with it before recording the vocal track. A few weeks later, the Staples came to John Fry's Ardent Studios in Memphis, where I always recorded with engineer Terry Manning. Mavis went into the isolation booth with Pops, Yvonne, and Cleotha and recorded their vocal while listening to the Muscle Shoals rhythm track on headphones.

**STAPLES:** My ad-libs during the song were inspired by the music. It's the gospel in me. I can't leave space alone. Toward the end of a song, I had to put some fuel in it, to keep it going. That's the seasoning. I never stopped a song where it was supposed to end. Pops liked that I did that. He'd say, "Go ahead, Mavis, take it," and I'd go crazy.

**BELL:** After the master vocal track was recorded, Terry and I added a few more things for color. Terry played that rock-sounding electric guitar on the last verse. I also wanted a sound in there that kids could relate to, like what they heard on cartoons. So Terry added a Moog synthesizer on the bridge, starting at around 1:10. We put in some horns, too, for texture. The ascending and descending lines that the Staples chant—"Dah dah dah, dah-dah/dee, dee, dee, dee"—that was the horn line Mack had improvised while singing on his original demo.

**STAPLES:** After the song came out and was a big hit, Al wanted us to appear at Wattstax, a large outdoor concert he was producing in August 1972 at the Los Angeles Coliseum. It was a benefit by Stax artists for Watts, a neighborhood that was struggling after the riot of '65. But we almost didn't make it.

At the time, we were opening for Sammy Davis Jr. at the Sands in Las Vegas. But on that particular day, Sammy suddenly had to be someplace for a thing for President Nixon. So he shut down his show at the Sands. When we realized we were going to be off, Pops called Al and told him we could come to his concert.

Al sent a car for us, and we made the five-hour trip. When we got to Los Angeles, we didn't check into a hotel—we went straight to the Coliseum, where they had a dressing room for us. When we got out, mercy, we saw all of these people. We couldn't believe it. There were 112,000 people there.

We went on around 3:30 p.m. and sang five songs. But "Respect Yourself" was the high point. It was just me, Pops, and Cleo with the Stax band. Yvonne wasn't well and was in the hospital. When we came on stage, the sun was shining and people cheered us. Then you didn't hear a peep. You could see people were listening and thinking.

After we finished and reached the dugout, we had a little crying session. We were so happy. In our dressing room, Al Bell and Rufus Thomas were impressed. Rufus said, "Roebuck, you got down, man. Ya got down! Talking that kid talk—ya got down." Pops said, "Maybe, Rufus, but I know what you gonna do." Rufus said, "Yeah, Pops. Now I gotta go out and take 'em there." Everyone laughed. And he did, in those pink Bermuda shorts of his [laughs].

**BELL:** When I first played Mack Rice the finished single, he looked at me and shook his head, saying, "Man, you destroyed my song." Several months later, when the song was a huge hit, Mack stuck his head in my office and said, "Doc, I just dropped by to really thank you for destroying my song."

Jimmy Cliff (c. 1971) in a promotional still for the film *The Harder They Come*.

*Michael Ochs Archives/Getty Images*

# 30: The Harder They Come

**JIMMY CLIFF**

*Released: February 1973*

Jamaican ska and rocksteady were hardly foreign to the American ear in 1973. The lurching beat, stuttering bass, and horns had already surfaced in a wide range of hits, among them Millie Small's cover of "My Boy Lollipop" (1964), Desmond Dekker's "The Isra-elites" (1968), the Beatles' "Ob-La-Di, Ob-La-Da" (1968), Johnny Nash's "Hold Me Tight" (1968) and "I Can See Clearly Now" (1972), and Paul Simon's "Mother and Child Reunion" (1972). What many Americans didn't know at the time was that the rhythm they heard on all of those songs had originated in Jamaica. For most people unaware of the music's roots, the calypso-tinged style just seemed like a Caribbean beat added to folk songs.

Jamaica's emerging socially conscious reggae sound and poly-rhythms would become better known after the North American release of *The Harder They Come* and the movie's soundtrack in February 1973. The album was a twelve-song compilation of reggae singles recorded between 1967 and 1972 by leading Jamaican art-ists. The title track was written and recorded specifically for the movie by Jimmy Cliff, a leading Jamaican reggae singer and the film's star. Cliff appeared on three other songs on the album, which included reggae singles by Desmond Dekker, Toots and the May-tals, Scotty, the Slickers, and the Melodians.

The cover illustration—featuring Cliff in cap and sunglasses with two guns drawn—was timely. The imagery fit in perfectly with other U.S. crime-drama films with African-American casts being released then, including *Shaft, Sweet Sweetback's Baadas-ssss Song, Hit Man, Super Fly, Across 110th Street,* and *Trouble Man.* Unfortunately, neither the film *The Harder They Come* nor the movie's soundtrack did especially well in the U.S., with the soundtrack peaking at No. 140 on the *Billboard* album chart. But they did give Cliff and reggae wide international exposure, particularly among American and British rock musicians. What followed was a wave of reggae-infused rock hits, including Eric Clapton's cover of Bob Marley's "I Shot the Sheriff" (1973), Elvis Costello's "Watching the Detectives" (1977), the Clash's "(White Man) in Hammersmith Palais" (1978), the Police's "Roxanne" (1978), and Blondie's cover of John Holt's "The Tide Is High" (1980). The *Harder They Come* soundtrack was inducted into the Grammy Hall of Fame in 2008.

## Interviews with JIMMY CLIFF (singer-songwriter and producer), JACKIE JACKSON (bassist), and HUX BROWN (lead guitarist)

**JIMMY CLIFF:** In 1969, I was at Dynamic Sounds Studio in Kingston, Jamaica, recording one of my songs, "You Can Get It If You Really Want." When we finished, I walked outside and met a gentleman named Perry Henzell, who had been waiting for me. He said he was making a movie and asked if I could write music for it.

I had already recorded quite a few hits and was already pretty well known in Jamaica and the U.K. I had always wanted to be a movie actor, so I asked Perry to send me the script. When I read it, I felt I had known the main character, Ivanhoe Martin, all my life. In the script, he was a guy from the country who came to the city to make it as a musician but was held back by the trickery of a record-company owner. Eventually Ivan turns to crime, and is killed at the end. I hope I didn't give anything away [laughs].

I told Perry that the script was great, and he decided to cast me as Ivan. The film at the time was called *Hard Road to Travel,* after one of my songs, and we filmed over the next year or so. When we shot the scene where Ivan cuts the bicycle-store owner who came on really hard, a line came to my mind—"the harder they come." In real life, if you come on hard like that, you're going to die hard. When I told Perry my line, he loved it. He thought it was a stronger film title and asked me to write a theme song to go with it. He didn't give me much time—just two days. He wanted to film me singing the song in the studio with the band for the movie.

The first development of my song is actually in the movie—when the guitarist and I are rehearsing in the church. That's an early draft of "The Harder They Come." The rest of the music came fast. When I have a title, the rest always comes fast. I'm quite good at melodies. The lyrics came from my past. I grew up in the church and had always questioned what they were telling me. Like the promise of a pie in the sky when you die. The second verse about oppressors trying to keep me down kind of reflected my own life—coming out of the ghetto in St. James, Jamaica, and fighting the system. I wanted the song to have a church feel and to reflect the environment I grew up in—the underdog fighting all kinds of trickery.

What you see in the movie's recording studio scenes is the song being recorded. You're watching the real thing. Gladstone Anderson was on piano, Winston Wright was on organ, Hux Brown was on lead guitar, Ronny Bop played rhythm guitar, Winston Grennan was on drums, and Jackie Jackson played that unbelievable bass.

**JACKIE JACKSON:** We were studio musicians of that era and had recorded with Jimmy many times before. For the theme song, we got together at Dynamic Sounds around 8 p.m. Usually the band started the day at 10 a.m. and recorded about ten sessions. That's how you made your money. But on this day, we didn't have any sessions, and we were fresh. The energy was flowing and we were champing at the bit.

**HUX BROWN:** When Jimmy arrived, he strummed the song on his acoustic guitar to give us the lowdown. The song's instrumental intro was his. Then Gladdy [Anderson] told us the key and chord progressions, and we spent a half hour getting around it and setting the tempo. Then we were ready to record.

**CLIFF:** I just sang along with the band and improvised the lyrics. I didn't have them all together or fixed in my head when the cameras started. I wasn't one of those writers who jotted down lines on paper. Now I do that, of course. But back then, expressing how I felt off the top of my head created more exciting results. You had the pressure on you.

**BROWN:** We weren't concentrating on the movie cameras—we were focusing on giving the promoter a hit. The band's job always was to sell a song. I was supposed to play what Jackie was playing, but I used a slightly different line—more bouncy, for texture and contrast. Ronny Bop and Winston Wright played off of what Gladdy was doing. And Winston Grennan went in between.

**JACKSON:** We wanted to do it in one take, so the music would be alive. Originally the song ran for about twenty minutes, but we could have kept going all night. They must have cut down the tape for the single and album.

**CLIFF:** The song for me was about social and artistic change. When I lived in the U.K., I recorded a lot of ska and rock steady styles of Jamaican music. But people there weren't accepting it. So I began using a faster reggae beat. On the record, the title song ends with those odd organ chords. That was Winston. He was a brilliant keyboard player. It was his decision to do that. He was good at adding those strange things you weren't expecting. When we finished, we all said, "Brilliant, wow, great!" What you see on my face in the movie was genuine. I felt good. We all felt good. We knew the song was special.

**JACKSON:** The first time I heard the song I was at the movie's premiere at the Harbour View Drive-In in East Kingston. The place was packed. I took my girlfriend in my Vauxhall Viva GT. We sat outside on the grass, very cool and relaxed. Some of the other guys from the band were there. When Jimmy and the song came on, we began jumping and screaming. That was us up there.

Gladys Knight performing with the Pips during an August 1973 Detroit concert that aired weeks later on ABC's *In Concert*.

*ABC Photo Archives/© ABC/Getty Images*

# 31 : Midnight Train to Georgia

**GLADYS KNIGHT AND THE PIPS**

*Released: August 1973*

In the late 1960s and early '70s, soul moved in two directions. Artists whose recordings addressed social issues tended to blend elements of rock and funk to harden their attack and widen their appeal. Other artists continued soul's romantic tradition, appealing to listeners involved in a relationship or trying to salvage one. Romantic soul's formula during this period tended to include a dramatic orchestral introduction followed by a vocal group harmonizing behind a lead singer. The approach was an updating of the harmony group tradition of the 1950s, when vocal ensembles such as the Ravens, the Moonglows, the Dominoes, the Channels, and the Platters had hits.

But instead of using the chord changes to Hoagy Carmichael's "Heart and Soul" as a foundation, as so many groups did, romantic-soul vocal groups in the early '70s were framed by new elaborately written and arranged songs that often included strings. These included "Baby I'm for Real" by the Originals (1969), "Love on a Two-Way Street" by the Moments (1970), "Have you Seen Her" by the Chi-Lites (1971), and Al Green's "Let's Stay Together" (1972). Many of these songs were delivered from the male perspective and featured lyrics about men trying to win over women or sweet-talking their way out of romantic trouble. This male-based model was altered in 1973 when Gladys Knight and the Pips recorded "Midnight Train to Georgia."

From the opening lyric, "L.A. proved too much for the man," the song told the story of a boyfriend's inability to make it in Hollywood as a superstar. What followed was the story of his decision to head home to a "simpler place in time" and the female protagonist's decision to give up her high-profile career to be with him, preferring to "live in his world than live without him in mine." When the song was released in August 1973, it became a No. 1 hit on *Billboard*'s pop chart for two weeks and on *Billboard*'s soul chart for four weeks. It was inducted into the Grammy Hall of Fame in 1999.

**Interviews with JIM WEATHERLY (songwriter), CISSY HOUSTON (singer), TONY CAMILLO (producer), and GLADYS KNIGHT (lead singer)**

**JIM WEATHERLY:** In the late 1960s I was living in Los Angeles in a one-bedroom apartment, trying to get recording artists to pay attention to my songs. One evening in 1970, I called Lee Majors, an actor friend who had just started dating model Farrah Fawcett. Lee and I had played college football and we were in a flag-football league together. Farrah answered the phone. She said Lee wasn't home and that she was packing to take a midnight plane to Houston to visit her folks. "What a great line for a song," I thought.

After I got off the phone, I grabbed my guitar and wrote "Midnight Plane to Houston" in about forty-five minutes—the music and lyrics. The line "I'd rather live in her world than live without her in mine" locked the whole song. I also used a descending bass pattern, which was the song's natural movement. Then I filed away the song.

In 1971 I signed with manager-publisher Larry Gordon, who urged me to record an album of my songs—to improve my chances that top artists would record them. I put "Midnight Plane" on there, along with "Neither One of Us" and a bunch of other songs.

Larry's strategy worked. When the album came out on RCA in 1972, Larry sent Gladys Knight's producer "Neither One of Us," which she loved. We also got a call from producer Sonny Limbo in Atlanta. Cissy Houston wanted to record "Midnight Plane" but felt it needed an R&B title. They wanted to change it to "Midnight Train to Georgia." I was fine with that.

**CISSY HOUSTON:** When Sonny played me Jim's song, I loved it right away. It was a country ballad that told a good story—about two people in love. But I wanted to change the title. My people are originally from Georgia, and they didn't take planes to Houston or anywhere else. They took trains. We recorded the single in Memphis in 1972 with a country-gospel thing going, and I arranged the background singers. But Janus, my label, didn't do much to promote it, and we moved on.

**WEATHERLY:** After Cissy's single came out, Larry sent it to Gladys, who's from Atlanta. She and the Pips loved it. The next step was for Gladys to find an arranger and producer.

**TONY CAMILLO:** In the late '60s, I owned my own studio in New Jersey and produced records for George Clinton; Freda Payne; Blood, Sweat & Tears; the Honey Cone; the Dramatics; and others. In 1973, Buddah Records offered me a multiyear exclusive contract, and I took it. Two weeks later, Buddah signed Gladys Knight and the Pips, and Neil Bogart, who ran the label, called and asked if I wanted to produce them. The song was "Midnight Train to Georgia." Initially I wrote two arrangements for the song, but I wasn't happy with them. The music needed to be catchier, to jump out of the radio.

**GLADYS KNIGHT:** I listened to Cissy's version and loved it—but I knew I wanted to do something different. I wanted an Al Green thing going, you know? Something moody, with a little ride to it. I've always liked my tracks full—horns, keyboards, and other instruments—to create texture and spark something in me. I also wanted to change a few of Jim's original lyrics—add a word or two and take out a few. So I'd call him every day. I'd say, "Hey Jim, what do you think of 'So he's leaving a life he's come to know' instead of '*we've* come to know'?" Jim was cool with everything. He allowed us that freedom.

**CAMILLO:** After I spoke with Gladys about what she wanted, I kept the rhythm section spare and used horns. For the rhythm tracks, I called in Jeff Mironov on guitar, Bob Babbitt on bass, and Andrew Smith on drums. I played the Wurlitzer electric piano. Then I brought in top guys to play the horns—Randy Brecker and Alan Rubin on trumpets, Michael Brecker and Lewis Del Gatto on saxes, and Meco Monardo and Dave Taylor on trombones. After I mixed the rhythm and horn tracks together, I took the tape to Detroit, where Gladys and the Pips recorded their vocal tracks.

**KNIGHT:** When Tony came to Detroit, our whole team came down to the studio—managers, label executives, Tony's crew. The place was jammed. At the studio, I recorded a scratch vocal—sort of a demo of my vocal that the Pips could hear in their headsets while they recorded their background parts. I had worked out those parts with them earlier. Then we rehearsed.

When they finished their master background tracks, it was my turn. Now, I'm not a scatter or an ad-libber—the inspirational things that are typically improvised along the way. I had this mental block about doing that freely. After my first take, my brother [Merald] "Bubba" Knight, who led the Pips, said I had to put in some gospel ad-libs. "Gladys," he said, "the song is begging for it. You can do it."

But when I got to the ad-lib section on the second take, I got stuck, I was struggling with it. So Bubba went into the booth and fed them to me through my headset. He told me, "Just sing what I say in your headset." So we did another take, with Bubba feeding me lines—things like "Gonna board, gotta board, the midnight train" and "My world, his world, our world," and "I've got to go, I've got to go" and "My world, his world, my man, his girl" at the fade. Well, it worked.

**CAMILLO:** After the vocals were recorded, I took the tapes back to my studio in New Jersey. I overdubbed a string section for sweetening, as well as Barry Miles on acoustic piano and me on Hammond organ and hand percussion to fill out the background.

**KNIGHT:** While recording that single, I was thinking about my own situation. My husband at the time was a beautiful saxophonist, and so gifted. But he was unhappy that we didn't have a more traditional marriage, because I was often on the road or recording. Ultimately it all proved too much for him, like the song said, and we divorced later, in '73. I was going through the exact same thing that I was singing about when recording which is probably why it sounds so personal.

The Allman Brothers Band, from left—Butch Trucks, Gregg Allman, Berry Oakley, Jai "Jaimoe" Johanny Johanson, and Dickey Betts.

*Photo by Twiggs Lyndon/Courtesy of the Lyndon Family*

# 32: Ramblin' Man
## THE ALLMAN BROTHERS
### *Released: September 1973*

In the late 1960s, Nashville's popular "countrypolitan" sound was in constant need of well-crafted story songs, accomplished studio musicians, and singers with voices that could sound hurt, despondent, or unloved. Many young Southern studio musicians in the early 1970s viewed rock as a way out of the relentless grind of Nashville's recording work. For a studio musician, there was little fame or reward for appearing on a singer's record date, just more anonymous work. As Gregg Allman told me during an interview, his late brother Duane, who worked extensively in studios as a slide guitarist, wanted to form the Allman Brothers Band because "he was tired of being a robot and hearing who had the biggest fucking TV set."

In all likelihood, the turning point for many Southern rock musicians came in February 1969, when Columbia signed Johnny Winter to a lucrative deal that paid the Texas blues guitarist $50,000 an album for six albums over three years, with an option for four more. A year later, several Southern rock bands comprised of former studio musicians formed and began recording, including the Allman Brothers, guitarist Charlie Daniels, and Barefoot Jerry. The Allman Brothers' distinct blues-rock sound began to catch on nationally with the release in July 1971 of its *At Fillmore East,* an electrifying live blues-rock album that proved Southern bands had plenty of soul and bite.

But the Allman Brothers almost had to call it quits—twice. In October 1971, Duane Allman was killed in a motorcycle accident, leaving the band without its star slide guitarist. Then in the summer of 1972, when the band was preparing to record what would become *Brothers and Sisters*, its fifth album, they needed songs and a stand-out guitarist to replace Duane. Dickey Betts offered up a song he had written called "Ramblin' Man," and brought in guitarist Les Dudek to play a guitar duel with him on the song when the band recorded it in October 1972. But tragedy struck the band a month later when bassist Berry Oakley died in a motorcycle accident. When "Ramblin' Man" was released as a single in September 1973, it became the band's biggest all-time hit—climbing to No. 2 on *Billboard*'s pop chart—and helped *Brothers and Sisters* remain at No. 1 on the album chart for five straight weeks.

**Interviews with DICKEY BETTS (Allman Brothers guitarist and songwriter), CHUCK LEAVELL (pianist), and LES DUDEK (guitarist)**

**DICKEY BETTS:** In 1969, I was playing guitar in several rock bands that toured central Florida. Whenever I'd have trouble finding a place to stay, my friend Kenny Harwick would let me crash at his garage apartment for a few days in Sarasota. Kenny was a friendly, hayseed-cowboy kind of guy who built fences and liked to answer his own questions before you had a chance. One day he asked me how I was doing with my music and said, "I bet you're just tryin' to make a livin' and doin' the best you can."

I liked how that sounded and carried the line around in my head for about three years. Then one day in 1972, I was sitting in the kitchen of what we called the Big House in Macon, Georgia—where everyone in the band lived—and decided to finish the lyrics. The words came fast, like I was writing a letter. When [producer] Johnny Sandlin asked later if I had any songs for our upcoming album, I ran down "Ramblin' Man" on my acoustic guitar. Everyone in the room went nuts.

My inspiration was Hank Williams' "Ramblin' Man," from 1951. His song and mine are completely different, but I liked his mournful, minor-chord feel. Except for Kenny's line, the rest of the lyrics were autobiographical. When I was a kid, my dad was in construction and used to move the family back and forth between central Florida's east and west coasts. I'd go to one school for a year and then the other the next. I had two sets of friends and spent a lot of time in the back of a Greyhound bus. Ramblin' was in my blood. But the song, as I originally wrote it, had a country flavor and needed to be Allmanized —given that rock-blues feeling. I thought of Eric Clapton's "Layla"— which had come out a year earlier—with its long jam at the end. I figured something like that might work.

When we went into Capricorn Sound Studios in Macon in October '72, "Ramblin' Man" was the first song we recorded—and it would be [bassist] Berry Oakley's last song before he died in a motorcycle crash a month later. I knew "Ramblin' Man" needed a solid intro to grab the listener. My daddy had been a fiddler, and I heard a lot of fiddle music as a child. I had a ukulele and had played along with him. What I came up with for the intro was a fiddle-like opener built on a pentatonic scale—but with me on guitar and Chuck [Leavell] on piano exchanging lines.

**CHUCK LEAVLLL:** Dickey had a cool country-rock lick for the intro, and he and I created a call-and-response on guitar and piano to round it out. I came up with my line answering Dickey's, and then we worked on the harmonies on the lines we played together.

**BETTS:** After we had the intro down, I played rhythm and sang the song's verse and chorus, and Chuck played bluesy piano fills. On the break between the song's verses and chorus, I took a solo. Then I had an idea that threw everyone for a loop. For that "Layla"-like instrumental part, I asked everyone to play the same line over and over again as I sang, "Lord, I was born a ramblin' man." This set up the next part. I wanted to overdub guitars in harmony—two playing high notes and two playing low notes. I planned to overdub a solo over all those guitars stacked together.

**LEAVELL:** I played rhythm piano on the studio's nine-foot Steinway grand, listening to drummers Butch [Trucks] and Jaimoe [Johanson] so I'd be in sync with what they were doing. I was also trying to complement Dickey's vocals, answering him with a line or two on piano and singing the lower harmony parts on the chorus.

**LES DUDEK:** I was up in Macon that fall, when Dickey invited me to the studio. When I entered the control room, the band was rehearsing "Ramblin' Man." They'd record parts and listen back to hear how the song was developing. Dickey kept asking what I thought of his overdubs, and I'd tell him. Finally he said, "Hell, why don't you come out in the studio and play it with me?" So I did. I played the high harmony parts and Dickey played the low ones. After we recorded the first set in the lower register, we overdubbed the same harmonies in the higher register. Then they stacked them all together on the tape. You hear us where the riff starts to repeat and there's a wall of guitars playing harmonies in two octaves. Quite cool, actually.

But a transition was needed entering the instrumental section, so I suggested a drum fill to introduce the higher-octave guitar parts. The section itself had four guitar parts playing harmonies in two octaves. Toward the end, Dickey overdubbed a slide guitar solo by placing his guitar flat and playing it like a lap steel.

**BETTS:** All of it together had a big, symphonic sound. It was like Benny Goodman's stuff in the '30s. His band was arranged so it would have this big, broad sound, with Benny's high clarinet weaving in and out. The contrast was exciting. Once we had all the guitar parts recorded, I did the same. I put on a headset and added my solo, weaving in and out.

**DUDEK:** The control room was packed the night we listened to the final playback. Phil Walden and all the executives from Capricorn were there, along with the band's road crew. It was Duane's band, and everyone was just trying to survive his death. The band's signature sound was the double-guitar harmony thing, with Duane and Dickey—and Dickey and I had just carried on the tradition, with the guitar harmonies—a salute to Duane. When the playback stopped, you could hear a pin drop. Then Red Dog [roadie Joe Campbell] said, "Damn. That's the best I've heard since Duane."

The Hues Corporation recording in 1973, from left—Bernard St. Clair Lee, Hubert Ann Kelley, and Karl Russel.
*Michael Ochs Archives/Getty Images*

# 33: Rock the Boat
## THE HUES CORPORATION
*Released: May 1974*

The riots outside New York's Stonewall Inn in June 1969 marked the start of the national gay rights movement. But despite media coverage of the gay community's violent clashes with police near the Greenwich Village bar, many of the city's laws prohibiting establishments from serving openly gay customers remained unchanged for years. To circumvent these laws, a growing number of gay-friendly New York bars and bathhouses stopped selling alcohol to walk-ins. Instead, they charged a membership fee or sent out invitations to be presented at the door. In effect, they became private clubs. Unlike Miami, where the 1972 Democratic Convention had been held and activists managed to change the laws governing the establishment of openly gay bars and clubs in South Beach, New York's "underground" gay bars and clubs still had to take steps to remain off the city's radar while providing sufficient entertainment to draw customers and compete with each other for business.

As private clubs, these sub-rosa establishments had an easier time obtaining a state liquor license and selling drinks to members and invited guests. Since clubs traditionally thrive when bar tabs are high, the job of keeping patrons entertained fell to disc jockeys, who sustained a high-energy vibe with new and little-known soul records with a strong beat. Live bands were too costly and jukeboxes were impractical, since singles were too short and the breaks between records too long. Disc jockeys at these clubs discovered dance tracks on obscure 45s or buried on soul LPs. The continuous play of records was possible using two turntables and a mixer, while the more popular singles could be extended for fifteen minutes or longer by using two copies and switching back and forth between turntables. By 1973, New York's gay clubs had become unintended labs and focus groups for vinyl-driven dance music, and record companies took notice.

If disco is defined as beat-centric, soul-based recordings specifically produced for club dancing, then one of the first examples of this emerging genre was the Hues Corporation's "Rock the Boat." At the heart of "Rock the Boat" was a rumba-like beat and a light reggae bass line, which when combined was ideal for partner dancing. Though the O'Jays' "Love Train" had come out at the end of 1972, it was really an up-tempo soul-gospel message song more geared to individual freestyle dance. "Rock the Boat" initially appeared on the Hues Corporation's first album, released in the spring of 1973. but it was passed over by radio. In early 1974, when RCA executives heard that the record had become a cult favorite at New York's gay clubs, it was remixed for club dancing, and a single was released, climbing to No. 1 on *Billboard*'s pop chart by July. The remix raised the impact of the record's sensual washing-machine beat, soulful vocals, and glittery brass and strings, and the record launched a dance craze that would last ten years and raise the standards of music production.

**Interviews with WALLY HOLMES (songwriter),
JOHN FLOREZ (producer), JOE SAMPLE (pianist),
and H. ANN KELLEY (Hues Corporation singer)**

**WALLY HOLMES:** I was a trumpeter, songwriter, and surfer living in Los Angeles in 1968 when I formed a soul-pop group called Brothers and Sisters. My plan was to manage the two black male and two black female singers and book them into Las Vegas clubs with an eight-piece band. But in 1969, the group broke up. We had the wrong mix of singers. St. Clair Lee, the lead singer and a surfing pal of mine, suggested we start another group. We found H. Ann

Kelley at a radio talent show, and she found singer Fleming Williams.

I was a rebel then and disliked wealthy people. So I named the new trio the Children of Howard Hughes, since they obviously weren't. When we began playing gigs at the lounge at Circus Circus in Las Vegas in 1969, some guy said, "If you use Howard Hughes's name, you're going to get sued unless you have a contract with someone named Howard Hughes." I saw the complications and changed the group's name to the Hues Corporation. We caught a break in early '72 when a friend—arranger Gene Page—orchestrated the score for *Blacula,* a cult film. He asked the Hues Corporation to record three songs for the soundtrack.

My business partner, Norm Ratner, and I quickly went looking for a record deal. RCA had just had hits with the Friends of Distinction, a soul-pop group, so the label gave us a shot, pairing us with John Florez, Friends' producer. For our first RCA album, we came up with a bunch of soul-funk songs, including Allen Touchsaint's ballad "Freedom for the Stallion."

**JOHN FLOREZ:** I was in my twenties then and didn't really know what I was doing. I knew that Gene Page, who arranged "Stallion," was superb, and I was convinced that the song would be the album's hit.

**HOLMES:** But too much of the material for the album sounded similar. I wanted to include a song that was more upbeat and pop. At home, I sat down at the piano and wrote "Rock the Boat" in about fifteen minutes. When I write, I always think in terms of "do, re, mi" and so on—without using sharps or flats. Those kinds of songs, like "Row, Row, Row Your Boat," tend to stick around for a long time. But I originally wrote the song on the beat, so it was stiff.

**FLOREZ:** The first version of "Rock the Boat" was a dog. It had nothing going on. But Don Burkhimer, RCA's head of talent acquisition in L.A., insisted we work with it, since the group was gaining clout.

**HOLMES:** During this time, RCA in L.A. hired David Kershenbaum, a young executive who liked to go out to hear new music. The Hues Corporation was at the Starlight on Santa Monica Boulevard one night when David was there. He liked "Rock the Boat," so we had one more shot. By the album's second recording session, I had added horns to the ending, and John reluctantly agreed to include the song. But he insisted on a punchier arrangement.

**FLOREZ:** Wally's original production started with the line "Ever since our voyage of love began." But it sounded too straight, so I asked if we could open instead with "So I'd like to know where, you got the notion." It had much more attitude. He agreed.

**HOLMES:** A friend told me about arranger Tom Sellers, who lived in the San Fernando Valley. I called Tom and brought him in for the session. Tom had just come back from the Caribbean and had heard a dance beat down there that had an upbeat at the end of each measure and a light reggae bass line on top of it.

**FLOREZ:** For the recording session, I brought in pianist Joe Sample, bassist Wilton Felder, and guitarist Larry Carlton from the Jazz Crusaders. Horns and strings were added later, after we had the rhythm and vocal tracks down. Jim Gordon was my first-call drummer for everything, and Grover Helsley was the engineer.

**JOE SAMPLE:** The song's feel started with Jim's new beat and my strong piano chords. Then Wilton's bass picked up on what my left hand was doing, Larry's rhythm guitar built out my right hand, and everything fell into place. And Larry had that wailing rock solo at the end. We killed it.

**H. ANN KELLEY:** What sold the song was the melodic beauty of the verse, which burst into a romp. I had never heard a beat like the one Tom had come up with. It was a backward beat, like a rumba. And Wally wrote and played that wonderful trumpet line at the end. [Singers] St. Clair, Fleming and I went in the isolation booth and listened as the band played the song several times in our headsets. Then we recorded together, but I had to stand on a box. I had this big voice for a little girl and needed to be on the same level in front of the mikes. Fleming's lead vocal was just fantastic.

**FLOREZ:** At the end of the final take, my jaw dropped. I ran up to Wally to hug him and said, "My God, you were right." It was still a lousy tune, but now it was commercially viable. Wally said to me, "Your issue, John, is that you want to make special, meaningful records. Instead, you should feed the market." Then I made a terrible mistake. I mixed the entire first album at once, which left the song's new beat sounding flat.

**HOLMES:** When "Rock the Boat" was mastered, a demo went up the chain at RCA, but they decided instead to release "Stallion" in the summer of '73 as the album's first single. "Rock the Boat" was planned for February 1974.

**FLOREZ:** Then something crazy happened. Tom Draper, RCA's vice president of A&R in New York, called in late '73 and said the track was the rage at the city's underground gay dance clubs. They were putting on two copies of the album and looping them to extend the song. Almost overnight, demand was climbing for a single. Anticipating radio interest, I took the tapes back into the studio and remixed "Rock the Boat" to make the bass drum, electric bass, and the other rhythm instruments sound bigger and snappier.

**HOLMES:** RCA released the newly remixed single in February, just as radio picked up on the song. Deejays jumped on it. By May, the song was No. 1 on *Billboard*'s pop chart—the dance chart didn't exist yet. After "Rock the Boat" hit, dozens of records followed that had a similar Tom Sellers–Jim Gordon beat. We put the newly mixed version on the Hues Corporation's second album, *Rockin' Soul*.

**FLOREZ:** Wally knew his stuff. He knew which simple things worked. My mistake was trying to turn the Hues Corporation into the Friends of Distinction. It was a new era, and "Rock the Boat's" sound came out of a divine moment. It wasn't manipulated. It just happened, and the studio musicians there were everything. Within weeks, singles with a chunky beat followed—like George McCrae's "Rock Your Baby." Everyone wanted a dance hit.

**THE HUES CORPORATION**
Arr. by Thomas Sellers

Produced by John Florez

RC٨

STEREO
APB0-0232
APB0-0232A

Victor

High Ground
Music, BMI

3:05

**ROCK THE BOAT**
(from the "Freedom for the Stallion"
album) (W. Holmes)

TMK(S) ® REGISTERED • MARCA(S) REGISTRADA(S)
RCA CORP. MADE IN U.S.A • ℗ 1974 RCA RECORDS

Aerosmith's Steven Tyler and guitarist Joe Perry performing in Pontiac, Michigan, in May 1976.

*Fin Costello/Getty Images*

# 34: Walk This Way
**AEROSMITH**
*Released: August 1975*

Hip-hop began in New York in the mid-1970s when teens lugged boom boxes to vacant lots and burned-out buildings in the Bronx and began break-dancing to looped beat clips. The first single to popularize hip-hop was the Sugarhill Gang's *Rapper's Delight*, released in 1979. But as "Rapper's Delight" climbed the charts, success landed the Sugarhill Gang in hot water. The song sampled the instrumental riff track from Chic's "Good Times," a lift that soon came to the attention of "Good Times's" songwriters—Chic's Nile Rodgers and Bernard Edwards. Legal action was threatened, and a settlement was reached, with Rodgers and Edwards being credited as cowriters of "Rapper's Delight."

Despite hip-hop's street credibility and Blondie's No. 1 hit with "Rapture" in 1981, the genre wasn't immediately accepted by leading record labels. When MTV began broadcasting in August 1981, hip-hop was virtually ignored, with the cable channel focusing instead on major rock and pop acts whose labels provided MTV with music videos. Many of those acts also happened to be white. As MTV's popularity and influence grew with the increasing number of cable subscribers, a rift widened between hip-hop and rock over rap's exclusion. Rappers viewed rockers as little more than video actors, and rockers viewed rappers as glorified disc jockeys and music thieves, not bona fide artists or musicians.

In 1985, when Run-D.M.C. considered remaking Aerosmith's 1976 hit "Walk This Way," they asked cowriters Steven Tyler and Joe Perry to join them. Hesitant at first, Tyler and Perry eventually agreed. They also appeared in the Run-D.M.C. music video. When the video aired in '86, it helped Run-D.M.C.'s version become a crossover hit, mending fences between hip-hop and rock and clearing a path for the Beastie Boys and other white hip-hop artists who followed. Interestingly, "Walk This Way" by Aerosmith was released twice. When the Aerosmith single first came out in 1975, the band wasn't well known and the single failed to chart. After the popularity of the band's *Rocks* album in 1976, "Walk This Way" was rereleased and reached No. 10 on *Billboard*'s pop chart. Ten years later, when the version with Tyler, Perry, and Run-D.M.C. was released, the rap remake reached No. 4 on the pop chart, and it was inducted into the Grammy Hall of Fame in 2014.

### Interviews with JOE PERRY (Aerosmith lead guitarist and cowriter) and STEVEN TYLER (lead singer and cowriter)

**JOE PERRY:** When Aerosmith played its first gig in November 1970, we were heavily into funk and soul. Joey Kramer, our drummer, had been putting himself through Boston's Berklee College of Music playing in an R&B band at seedy clubs in the city's "Combat Zone." So he knew all the Motown stuff, while the rest of us were into James Brown and Sly Stone. Guitarist Jeff Beck had turned me on to the Meters, and I loved their riffy New Orleans funk, especially "Cissy Strut" and "People Say."

In December 1974, we flew to Honolulu to open for the Guess Who. During the sound check, I was fooling around with riffs and thinking about the Meters. I asked Joey to lay down something flat with a groove on the drums. The guitar riff to what would become "Walk This Way" just came off my hands. I heard the start of a song and knew I'd need a bridge, so I played another riff and went there. But I didn't want the song to have a typical, boring 1, 4, 5 chord progression. After playing the first riff in the key of C, I shifted to E before returning to C for the verse and chorus. By the end of the sound check, I had the song's basics.

**STEVEN TYLER:** When I heard Joe playing that riff during the sound check, I ran out and sat behind the drums and we jammed. I rattled off the beat and just felt the song. Joe and I did this all the time when we wrote. I was originally a drummer, so playing along with Joe's riff gave me this extra vibe when writing lyrics. I scat nonsensical words initially to feel where the lyrics should go before adding them later.

**PERRY:** The following year, halfway through recording our *Toys in the Attic* album in early '75 at New York's Record Plant, we were stuck. Writing was a long, tough process for us in those days. Our first two albums were mostly songs we had played at clubs. For *Toys,* we had written three or four songs and then had to write the rest in the studio. That's when we decided to try the song I had come up with in Hawaii. We didn't have lyrics or a title yet, so we took a break.

Steven, Joey, [bassist] Tom [Hamilton], [guitarist] Brad [Whitford], and [producer] Jack [Douglas] went down to Times Square to see Mel Brooks's *Young Frankenstein,* which was in theaters then. I had already seen it, so I stayed behind and hung out on the roof. When the guys returned, they were throwing lines back and forth from the film. They were laughing about Marty Feldman greeting Gene Wilder at the door of the castle and telling him to follow him. "Walk this way," he says, limping, giving his stick to Wilder so he can walk that way, too. While all this was going on, Jack stopped and said, "Hey, 'Walk This Way' might be a great title for the song." We agreed. But we still needed lyrics.

**TYLER:** That night at the hotel, I wrote lyrics for the song and stuck them in my cloth shoulder bag. But when I arrived at the studio the next day, I didn't have it. I had left the bag in the cab. I must have been stoned. All the blood drained out of my face, but no one believed me. They thought I never got around to writing them.

**PERRY:** Steven was pretty upset, but we still needed lyrics. He took a cassette tape of the instrumental track we had recorded, popped it into his portable tape player, and walked around with head-phones on trying to get the feel. Then he disappeared into the stairwell.

**TYLER:** I grabbed a few No. 2 pencils and went up to the Record Plant's top floor and then down a few stairs of the back stairway so I wouldn't be disturbed. The lick Joe had written was so groovy, and I was scatting with the headset on. When the words started coming, I realized I had forgotten to bring paper with me. So I wrote them on the wall. It took two or three hours. When I finished, I ran downstairs for a legal pad and ran back up and copied them down.

**PERRY:** When Steven returned, we ran down the song. His lyrics were so great. Being a drummer, he likes to use words as a percussion element. The words have to tell a story, but for Steven they also have to have a bouncy feel for flow. Then he searches for words that have a double entendre, which comes out of the blues tradition.

After the run-down of the music and vocal, Steven and I had this big tug-of-war over whether I'd overdub my lead guitar solos first or he'd do his vocal. I always liked to wait until Steven recorded his vocal so I could weave around his vocal attack. In many cases, his vocal line would inspire my solo. He wanted me to record first for the same reason—so he could play off my solo. But on "Walk This Way," Steven's vocal was recorded first, and I came back with the guitar.

**TYLER:** At first, I wasn't sure where I wanted to put the song's title in the lyrics. I decided to put it where Joe hits the guitar. It was a natural chorus. I also added a little screech to my voice on the chorus [sings to illustrate]: "Walk this way, talk this way." I wanted to match the sound of Joe's basic guitar track, sort of like a call-and-response thing.

**PERRY:** I wanted my guitar to sound like an electric razor. For "Walk This Way," I used a late-'50s Stratocaster Tobacco Sunburst plugged into a stand-alone Ampeg V4 amp on top and a Marshall 4-by-12 speaker cabinet on the bottom. I also used a Gibson Maestro Fuzz-Tone to give the notes a little distortion. At some point, Steven suggested the double-kick drum, which gave us our trademark sound.

I had no idea the song was hot until our *Toys in the Attic* tour, when audiences spontaneously jumped up and started dancing to it. That's what I had set out to do, to channel the funk, and Steven's lyrics were so edgy. David Johansen of the New York Dolls told me it was the dirtiest song he had ever heard on the radio. Coming from David, that was high praise.

By 1985, we had eight albums out and a growing fan base. Between tours, when I was home in the Boston area, I heard a Run-D.M.C. song coming from my son Aaron's room. They were new to me and I liked it—the sound was like a freight train. A month later, I got a call from Run-D.M.C.'s producer, Rick Rubin, who said he wanted the guys [Joseph "Run" Simmons, Darryl "D.M.C." McDaniels, and Jason "Jam Master Jay" Mizell] to rap over our song "Walk This Way."

Rick said our original version from '75 was "proto-rap"—since Steven's lyrics were half-spoken, half-sung, and we had this solid beat. Rick asked if I'd be willing to put some guitar on it and if Steven would sing new vocals. We said, yeah, why not. They were sampling our kick-drum beat anyway. It was going to be radical, since up until then most rappers had avoided electric guitars.

**TYLER:** When we got to the studio, I wasn't happy that they had changed my lyrics in places. But Joe and I agreed it was their interpretation, so the changes were fine.

**PERRY:** Once we had the basic track down, Rick wanted me to add a bass part. But I hadn't brought one along. A guy who was in the booth watching the session with a bunch of his friends went home to get one. It turned out those guys were the Beastie Boys, and Rick was producing them. Once the session was over, Steven and I left and forgot about it. Weeks later, Rick called again and said they were shooting a video for the song and asked if we wanted in.

TYLER: I hated rock videos that were literal interpretations of songs. But when I saw the "Walk This Way" script, I liked it. It called for a wall between us and Run-D.M.C. They'd be complaining about the noise we were making playing "Walk This Way," and when they cranked up their speakers and began scratching our record and singing over it, we'd act surprised and want to see what was going on. It sounded like fun.

PERRY: We flew to New York and director Jon Small explained what he wanted. At the time, a rock-rap video was unheard of. Rap wanted to do its own thing, and MTV hadn't really featured too many videos by black artists then except for Michael Jackson. In the video, my wife Billie, who was pregnant with our first child, and Teresa, who was with Steven at the time, are seated behind us listening, which was cool.

TYLER: The script called for me to break through the wall with my mike stand to see what was going on next door. The set guys were supposed to make a phony hole in the wall so breaking it would be easy. But when I hit it with everything I had, nothing happened. I pulled every muscle in my back. I finally bashed it in.

PERRY: I loved the video's metaphor—that the wall between rock and rap was coming down and that the two music styles actually worked well together. It was glitter meets gold. Everyone who watched MTV then—rock and rap fans—got the message. For me, it was validation. "Walk This Way" was recognized for being funky—the heart and soul of what we had intended from the start.

Stevie Wonder at age twenty-six in 1976, the year that *Songs in the Key of Life* was released.
*Courtesy of Johnson Publishing Company, LLC*

# 35: Love's in Need of Love Today

**STEVIE WONDER**

*Released: September 1976*

In 1970, under mounting pressure from Motown's leading artists to record socially aware songs and concept albums, Berry Gordy was torn. While he fully understood that times had changed and that other artists on other labels were making political statements in their works, Gordy was never comfortable following the crowd. Besides, there were huge risks. Allowing Motown's major artists to deviate from its upbeat sound and brand could backfire and leave the label without its core audience. Ultimately he let Marvin Gaye roll forward with his single and album *What's Going On,* which became a huge success in early 1971.

But when Stevie Wonder approached Gordy with a similar request, Gordy resisted. In May 1971, Wonder decided to leave Motown to produce and record independently. The following year, Gordy lured Wonder back to Motown with a significant deal that gave him full creative control and the rights to his own songs. The first two albums—*Music of My Mind* (1972) and *Talking Book* (1972)—were experiments with love songs and mysticism. *Innervisions* (1973) was Wonder's first concept album, intermingling love songs with songs of social criticism, and *Fulfillingness' First Finale* (1974) blended songs about faith, beauty, and spiritualism.

When *Songs in the Key of Life* was released in 1976, the double album couldn't hold all of Wonder's musical ideas. Refusing to cut songs from the release, Wonder included four additional songs on an EP that was added to the package as a bonus. Like a suitor hoping for a positive outcome, Wonder worked to seduce his audience—not to induce sales but to overwhelm their senses. The album's opening song, "Love's in Need of Love Today," almost pleads with the listener to love more. Though "Love's in Need" was never released as a single, it helped the double album reach No. 1 for thirteen weeks and remain on the *Billboard* chart for eighty weeks in all. *Songs in the Key of Life* was inducted into the Grammy Hall of Fame in 2002.

### Interview with STEVIE WONDER (singer-songwriter)

**STEVIE WONDER:** "Love's in Need of Love Today" wasn't the first song I wrote for my album *Songs in the Key of Life*, but there was something about it that insisted on being the album's opening song. I wrote the song's basic idea in late 1974 in my hotel room in New York, when Yolanda [Simmons] was pregnant with our daughter Aisha. I remember it was so cold outside that day. The concept I had in mind was that for love to be effective, it has to be fed. Love by itself is hollow. I recorded the song's demo in my hotel room on a Fender Rhodes using a portable Nakamichi cassette recorder. I used to take that recorder with me everywhere, like a notebook.

Capturing the song's basic feel this way was like a sketch. The cassette recorder let me save my original thinking so I could get back into the same groove later in the recording studio. I didn't have all the words for the song at first, only the title phrase. I started at the hotel by playing chords on the keyboard and humming along, adding just a few words where they felt right.

To this day, I never sit down and formally write songs. They emerge from the process of listening to what I'm doing on the keyboard. I just play, and songs sort of happen. Like a painter, I get my inspiration from experiences that can be painful or beautiful. I always start from a feeling of profound gratitude—you know, "Only by the grace of God am I here"—and write from there. I think most songwriters are inspired by an inner voice and spirit. God gave me this gift, and this particular song was a message I was supposed to deliver.

"Love's in Need" really began to take shape when I took the cassette demo into Crystal Sound in Hollywood the following year, in 1975, and began recording. At Crystal Sound, I was playing chords and humming along, adding lyrics and phrases as I heard the music evolve. I wanted to feel the song and move with the music rather than try to control it. The cadence and melody came first, and then by humming harmony up high like this [illustrates by singing], I was inspired to add lyrics. Though I had recorded the demo on a Fender Rhodes in the key of D, I decided to record the song at Crystal Sound in E-flat. The slightly higher key was better for my voice and felt better, spiritually. [Over the phone from his home in Los Angeles, he illustrates by humming the melody and singing lyrics in select places, accompanying himself on a *harpejji,* an electric stringed instrument.]

Almost immediately, the song felt significant, so I wanted to do something different with it. Rather than start with an instrumental, I developed a choral introduction to set the song's tone, and the gospel harmony I wrote came naturally. When I overdubbed my voice singing all the choir's vocal parts, I knew my harmonized voices had to be clear but that my lead vocal had to be heard above the rest, not tucked in the back. The song was going to be a sermon, telling people that love was in need of love.

As I worked on the introduction, it began to feel like one of those gospel radio shows I heard as a child. So after the choir introduction, I came up with this [sings]: "Good morn or evening friends/Here's your friendly announcer." I was thinking about those churches that had radio programs back in the day and how an announcer would come on and say, "Good morning or good evening everyone in radioland. I want to give you a message"—the whole deal, you know. My inspiration was the gospel quartets of the 1950s, like the one Sam Cooke was in. When I sang my final vocal on top, I imagined Sam in the studio with me—his spirit and energy.

While developing the song in the studio, I began to play and record all of the other instruments and layer them in—including the clavinet, bass synthesizer, and drums. Eddie "Bongo" Brown played the congas. Eddie was an African drummer who played on many Motown songs and had recently moved to L.A.

I also added the sound of strings using a Yamaha GX-1. I used to call it "the Dream Machine." I didn't want full strings, just a light Al Green feel. I wasn't thinking of Al's vocal, just the single-note unison string sound on his records. After adding the strings, I decided that was enough. The rest of the process was fitting everything together like pieces of a puzzle. I always like my songs to fit right.

Finalizing "Love's in Need" was just a matter of listening back and deciding what should stay in and what should come out. It's about creating a marriage of all the instruments and vocals, bringing them together to make a statement. It's similar to the way arrangers hear all the parts in their head. Whether it's the Beatles, Sly Stone, Prince, or Ed Sheeran, you start with an idea or vision and bring what you hear in your mind to reality. When I'm doing this, I become all the different musicians and approach the song from each musician's understanding.

Fine-tuning also was key. For example, I originally sang an ad-libbed solo toward the end and then decided my ad-lib alone wasn't enough, so I added the keyboard to play the melody I was singing. In another case, on a playback, I noticed that my bass notes weren't deep enough. I sped up the tape a little when recording, which let my voice hit the lower notes when the tape played back at the normal speed.

When I was finished, I listened to the playback and realized the song was perfect to open the album, to set the entire tone. As for the album's title, I actually dreamed it. The point is that life is endless, so there will forever be songs about things that happen in life. But hearing the song back in the studio also hurt, because it was so emotional. It's still emotional for me. When I performed it in New York recently, I broke down. I've seen people come and go, and live and die, cry and laugh. It all came rushing back.

Steely Dan's Walter Becker, left, and Donald Fagen at the Bel Air Hotel in Los Angeles in October 1977.

*Chris Walter/Getty Images*

# 36: Deacon Blues
## STEELY DAN
*Released: September 1977*

In addition to duffel bags of clothes and bedding, most students who entered college in the mid-1970s brought along audio systems and milk crates of LPs and eight-track tapes. Once settled in dorms, students who thought they knew everything about music were in for a shock. No two students on their floor were likely to be blasting the same artists from their rooms, and album collections rarely overlapped. Strolling down a hall past open doors, one could hear punk, glam, pop, jazz, hard rock, soul, female folk, funk, and disco, among other genres. Two factors contributed to the improvement in choice and sound: the proliferation of discount record superstores such as Tower that stocked a large, eclectic mix of offerings, and significant advancements in studio technology that enabled producers and engineers to record better-sounding albums.

Compared with most rock stars of the era, who thrived on stage and loved the attention of the media, celebrities, and fans, Donald Fagen and Walter Becker of Steely Dan were virtual homebodies. While their quirky blend of R&B and jazz attracted a sizable following of sophisticates, Fagen and Becker were shadowy figures who remained out of the public light. Self-described music nerds, Fagen and Becker spent much of their time holed up in recording studios fiddling and fussing with original songs. Once they had written enough material for an album, they'd match specific musicians to songs and layer track upon track until they reached the desired effect and sound.

Steely Dan's obsessive experiments paid off in 1977, after Fagen and Becker spent six months recording *Aja*. The album—with its mystical, dreamlike feel, jazzy layers, and songs celebrating hapless losers and hopeless dreamers—would become Steely Dan's crowning achievement. As midlife-crisis songs go, the album's "Deacon Blues" ranks among their most melodic and existential. The song details the bored existence of a ground-down suburbanite and his romantic fantasy of life as a jazz saxophonist. The escapist song helped *Aja* reach No. 3 on *Billboard*'s album chart, where it remained for seven consecutive weeks. The song also became a hit single in early 1978, reaching No. 19. The album *Aja* was inducted into the Grammy Hall of Fame in 2003.

**Interviews with DONALD FAGEN (Steely Dan keyboardist and cowriter), WALTER BECKER (guitarist and cowriter), LARRY CARLTON (guitarist), TOM SCOTT (saxophonist), and PETE CHRISTLIEB (saxophone soloist)**

**DONALD FAGEN:** Walter and I wrote "Deacon Blues" in Malibu, California, when we lived out there in '76. Walter would come over to my place and we'd sit at the piano. One day I had an idea for a chorus: If a college football team like the University of Alabama could have a grandiose name like the "Crimson Tide," the nerds and losers should be entitled to a grandiose name as well.

**WALTER BECKER:** Donald had a house that sat on top of a sand dune with a small room with a piano. From the window, you could see the Pacific in between the other houses. "Crimson Tide" didn't mean anything to us except the exaggerated grandiosity that's bestowed on winners. "Deacon Blues" was the equivalent for the loser in our song.

**FAGEN:** When Walter came over, we started on the music and then filled in more lyrics to fit the story. At that time, there had been a lineman with the Los Angeles Rams and the San Diego Chargers, Deacon Jones. We weren't serious football fans, but Deacon Jones's name had been in the news a lot in the 1960s and early '70s, and we liked how it sounded. It also had two syllables, like "Crimson," which was convenient. The name had nothing to do with Wake Forest's Demon Deacons or any other team with a losing record. The only Deacon I was familiar with in football at the time was Deacon Jones.

**BECKER:** Unlike a lot of other pop songwriting teams, we worked on both the music and lyrics together. It's not words and music separately, but a single flow of thought. There's a lot of riffing back and forth, trying to top each other until we're both happy with the result. We've always had a similar conception and sense of humor.

**FAGEN:** Also, Walter and I both have jazz backgrounds, so our models are different than many pop songwriters. With "Deacon Blues," as with many of our other songs, we conceived the tune as more of a big-band arrangement, with different instrumental sections contributing a specific sound at different points. We developed "Deacon Blues" in layers: First came the rhythm tracks, then vocals, and finally horns.

Many people have assumed the song is about a guy in the suburbs who ditches his life to become a musician. In truth, I'm not sure the guy actually achieves his dream. He might not even play the horn. It's the fantasy life of a suburban guy from a certain subculture. Many of our songs are journalistic. But this one was more autobiographical, about our own dreams when we were growing up in different suburban communities—me in New Jersey and Walter in New York's Westchester County.

**BECKER:** The protagonist in "Deacon Blues" is a triple-L loser—an L-L-L Loser. It's not so much about a guy who achieves his dream, but about a broken dream of a broken man living a broken life.

**FAGEN:** The concept of the "expanding man" that opens the song ["This is the day of the expanding man/That shape is my shade there where I used to stand"] may have been inspired by Alfred Bester's *The Demolished Man*. Walter and I were major sci-fi fans. The guy in the song imagines himself ascending the levels of evolution, "expanding" his mind, his spiritual possibilities, and his options in life.

**BECKER:** His personal history didn't look like much, so we allowed him to explode and provided him with a map for some kind of future.

**FAGEN:** Say a guy is living at home at his parents' house in suburbia. One day, when he's thirty-one, he wakes up and decides he wants to change the way he struts his stuff.

**BECKER:** Or he's making a skylight for his room above the garage and when the hole is open he feels the vibes coming in and has an epiphany. Or he's playing chess games against himself by making moves out of a book and cheating. A mystical thing takes place and he's suddenly aware of his surroundings and life, and starts thinking about his options. The "fine line" we use in the song ["So useless to ask me why/Throw a kiss and say goodbye/I'll make it this time/ I'm ready to cross that fine line"] is the dividing line between being a loser and winner, at least according to his own code. He's obviously tried to cross it before, without success.

**FAGEN:** By the mid-'70s, we were using session players in the studio. Steely Dan became just Walter and myself. We'd handpick musicians for the sound we were looking for on each song. We tended to go through quite a few musicians looking for the results we wanted. Soundwise, we were influenced by the jazz albums of engineer Rudy Van Gelder, the engineer who recorded many of those legendary Prestige and Blue Note albums in the 1950s and '60s.

**BECKER:** The thing about Rudy's recording technique is how he got each instrument to sound intimate, with musicians playing close to the microphones. The way he recorded, you had the continuity of lines and the fatness of tone that made solos jump out. We wanted all of our recordings to sound that way.

**LARRY CARLTON:** When I met with Donald, he gave me demos of him singing and playing "Deacon Blues." I transcribed the chords and built an arrangement for the rhythm section that was tight but left plenty of space for other layers—like horns and background vocals that I knew they would add later. The song's famous opening is my guitar and Victor Feldman's Fender Rhodes electric piano playing the exact same chords and voicings, plus drummer Bernard Purdie's cymbal figures. To keep the song's rhythm-section arrangement from sounding stiff, I added guitar ad-libs here and there to create contrast after Donald's vocal was in place. They were there to frame his voice.

**FAGEN:** Once the rhythm track and my vocal were set, horns were added to give the song a dreamy, reedy sound. We brought in saxophonist Tom Scott to write the arrangement. We told him we wanted the horns to have a tight, romantic "Duke Ellington cloud" feel.

**TOM SCOTT:** When I arrived at the Village Recorder in West Los Angeles, where Donald and Walter were recording, they played me the rhythm track. Donald said he wanted to add four reeds, two trombones, and a trumpet—but not a high-note trumpet. I heard right away how I'd arrange the horns—adding ninths and elevenths and other jazz dissonances that were implied but not there. I had about a week and a half to write arrangements for all the songs on

*Aja* where they wanted horns. For "Deacon Blues," I used a sound that mirrored Oliver Nelson's orchestral style. I wrote in these "rubs"—two notes close together in the middle register played by the tenor and baritone saxophones. This produces a really thick, reedy sound.

**FAGEN:** When everything was recorded—the rhythm section, the horns, and the background vocals—Walter and I sat in the studio listening back and decided we needed a sax solo, someone to speak for the main character. We liked the sound of a tenor saxophonist who played in Johnny Carson's *Tonight Show* band, a cat who blew like crazy when the show went to a commercial. He had this gutsy sound, but we didn't know who it was.

**BECKER:** We had our producer Gary Katz ask around and he found out it was Pete Christlieb. Pete had invented any number of cool harmonic devices that made his playing sound unique. He just sounded like a take-charge soloist, a "gunner."

**PETE CHRISTLIEB:** I went over to the studio one night after *The Tonight Show* finished taping at 6:30 p.m. When I listened on headphones to the track Tom had arranged, there was just enough space for me to play a solo. As I listened, I realized Donald and Walter were using jazz chord changes, not the block chords of rock. This gave me a solid base for improvisation. They just told me to play what I felt. Hey, I'm a jazz musician—that's what I do. So I listened again and recorded my first solo. We listened back and they said it was great. I recorded a second take, and that's the one they used. I was gone in a half hour. The next thing I know I'm hearing myself in every airport bathroom in the world.

**FAGEN:** The song's fade-out at the end was intentional. We used it to make the end feel like a dream fading off into the night.

**BECKER:** "Deacon Blues" was special for me. It's the only time I remember mixing a record all day and when the mix was done feeling like I wanted to hear it over and over again. It was the comprehensive sound of the thing: the song itself, its character, the way the instruments sounded, and the way Tom Scott's tight horn arrangement fit in.

**FAGEN:** One thing we did right on "Deacon Blues," and all of our records: We never tried to accommodate the mass market. We worked for ourselves, and still do.

Elvis Costello with a Fender Jazzmaster guitar in March 1977 during a photo shoot for his first album, *My Aim Is True*.

*Estate of Keith Morris/Getty Images*

# 37: (The Angels Wanna Wear My) Red Shoes

**ELVIS COSTELLO**

*Released: November 1977*

Glam rock wasn't universally appreciated in the U.K. in the early 1970s. Artists such as David Bowie, T. Rex, Mott the Hoople, and Gary Glitter had plenty of detractors, among them fans of pub rock. The stripped down pub-rock movement developed in North London, and artists and fans rejected glam's theatrical flamboyance and soul-pop eccentricity. Glam, for many of them, was slickly superficial and inaccessible, more glitz and icy pretension than heartfelt expression. Leading glam artists were performing in arenas, which also didn't necessarily sit well with pub rockers or their fans, who equated intimate club space with musical honesty and artistic authenticity.

Tearing a page from Britain's skiffle movement of the 1950s, which embraced traditional jazz and folk and the acoustic guitar, pub rockers tended to dress down, eschewing flash or gimmickry. Instead, their music was inspired by the high-strung rockabilly energy of Jerry Lee Lewis and geek-country innocence of Buddy Holly. Pub rockers in the early and mid-1970s, such as Mickey Jupp, Eggs Over Easy, Dr. Feelgood, Ducks Deluxe, and Nick Lowe, typically performed in pubs and clubs, developing a loyal and enthusiastic following. While the U.K.'s pub rockers retained punk's driving attack, their songs tended to be more poetic and romantic, with a retro feel.

While holding down a job at a London cosmetics company, Elvis Costello wrote songs in a small notebook and performed them in the mid-1970s at pub-rock venues at night. One of these songs was "(The Angels Wanna Wear My) Red Shoes," which he dashed off in the last ten minutes of a train trip. The song was a surrealist tale about an imagined jilting and the appearance of earthbound angels offering the song's protagonist immortality in exchange for his footwear. Months after completing the song, Mr. Costello recorded "Red Shoes" for his first album, *My Aim Is True*, released in 1977. As a single, "Red Shoes" charted briefly in the U.K., while *My Aim Is True* peaked on *Billboard*'s album chart at No. 32. The album was inducted into the Grammy Hall of Fame in 2007.

## Interview with ELVIS COSTELLO (singer-songwriter and guitarist)

**ELVIS COSTELLO:** In mid-1976, I was on holiday from my London office job when I decided to take the train up to Liverpool to visit my mother. I was still working as a computer operator for the cosmetics firm Elizabeth Arden and had begun taking sick days to rehearse and record what eventually would become an entire album, completed before I even turned professional.

Back then the journey from London to Liverpool took around three hours, and Runcorn was the last stop before the train continued another ten minutes to its final destination—Liverpool Lime Street. At Runcorn station, I took out a little blue pocket-sized notebook that was supposedly where I wrote the names of people who had crossed me, but, in truth, contained only phone numbers and lyrics to songs I was writing. I'd write drafts of songs from page to page, rewriting them over and over until they made sense.

As the train pulled out of Runcorn, I began to write. The idea for "Red Shoes" came to me fully formed, with the song's summarizing chorus line—"The angels wanna wear my red shoes"— appearing first. So in the minutes that followed, I worked backward from the chorus line on the rest of the lyrics. I could write snappy lines like "Oh I used to be disgusted/and now I try to be amused" in my sleep, but it perplexed me a little to be suddenly writing this song about mortality at only twenty-two. The verses were a pretty routine tale for me of romantic letdown. What surprised me was the visitation by angels with rusted wings offering a deal for my shoes. I couldn't figure out if they were gatekeepers to immortality or fame, which seemed so far off at that point in my career.

When the train arrived at Lime Street ten minutes later, the song's words were finished and the music was in my head. I have no idea where the song's inspiration came from. There wasn't much to see out the train windows. And I didn't own red shoes, only a pair of oxblood Doc Martens, which you might say were red. I had only one pair of shoes, but I didn't think of them as red. The song's only connection to my past was the woman in the song who tells me to drop dead and leaves with another guy. Something like that had happened to me three years earlier on the same London-to-Liverpool train.

Back then, I was seated in a compartment with a sophisticated-looking girl my age in a business suit and a soldier on leave. At some point, the three of us started talking, and eventually wound up sharing a bottle of whiskey that the soldier produced from his bag. Not being a terribly experienced whiskey drinker, I became convinced that I was irresistible. As is the case when one drinks too much, things became "all for one and one for all" pretty quickly. I was convinced the girl had eyes for me, but I quickly discovered that this wasn't the case when she disappeared with the soldier ["I said 'I'm so happy, I could die'/She said 'Drop dead,' then left with another guy"]. Eventually I woke up on a bench on Lime Street, having fallen asleep. I'm just thankful no one stole my guitar.

Three years later I was on the same train writing "Red Shoes." When I got off at Liverpool Lime Street, I worried I'd forget the melody before it was fixed in my head. I couldn't write music, and I had no way of recording the song on the fly like you can today with all the new technology. What's more, the slightest distraction could distort the song or erase it from my mind completely. But I wasn't in panic mode. I typically resisted going to an instrument too quickly. You have to let a song live in your head for a while. Otherwise, you'll settle for a melody or harmony that's a bit predictable.

Maybe that's why I've written so many unevenly proportioned songs. For example, on "Red Shoes," the verse ["Oh, I know that she's disgusted/Cause she's feeling so abused/She gets tired of the lust,/but it's so hard to refuse"] is sort of like a verse but it's also like a bridge. If the song had come to me when I had a guitar in hand, it might have wound up too polished.

As I walked through the Liverpool Lime Street station to find a cab, I must have looked deranged. I was muttering and singing the song to myself over and over, trying to block out noise and distractions. Fortunately, the cab ride was quiet—the driver wasn't playing the radio or eager to talk. When I arrived at my mother's house, I shouted a brief hello and rushed upstairs to my old room. I pulled out my old Spanish guitar and tuned the steel strings carefully, since I didn't have spares if these snapped. I also didn't have a tape recorder to capture what I was playing. By playing it over and over, I had it down.

Soon after I completed "Red Shoes," I was signed to Stiff Records, a British independent label. Stiff sent me off to Headley Grange, about an hour and a half southwest of London, to rehearse backed by members of Clover, an American country-rock band that was in the U.K. to record an album. Headley Grange was a former poorhouse that became a rock 'n' roll safe house where record companies lodged their bands and had them work on material before recording. It was cost-effective for them.

We recorded "Red Shoes" and the rest of *My Aim Is True* in late 1976 and early '77 at Pathway Studios in London. Nick Lowe produced. The studio was a small space with an eight-track board and a bit of magic in the sound. The beauty of that studio is you didn't have room to overcomplicate your ideas. I was right on top of the music, which meant I couldn't get further away from anyone else or myself to gain perspective on what was going on.

Clover liked "Red Shoes" and could remember it from one end of the day to the next. Musically, I didn't know how to get an audience's attention then, and what the guys from Clover were doing with the song instrumentally sounded bold from the start. John Ciambotti, Clover's bassist, referred to "Red Shoes" as "the song that sounds like the Byrds." I said to myself, "Well, OK, if it sounds like the Byrds, that's a good thing." Guitarist John McFee opened the record with a figure that almost sounded like a twelve-string guitar, which was good, since we didn't own one between us. I was playing rhythm guitar, but in truth I didn't know what I was playing, really.

Soon after *My Aim Is True* was released in the U.K. in July '77, I quit my day job and formed the Attractions. The way we approached "Red Shoes" and the rest of my songs changed quickly. After a tour of theaters in Britain and then clubs in America after the song's release in the States in December, we played "Red Shoes" and the other songs almost twice as fast as I had recorded them with Clover. But what we lost in the swing we gained in the attack. It was our natural disposition to be argumentative, so we sped them up to stand out.

Today, I start most of my concerts with "Red Shoes." I always want a strong starting point. My shows open with a reel of my music videos on a large screen. I figure no one else is going to show them, so why not me. But today, they look like Buster Keaton films. So much time has passed. Since the audience already heard many of my hits in the opening series of videos, that anxiety has been removed. As a result, "Red Shoes" doesn't have to obliterate everything. I'm able to tell a much longer, more diverse story with the song that's closer to the way I intended it on that ten-minute train ride between Runcorn and Liverpool Lime Street.

Blondie's Debbie Harry and Chris Stein at New York's Media Sound Studios in May 1979.

*Allan Tannenbaum/Getty Images*

# 38: Heart of Glass
**BLONDIE**
*Released: January 1979*

Punk rock in New York had run its course by the late 1970s. Too much was happening on the city's music, art, and fashion scenes for any one style to last long without trying to become something else. In fact, by decade's end, all three cultural spheres were beginning to intersect as they embraced media exposure and stardom. Andy Warhol had encouraged the overlap, building bridges between musicians at Max's Kansas City and celebrities at Studio 54, and between the city's art galleries and catwalks. Warhol, with his *Interview* magazine and Rolodex, saw value in the unification of performance and exposure, and between status and mingling. For Warhol, New York's cultural scene had a singular beauty, even as the city itself decayed.

But punk's ethos and Warhol's vision never quite gelled. Punk celebrated the written-off and badly behaved and was largely subterranean, damaged, and monochromatic, with many of its artists projecting the same general post-Ramones look and rage. Though Warhol had been instrumental in helping to launch the proto punk Velvet Underground in the 1960s, punk culture in the late 1970s was an indistinguishable swarm of dark conformity rather than a collection of pretty characters and individualists. Warhol's vision was more tightly connected to trashy decadence and the commerce of color and manipulation, the industriousness of producing rather than just doing or ranting. As he wrote in his 1975 manifesto, *The Philosophy of Andy Warhol (From A to B and Back Again)*, "I like working better than relaxing." When the new-wave movement emerged in the late 1970s, the music seemed to have Warhol's fingerprints all over it. New wave upgraded punk, retaining the music's high-strung impatience but adding pop glamour and cool-toned disinterest. In 1978, upwardly mobile post-punk artists such as the Talking Heads, Malcolm McLaren, Elvis Costello, and the B-52s were artfully camp in their jittery nerdiness and jaded sophistication. Their music was also more accessible and less taunting than punk, making the shift from gothic bleakness to art rock.

Unlike many female punk singers at the time, Debbie Harry didn't look like a corpse. With bleach-blond hair and a model's features, she seemed to have more in common with the fashion and graffiti art scenes than with the music of the Lower East Side. Yet there was something about her that was damaged goods—a quality Warhol fully appreciated. Up until 1978, Harry's band, Blondie, had a narrow following, largely held to New York's CBGB, Max's Kansas City, and other assorted downtown bars and joints. By '78, the band had grown tired of kicking around and was eager to record a hit. So the group's label, Chrysalis, paired them with producer Michael Chapman for their third album. The result was *Parallel Lines,* which included "Heart of Glass," a seemingly impossible mash of punk and disco. When the single was released in January 1979, it became Blondie's first *Billboard* pop-chart hit, climbing to No. 1 in April, largely thanks to Harry's leveraging of Donna Summer's sighing falsetto and a Giorgio Moroder Euro-techno sound. The single was inducted into the Grammy Hall of Fame in 2016.

**Interviews with CHRIS STEIN (Blondie cofounder, guitarist, and cowriter), DEBBIE HARRY (cofounder, lead singer, and cowriter), and MICHAEL CHAPMAN (producer)**

**CHRIS STEIN:** When Debbie and I lived together in a top-floor apartment at 48 West 17th Street, I often messed around on a borrowed multitrack tape recorder. It let me record a rhythm guitar track and then layer melody and harmony lines on top. I wrote and developed my songs this way. In the summer of 1974, I wrote a song that referenced the catchy feel of "Rock the Boat" by the Hues Corporation [see Chapter 33], which was a big hit then. Debbie and I began calling the music I wrote "The Disco Song."

**DEBBIE HARRY:** I used to keep a notebook to jot down lyrics and lyric ideas that came to me. On this one, Chris was constantly experimenting with the song, and the lyrics just floated into my head. The words I came up with expressed a very high school kind of thing—falling in and out of love and getting your feelings hurt. But instead of dwelling on the pain, the words sort of shrugged off the breakup, like, "Oh, well, that's the way it goes."

Chris and I both came from an art background, and we were familiar with existentialism, surrealism, abstractionism, and so on. The feeling I wanted to get across was, "Live and let live," like this is what happened and now it's not happening, you know? I threw in the "Ooo-ooo, ohhh-oh" fill when we started performing the song at CBGB. It was a 1960s "girl group" thing. Chris and I both loved R&B.

**STEIN:** The Shangri-Las were a huge influence on us. When I was a kid, I didn't get it. I thought they were commercial and weird. All those soap opera scenarios they sang about were strange. But after Debbie and I started Blondie in '74, I realized how fantastic and raw their music was and that their gang-related sensibilities were appealing.

**HARRY:** The whole Blondie thing was about a distinctive approach. In the mid-'70s, there weren't a lot of girls singing in a feminine way. The music was gritty. So we combined punk rock with an R&B feel. That's what gave us an identifiable sound and kept us going. Soon, the kids who came to our shows began asking for "The Disco Song."

**STEIN:** The hook was in the verse, when I had the song's key pivot from major to minor on the same chord. It was catchy. But we were always playing the song differently. We tried a calypso beat, a funk approach, and others. Nothing ever seemed to work comfortably. In 1975, we made a demo of the song that was pretty stripped down, calling it "Once I Had a Love." Then we forgot about it.

**HARRY:** In 1978, Terry Ellis, cofounder of Chrysalis Records, wanted Mike Chapman to produce our third album. Terry was very excited about us making a really commercial pop record. We had no problem with that, since we thought we were doing that already, you know? This was just taking it to another level. But we were neophytes and didn't have any experience making an intense, tight-sounding record for radio.

**MICHAEL CHAPMAN:** I first met Chris and Debbie in New York at the Gramercy Park Hotel. They played me tapes of new songs for the album. The music was great, but I wanted a song that would really pop. I asked if they had anything else. They said, "Well, we have this song we call 'The Disco Song.'" When they played it, I thought it was quite good, but the song wasn't 100 percent there yet.

At our first rehearsal for the album, all six members of the band were there. To break the ice, I wanted to start with a song that was most comfortable for them—"Once I Had a Love." It needed a new title.

**STEIN:** Originally, Debbie's second line of the song was, "Soon turned out, he was a pain in the ass." Mike thought that might not play well on the radio, so I threw out a phrase, "heart of glass," which everyone liked. Debbie worked it in as "Soon turned out, had a heart of glass." That's the new title we used on the song.

**CHAPMAN:** I asked Debbie which singer she liked most in the music business. She said, "Donna Summer," particularly on "I Feel

Love." I never expected that. I said to her and Chris, "Why don't we give this song a Giorgio Moroder feel?" Giorgio had produced Donna's great albums.

**STEIN:** We loved the idea. As a band, we had already been referencing the electronic-dance feel of Kraftwerk, which had released *Trans-Europe Express* a year earlier. We felt that would be a move forward. But getting that sound back then was a mystery to all of us. It had to be invented.

**CHAPMAN:** We went into New York's Record Plant in June 1978, but the sound I wanted turned out to be a Pandora's box of nightmares. The first step was to get the tempo right. I had this Roland drum machine that I wanted to use in sync with Clem Burke's drums. You hear the machine on the opening. To provide Clem with a track guide, I recorded the vocal in falsetto. After we had the kick drum pounding, I changed the arrangement so it would skip a beat along the way, to give it a dance feel. I had to get the Roland to skip the beat at the same time.

Then we recorded the rest of the drum parts individually—the high-hat, the snare, and the tom-tom. The eight tracks of drums took a week, and synchronizing them with the drum machine was the toughest part. We only had a twenty-four-track recorder, and we couldn't cut and paste digitally like you can today. What I was asking Clem to do was close to enslavement, and he was ready to kill me. I also brought in two EMT 250s, the first digital reverb machine. I had discovered the EMT in Montreux, Switzerland, a year earlier. They gave the snare drum—and later, the vocal—more dimension, and an electronic vibe.

Once we had the drum tracks, I turned to the bass. With my vocal track standing in for Debbie, bassist Nigel Harrison and I spent an entire day on it. In the end, we had the most amazing bass line. Next came Jimmy Destri on the keyboard. We didn't have sequencers then, so we ended up recording three different parts using a Roland SH-5 and a Minimoog, which we spent hours trying to figure out how to use. When we had the rhythm-section track complete, I turned to recording Debbie's vocal on top.

**HARRY:** I don't think there's one particular emotion that I connected to when recording the vocal. I don't really work like that. It's usually sort of in-the-moment. In those days, just being able to pull it off technically for me was a pretty major achievement. I think the emotional content and thinking came later, with experience.

**CHAPMAN:** I cleared the studio so it was just Debbie in the middle of the room alone with her headset on. I was in the control booth. Debbie sang three or four takes. Her pitch was beautiful and expressive, so you hear every aspect of her personality. But after listening back, I thought we should overdub Debbie singing a background vocal in places. To illustrate what I wanted, I came in early the next day and had my engineer, Peter Coleman, record me singing the background track. When Debbie arrived, I played it for her with her lead vocal. She thought it sounded great and wanted me to leave it. So I'm singing background on the record.

**HARRY:** Singing those lead-vocal takes was excruciating, especially the high notes. I wasn't singing in falsetto—that was the soprano part of my voice. Mike knew what he wanted, and I couldn't get away with a stinking thing.

**CHAPMAN:** The guitars were the last element. Chris provided the ambient sounds, and Frankie [Infante] came in next to do the aggressive guitar parts. Recording the song took a little over a week, leaving us four weeks to finish the album. Then came the editing process. We must have made thirty to forty edits for the final master.

**STEIN:** For years I thought some of the ambient swishing sounds on the recording were synthesizers. Then a couple of years ago we took the tracks apart for a TV documentary and I realized that a lot of the weird noises were actually coming from my guitar, which I had fed through a Roland tape-loop echo machine.

**CHAPMAN:** I always thought that if "Heart of Glass" could capture the mass market discreetly and tastefully, it would open the entire world to Blondie, and it did. The trick was to accessorize the band's coarse sound, not replace it or have them sell out. There was real danger in changing them too dramatically. Debbie's voice was key to the sound. I knew if I let Debbie be Debbie, listeners would feel what she was singing.

**HARRY:** I think many people connect with the sense of loss or sadness that's underneath the song. They also connect with the melody's descending scale, sort of an "Ahhh, yeah, oh well," like a musical sigh. A lot of people have things like that feeling in their lives.

When we were recording, we all went to Studio 54 at night. But the "Heart of Glass" video wasn't shot there. It was shot in some club on the West Side with palm trees. I still have the gray one-strap Stephen Sprouse dress I wore in the video and the gray scarf. The clear plastic shoes? They melted somewhere along the way.

Roger Waters in London in June 1990, weeks before recording *The Wall: Live in Berlin*.

*Tom Stoddart Archive/Getty Images*

# 39: Another Brick in the Wall

**PINK FLOYD**

*Released: November 1979*

One of the earliest multimedia rock performances was the first Exploding Plastic Inevitable screenings by Andy Warhol in 1966 at New York's Dom ballroom. As Warhol's films were projected on screens, members of his Factory danced to a performance by the Velvet Underground and Nico. The following year, Joshua White's Joshua Light Show was projected at a Frank Zappa concert in Mineola, New York, and in 1968 White's light shows began appearing regularly behind artists performing at New York's Fillmore East. Rock also found its way into the theater, starting with *Hair* in 1967 and followed by a succession of rock musicals and operas. Improvements in lighting design and sound-system technology in the early 1970s also led to more theatrical and thematic arena concerts by artists such as David Bowie, Alice Cooper, KISS, and George Clinton and Parliament-Funkadelic.

But all would pale in comparison with the art-rock extravaganzas staged by Pink Floyd, which pioneered special effects at live rock shows. Beginning in 1973, with the band's *Dark Side of the Moon* arena tour, Pink Floyd used props and pyrotechnics, and floated helium-filled characters above audiences. Such staging would reach a high point with Pink Floyd's concert tour for *The Wall* in 1980 and '81. The staging included a 160-foot-long, 35-foot-high wall made from 340 giant lightweight "bricks" erected between the audience and the band during the first half of the show.

Pink Floyd's tour started soon after the band released *The Wall* in late 1979. The anti-tyranny rock opera explored parental abandonment and teacher harassment, as well as the emotional isolation and mental breakdowns they produced. Among the twenty-six songs featured in *The Wall* was Pink Floyd's only No. 1 hit single in the U.S.—"Another Brick in the Wall, Part 2." The four-minute song—with its throbbing bass line, thumping beat, and teen chorus—has long been viewed as an anti-education mantra, a mischaracterization that still rattles Roger Waters, the song's composer and former Pink Floyd front man. "How easy it is for people to misinterpret stuff when they don't bother to actually think about what they're hearing and seeing," he told me. Nevertheless, the song's chant "We don't need no education" caught the imaginations of frustrated students, and in March 1980 helped lift the single to the top of *Billboard*'s pop chart, where it remained for four weeks. The album, *The Wall*, was inducted into the Grammy Hall of Fame in 2008.

### Interview with ROGER WATERS (Pink Floyd cofounder, lead singer, songwriter, and bassist)

**ROGER WATERS:** For much of my life, I have been defensive. My 2015 film [*Roger Waters: The Wall*] is the start of an attempt to come out from behind my defenses and declare my vulnerability and acceptance of others. I have this huge desire to nail my colors to the mast of something that isn't about confrontation but about cooperation.

The idea for *The Wall* came to me in 1977, during Pink Floyd's *Animals* tour. Toward the end of the tour in July, a few assholes in the audience at Montreal's Olympic Stadium set off fireworks, interrupting the show. It was more than distracting. It was—excuse my French—fucking rude, and I told the audience. Things got a bit out of hand, and famously, when some over-enthusiastic punter tried to scale the barriers at the front of the stage, I spat in his face.

Nothing personal, but it made me think about my relationship with the audience and the obvious wall between some of them and some of us on stage.

After the tour, when the band had had a chance to rest, I thought about what had happened, and developed an idea for a large-scale rock show: A huge theatrical brick wall would be erected between the band and the audience to express the alienation between those in the seats and what we were trying to do. As I thought about the idea, the wall became a metaphor for some of the mechanisms people and institutions use to keep the rest of us under their control and dictate how our lives should be led—without seeming conspiracy-theory about everything.

I also wanted this wall to stand for the emotional barrier we build around ourselves as individuals, with the bricks representing difficult things that have happened to us over time. At one point, I drew a brick wall on the back of a white envelope. The lyric for "Brick 2" was the progeny of that idea.

In late 1978, I called a meeting of the band at our Britannia Row Studios in London. By then, I had recorded two concept-album demos that were each about fifty minutes long. I also brought along texts that outlined the concepts I had in mind. At the studio, I told the band—Dave [Gilmour], Rick [Wright], and Nick [Mason]—that I had written two theatrical works. One was *The Pros and Cons of Hitch Hiking* and the other was *The Wall*. After we listened to the demos, they picked *The Wall*, which I thought was a good choice since it had more universal concepts.

I had already written what would become *Brick 2* at Bourne Hill House in Horsham, West Sussex, England, where I was living at the time. I had an old sixteen-track analog mixing board that came from Criteria Recording Studios in Miami. I used it to record my demo of "Brick 2" and a number of other songs for *The Wall*.

The words and music were written as I strummed on a six-string acoustic guitar. The song flowed straight out of me in a minute and a half. It only had a single verse and a chorus. On the demo, I accompanied myself. [He sings the rhythmic acoustic-guitar introduction and then the lyrics, "We don't need no education/We don't need no thought control."]

The lyrics were a reaction to my time at the Cambridgeshire High School for Boys in 1955, when I was twelve. Some of the teachers there were locked into the idea that young boys needed to be controlled with sarcasm and the exercising of brute force to subjugate us to their will. That was their idea of education.

When the band first recorded "Brick 2" in the studio in early 1979, I thought of it as just a short thematic interlude in *The Wall*. After we finished it, we realized the song was catchy and had bigger potential, but we weren't quite sure how to build it out. We tried a guitar solo over the verse, but the song was still too brief.

It wasn't until *The Wall* was almost finished that I thought it might be good to get a bunch of English kids to sing the chorus, to animate the lyrics. We were in Los Angeles at the time, finishing the album at Producers Workshop studio with [producer] Bob Ezrin and [engineer] Brian Christian. So we sent the twenty-four-track studio tape of "Brick 2" to [engineer] Nick Griffiths at Britannia Row Studios and asked him to find some kids to sing on it.

Nicky found the kids at the Islington Green School in North London, near our studio. He put together about twenty-five students between ages thirteen and fifteen and overdubbed them singing several times, so it would sound as if there were many more of them. I originally thought we'd use their voices as background for the lead vocals Dave and I had recorded, but the sound we heard on the tape when it came in was so emotionally powerful that we let them sing their part alone.

To hear those kids from a not-so-affluent part of London singing the lyrics took my breath away. By adding those voices, Nicky had made the song visceral and deeply moving in a very serious way. Letting them sing alone and adding David's guitar solo expanded the song to four minutes. In my recollection it was my idea to add the kids singing, but human memory is a fallible device. Bob Ezrin might say it was his idea. Other members of the band might say it was theirs. I have no interest in arguing with any of them about any of it, as what we do know now, for certain, is that we'll never know.

The song ran slow, almost like a chant or mantra, at a hundred beats per minute. To give it a bit of punch, Bob Ezrin added a kick drum on every beat, which made the song a different animal than something strummed on an acoustic guitar. It's not a disco beat, as many people have said, but more of a heartbeat. It's very cool.

Featuring the song once on the album was never my intent. My demo was meant as a thematic interlude that would appear in different forms in different places to transition from one section to another. I had written lyrics for three parts, with slightly varying orchestrations.

For example, "Brick 1" starts with the lyrics "Daddy's flown across the ocean/leaving just a memory." It's about my father's death, which was my first "brick." "Brick 2" is my educational thing. And "Brick 3"—"I don't need no arms around me"—was used after *The Wall*'s main character has a mental breakdown following his wife's betrayal. What can I tell you? In relationships, shit sometimes happens, and sometimes we get the feeling we are immune even to the healing power of loving arms. We don't always see straight.

Then again, sometimes we do see straight. When Nick Griffiths sent me the multitracks of the song from London, I was in Los Angeles and had Brian stick it on the tape deck. "OK," I said, "push all the faders up." As soon as the song came on, it was like, "Whoa." I knew instantly it was a hit.

After "Brick 2" was released as a single, even some intelligent writers thought it was an antieducation song and said it was disgusting and obscene. But the song was never that. It's a protest song against the tyranny of stupidity and oppression, not just in schools but universally. It's about the malign influence of propaganda. Obviously, I care deeply about education. I just wanted to encourage anyone who marches to a different drum to push back against those who try to control their minds, rather than to retreat behind emotional walls.

In 2011, during my most recent tour for *The Wall*, I was moved to write "Brick 4." I was sitting in a hotel room somewhere in the States when it occurred to me that the Hammond organ solo at the end of "Brick 2" was just filling time. I didn't want to do that anymore, so I wrote lyrics for a new "Brick." It became my homage to Jean Charles de Menezes, a Brazilian engineering student killed in London by the police in 2005 when they mistakenly thought he was one of the people involved in the failed Underground [subway] bombing attempt days earlier. This song appears in the movie right after "Brick 2."

Listening to "Brick 2" today, I wouldn't touch a thing. If you have something to do with a four-minute song that has proved to be as powerful as this one, you would have to be an idiot to tear the wings off to see what makes it fly. Looking back, however, I realize that whenever you collaborate with others on something special, you have to be grateful that you came together. This is true about all my colleagues in Pink Floyd, and Bob Ezrin, Nick Griffiths, and whoever else was involved. You have to say, "Hey, we were a team."

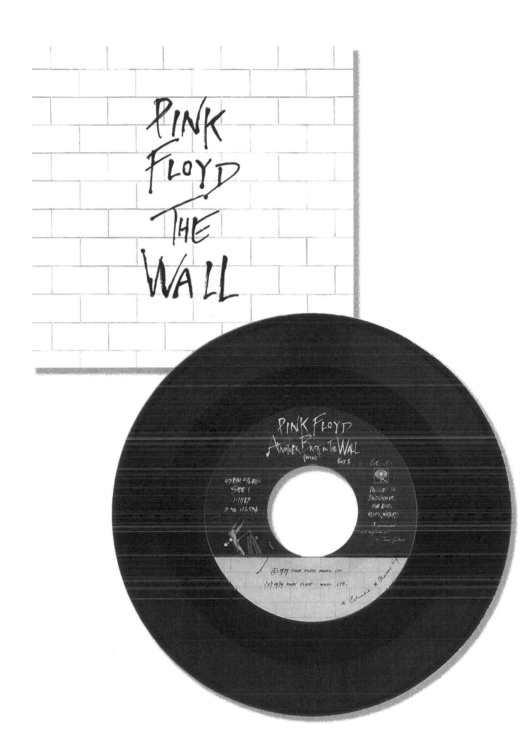

The Clash on New York's West Side in September 1978, from left—Nicky "Topper" Headon,
Mick Jones, Joe Strummer, and Paul Simonon.

*Michael Putland/Getty Images*

# 40: London Calling

**THE CLASH**

*Released: December 1979*

By mid-1977, a growing chorus of British punk rock artists voiced frustration over the music's stagnancy. The movement had arrived late in the U.K., catching on in 1976 after a Ramones concert. A year later British punk seemed to be moving in circles instead of evolving. On a radio show in London in July 1977, Johnny Rotten (John Lydon) of the Sex Pistols was interviewed by host Tommy Vance for *The Johnny Rotten Show: The Punk and His Music,* a program devoted to chat and Rotten's favorite records. Rotten soon began voicing disgust with punk's narrow imagination and most bands' unwillingness to surface new, more varied approaches to the music. "That's the trouble with most punk bands—you can predict what their next song is gonna be, and as soon as they start up you can sing along with the words," he said, disparagingly. In October 1977, British punk entered a new phase with the release of the Sex Pistols' *Never Mind the Bollocks,* a slickly produced album that seemed to have more in common with conventional hard rock. Rotten quit the band in January 1978.

Punk's internal struggles continued in 1978 over authenticity, which led the music to shift. As unemployment and social unrest mounted in Britain, some bands, like the Clash, developed songs laced with social protest that mirrored the critical tone taken by reggae bands in Jamaica. No longer content to merely rail against social norms or advocate for individual freedom, British punk bands experimented with social criticism, taking public policies, national officials, and even the Queen to task, along with the U.K.'s harsh economic conditions. Punk's new sociopolitical ire would come in handy when Margaret Thatcher, a Conservative, became prime minister in May 1979. When the Clash wrote and rehearsed "London Calling" early that year, the band addressed global warming, potential flooding by London's River Thames, and police beatings of demonstrators.

"London Calling" was released in December 1979 and became one of the era's most stirring and influential rock anthems. With its martial beat, radio warning beeps, rocksteady funk bass line, and lashing lyrics, the song warned of a world facing dire ecological risks. Cowritten by Mick Jones and Joe Strummer, the band's lead singer, the song "London Calling" never became a *Billboard* hit in the U.S., but reached No. 11 in the U.K. The album on which it appeared (and with which it shares a title) climbed to No. 9 in Britain, but to only No. 27 in the U.S. Nonetheless, it was inducted into the Grammy Hall of Fame in 2007.

**Interviews with MICK JONES (the Clash singer, guitarist, and cowriter), PAUL SIMONON (bassist), and TOPPER HEADON (drummer)**

**MICK JONES:** The initial inspiration for the song "London Calling" wasn't British politics—it was our fear of drowning. In 1979 we saw a headline on the front of the London *Evening Standard* warning that the North Sea might rise and push up the Thames, flooding the city. We flipped. To us, the headline was just another example of how everything was coming undone.

**PAUL SIMONON:** In the '70s, when we formed the band, there was a lot of tension in Britain, lots of strikes, and the country was an economic mess. There also was aggression toward anyone who looked different—especially the punks. So the name "the Clash" seemed appropriate for the band's name. Before "London Calling," we didn't really have a manager or rehearsal space, so we were drifting about. Our road crew found us space off Vauxhall

Bridge Road in the Pimlico section along the Thames. It was a thin, drafty, soundproof room upstairs in the back of a garage.

**JONES:** We rehearsed hard each day, taking a break in the afternoons to cross the road to a fenced-in playground where we played football. It was like a team-building thing. We had a strong sense of togetherness. [Lead singer] Joe Strummer was living in a building along the Thames and feared potential flooding. He did two or three drafts of lyrics that I then widened until the song became this warning about the doom of everyday life. We were a bit ahead of the global-warming thing, weren't we?

The line about phony Beatlemania biting the dust was aimed at all the touristy sound-alike rock bands in London in the late '70s. We were fans of the Beatles, the Who, and the Kinks—but we wanted to remake all of that. We wanted "London Calling" to reclaim the raw, natural culture. We looked back to earlier rock music with great pleasure, but many of the issues people were facing were new and frightening. Our message was more urgent—that things were going to pieces. Once we had most of the words down, I began creating music to fit the rhythm of the lyrics. I wanted the urgency of a news alert. The two guitar chords I used were a bit jumpy at first, but I figured out a trick with my little finger to change them smoothly.

**TOPPER HEADON:** When Mick started playing the chords, I began drumming. My music background had been jazz and soul, so I wanted to give my martial tempo a bit of variety. I played the intro straight, but when the band and Joe's vocal came in, I played sixteenths on the high-hat with my right hand for some shimmer. Then when we started the chorus that began with "The Ice Age is coming," I added a little swing thing.

**SIMONON:** I wanted my bass line to be like a big declaration—like "Here we are!" My influence was Leroy Sibbles, the bass player for the reggae band the Heptones.

**JONES:** The song's title came from Joe. When he was a kid, his family had moved to Germany, and that's where he first heard the phrase "London calling," on the radio. The BBC used it for years to open its news broadcasts abroad.

**HEADON:** "London Calling" took weeks until we got it right. We weren't in a great state financially and our third album had to sell or we were going to be in trouble with our record company. Making matters worse was our intention to do a double album, which didn't go over well with the label. We had a lot riding on the work.

**JONES:** After "London Calling" was set—along with a batch of other songs for the album—we went into Bill Price's Wessex Studios in August 1979. It was a former church in North London. Bill set us up in the studio in a tight circle.

**SIMONON:** Our producer Guy Stevens was really important to us for his musical and emotional contribution. He was once asked to describe his style and he said, "In this world there are two Phil Spectors, and I'm one of them." During the recording of "London Calling," Guy would come into the recording room to intensify the mood. One time he came in while we were recording and started smashing chairs against the wall to increase the atmosphere. But not everyone was able to get out of the way. Joe was singing and playing the piano, and Guy didn't want it in there. He picked up a bottle of red wine and poured it all over Joe's hands and onto the keyboard.

**JONES:** Most people aren't aware that my guitar solo in the middle of the song is backward. After I recorded it, I turned the tape over and overdubbed it onto the mix that way. That's why it whooshes. I wanted it to sound raw and unhinged.

**HEADON:** Guy added the fire of magic. Look, when someone's swinging a ladder around and you have to keep ducking, the music is definitely alive. At one point he said, "OK, that's a take." I said,

"No it's not. It speeds up a bit." He said, "All great rock 'n' roll speeds up. That's a take." And he was right. It made us realize that a good rock producer leaves imperfection in there someplace.

**JONES:** Bill Price is the one who added echo and the sound of cannons firing. We also added Joe making seagull cries that were influenced by Otis Redding's "(Sittin' on) The Dock of the Bay" [see Chapter 16]. As musicians, you take the past with you, don't you? The Beatles, Stones, Kinks, and Small Faces had done something new and different, and I wanted us to do that, too. The Morse code thing at the end was me. I turned off one of my guitar pickups and used the remaining pickup to tack out the radio signal—to give it that BBC sound on the fade-out.

**SIMONON:** The photo of me on the "London Calling" album cover was taken while we were performing at New York's Palladium Theater. The sound on stage was bad and I struggled to hear my notes. Also, most of the audience was sitting, so I assumed that either they didn't like the show or that security wasn't letting them dance. In frustration, I took it out on my bass guitar. Unfortunately, for the rest of the tour I had to use my spare bass that didn't sound as good as the one I had smashed.

Photographer Pennie Smith took the photo. It was so quick and sudden—which is why the image of me smashing my bass guitar is blurry. Joe suggested we use Pennie's photo for the cover of "London Calling," and we did. My temper? It's better now, but not cured. It's creative frustration triggered by whatever circumstance I'm in. I've got it almost under control, but things do happen. Sometimes it's hard counting backward from twenty.

The Neville Brothers (c. late 1970s), from left—Aaron, Cyril, Charles, and Art.

# 41 : Brother John/ Iko Iko

**THE NEVILLE BROTHERS**
*Released: April 1981*

Since the late 1800s, New Orleans musicians have prided themselves on being influenced by everything but sounding like nothing else. The music of New Orleans is a product of the city's many cultural cross-currents, long-standing traditions, and annual Mardi Gras parade, which serves as the city's musical core. The parade—with its Carnival roots, carnal abandon, and jazz feel—never seems to leave the souls of musicians, no matter how famous they become after leaving the city. Musicians such as Buddy Bolden, King Oliver, Louis Armstrong, Jelly Roll Morton, Professor Longhair, Fats Domino, Huey "Piano" Smith, Allen Toussaint, the Meters, Dr. John, and the Dixie Cups all left New Orleans at some point in search of fame, but the city's potent musical legacy managed to remain with them.

One of the most famous musical families in New Orleans are the four Neville Brothers. When the brothers first came together in 1978 to record the album *The Neville Brothers,* the result was an eclectic and highly unusual fusion of music styles steeped in the city's cultural history. Though the Neville Brothers collectively have never had a *Billboard* pop hit, vocalist Aaron Neville has had nine, including "Tell It Like It Is" and "Don't Know Much," both reaching No. 2, in 1966 and 1989, respectively.

One of the quartet's most critically acclaimed songs is "Brother John," recorded first in 1976 on *The Wild Tchoupitoulas*, an album by a Mardis Gras "Indian" tribe of the same name. The song was recorded again in 1981 combined with "Iko Iko," and it appeared on the Neville Brothers' *Fiyo on the Bayou* album. Over the years, "Brother John/Iko Iko" has become an important Mardi Gras anthem and is culturally linked to the chants of Mardi Gras "Indians," whose lineage dates back to the late nineteenth century. Back then, "tribes" were formed in New Orleans's African-American neighborhoods to pay homage to Native Americans and create an alternate Mardi Gras celebration. The customized African dress, masks, and rituals have since been passed down to successive generations. Like most songs born in New Orleans, "Brother John/Iko Iko" is a fusion of musical influences, including Creole, funk, R&B, doo-wop, and girl-group pop.

**Interviews with CYRIL NEVILLE (singer, keyboardist, and cowriter), AARON NEVILLE (singer), ART NEVILLE (singer and keyboardist), CHARLES NEVILLE (singer and saxophonist), BARBARA HAWKINS (Dixie Cups singer and cowriter), and MAC REBENNACK, also known as "DR. JOHN" (arranger)**

**CYRIL NEVILLE:** From the time I was six, I always carried a paperback dictionary, pencil, and paper. My mother insisted I learn to read early, so I wouldn't stumble into death. Down in New Orleans in the 1950s, if you drank from the wrong fountain because you couldn't read the sign that said "Whites Only," you could wind up beaten or dead.

In my teens, when I began singing and playing percussion, I'd use my pad to jot down things I heard that sounded interesting for songs. In the case of "Brother John," I wrote the lyrics in the early '70s with my Uncle Jolly [George Landry]. They're set to a song with an African rhythm that was popular with every Mardi Gras Indian tribe then. New Orleans is really the northernmost point of the Caribbean, so the African, island flavor has always been there. James "Sugar Boy" Crawford was first to popularize this rhythm on his 1954 hit "Jock-a-Mo." I wrote the lyrics for "Brother John" with my uncle as a tribute to a friend—John "Scarface" Williams—who had been killed a short time earlier.

**AARON NEVILLE:** I was close with Scarface when we were teens. He sang with Huey "Piano" Smith and the Clowns in the early 1950s and then with the Tick Tocks—both significant R&B groups in New Orleans. Scarface and I hung out a lot at the Dew Drop Inn on Lasalle Street. One night in March 1972, he was stabbed trying to stop a fight in front of a club on Dryades Street. His death was a big blow, not only because he was a well-known musician but also because he was the Big Chief of the Mohawk Hunters tribe and a friend of our uncle, Big Chief Jolly, who was chief of his Mardi Gras Indian tribe.

**CYRIL NEVILLE:** As a child, I was always curious about the Mardi Gras Indians. I used to follow Uncle Jolly all over town. Back then, all of the Indian tribes in the city's wards sang the same songs but played the African rhythms differently, giving the songs their own flavor. I learned all the inflections just by tagging along with him.

One day in the early 1970s, I was at my Uncle Jolly's house, where he and four of his friends were sewing their Indian suits for Mardi Gras. I had written some lyric ideas on my pad: "He was a mighty friend with a heart of steel/Brother John is gone/But he never would bow and he never would kneel/Brother John is gone." My uncle read them and laughed, saying how much he liked what I had done. That was one of the proudest moments of my life.

**ART NEVILLE:** My three brothers and I were all singers and musicians, but we didn't officially come together as a group until 1976, when we sang backup harmony on *The Wild Tchoupitoulas*—my Uncle Jolly's album. It was named after his tribe and featured Mardi Gras Indian call-and-response chants. Members of the New Orleans band the Meters were on there, and it was coproduced by

Allen Toussaint. That's the first time we recorded Cyril's "Brother John."

After that album, my brothers and I decided to stick together. It felt good. In 1978, we recorded our first album, *The Neville Brothers*, for Capitol, which didn't do much. We were without a label for a few years, until Bette Midler came down to New Orleans to perform at the Orpheum Theater. After she heard us play at Tipitina's, we spoke and she said she was going to tell Jerry Moss of A&M Records about us. She did, and we were signed to his label. Our first album for the label was *Fiyo on the Bayou*, released in 1981. We decided to record "Brother John" combined with "Iko Iko," which we had been doing at clubs for years.

**CHARLES NEVILLE:** Actually, three of us came together for the first time in New York in the early 1970s, when Cyril and Aaron stayed with me for a while. They had just started playing "Brother John." The three of us rehearsed it in Brooklyn before performing at the club Catch a Rising Star. The song went over great. There, we met David Forman, a singer-songwriter who was inspired by Aaron, and Bill Dicey, a harmonica player. So we put together a band.

**AARON NEVILLE:** Whenever we performed live in the late '70s, people in the audience liked to dance to "Brother John." To stretch out the groove so people could dance longer, we'd tack on other artists' hits, like Hank Williams' "Jambalaya" and Hank Ballard and the Midnighters' "Sexy Ways." They all sounded similar and fit right in with our funky Creole thing. Soon we added "Iko Iko," which went over so well we kept the two songs together. "Iko Iko" was credited to Barbara Hawkins and the other two Dixie Cups, and it was a big hit for them in 1965.

**BARBARA HAWKINS:** Growing up in New Orleans, my sister Rosa, my cousin Joan Johnson, and I learned a street song from our grandmother. We used to call it "Iko Iko." In 1965, we were in New

York recording for Red Bird Records. On a break in the studio, the three of us began jamming on the song, probably because we were homesick.

Someone in the control booth liked what we were doing and started recording us without our knowledge. Then he asked us to do it again. We kept jamming with our drumstick, Coke bottle, ashtray, and aluminum chair, and that second taping became the master vocal track for our 1965 hit. For publishing purposes, the three of us in the Dixie Cups became the songwriters. After "Iko Iko" came out and was a hit, the company that owned the rights to "Jock-a-Mo" sued on behalf of "Sugar Boy" Crawford, but everything was settled in 1967, giving him part of the royalties. At the time of the recording, we didn't even know his song existed. The harmony, flavor, and lyrics of "Iko Iko" were distinctly ours.

**CHARLES NEVILLE:** We recorded "Brother John/Iko Iko" along with the rest of *Fiyo on the Bayou* at Studio in the Country in Washington Parish, Louisiana, a couple of hours north of New Orleans. It was in the middle of nowhere. Food, beverages, and everything else were brought in, which kept us from wandering off on breaks. We were so far from town, nobody would drop in and distract us.

**ART NEVILLE:** I wanted to hook up the song the way we played it on gigs—with a live, party feel. Joel Dorn, the album's producer, agreed and wanted to use the band that backed Mac [Rebennack, also known as Dr. John]. Joel wanted the song and album to be more commercially accessible, which meant a bigger, punchier sound for FM radio and stereo systems. Mac wrote the arrangements. Using Mac's band was always part of the plan, before we even arrived at the studio. Those guys were great. Of course, our band didn't like that they weren't going to record on the song. But when we explained that Joel wanted a different feel, they understood. They were going to have plenty of time to play it on tour after I gave them Mac's arrangement.

**CHARLES NEVILLE:** We did a couple of takes of "Brother John/Iko Iko," plus some overdubs. It was mostly straight-ahead playing and recording. The cats in our band had a certain way of playing it, but Herman [Ernest III] from Mac's band had his way of playing the second-line drum with a Mardi Gras groove, and bassist David Barard had a Mardi Gras feel, too. Everyone liked it.

**AARON NEVILLE:** I sang high harmony on the record, while Art and Charles sang the lower notes and Cyril sang the lead. I loved singing the high notes. I'd listen to Art and Charles to make sure we sang the notes together and that I blended in. I was part of the group. That's what has always fascinated me about doo-wop—the harmony and falsetto.

**MAC REBENNACK:** "Scar" John, the guy the song was written for, was a special cat. He saved my life one time. We were standing outside the Robin Hood Club listening to Little Miss Cornshucks when he suddenly said, "Look out, man." So I looked out and half a St. Louis brick came sailing past my head. All the Nevilles singing about him was special on that record. But there's also something about that drum that Herman played that put a hurt on that sucker. The Nevilles' singing and Herman's drum always got folks wigglin.' And that's all right.

Merle Haggard at a small, downtown Los Angeles hotel in 1981 chosen for the *Big City* album cover shoot.

*Photograph by Norman Seeff*

# 42: Big City
**MERLE HAGGARD**
*Released: January 1982*

When Columbia, Decca, and RCA opened offices in Nashville in the 1950s, producers began replacing country's rural and cowboy traditions with a smoother pop sound. But not all country artists and fans appreciated Nashville's slick makeover of country music. In the late 1950s, a countermovement developed on the West Coast in Bakersfield, California, that retained more of country music's original twang and free-range quality. Missing from Nashville's country-pop sound, they believed, was the earthiness of honky-tonk, electric-guitar picking, a musician's individual talents rather than a silky backdrop provided by studio musicians, and the Western-swing tradition pioneered in the 1940s by Jimmie Rogers, Hank Williams, Milton Brown, and Bob Wills. These early artists and others represented the roots of country music, and many artists felt that their yearning voices and acoustic instruments had been lost in Nashville's pasteurization process.

Bakersfield wasn't as unlikely a bastion of resistance to Nashville's increasing dominance over country music as one would imagine. Many Bakersfield musicians were children of poor families who had moved west from the South and Southwest during the Depression and after World War II in search of jobs. Hugely influential was Buck Owens and the Buckaroos, whose country-rockabilly sound influenced a generation of rock bands, from the Beatles to Creedence Clearwater Revival. Merle Haggard also helped bring the new Bakersfield sound to national attention.

Born in Oildale, California, singer-songwriter and guitarist Haggard came to music by way of prison. He had been arrested in the late 1950s for trying to rob a roadhouse, and as a San Quentin inmate, he heard Johnny Cash perform there in 1958. By the time he was released in 1960, Haggard was committed to becoming a musician, and hits followed in the 1960s and '70s, including "Okie From Muskogee" (1969). His song "Big City," released in January 1982, tapped into blue-collar frustration over working on urban assembly lines, and it soon reached No. 1 on *Billboard*'s country chart. The album *Big City* reached No. 3. Haggard's "Big City" cowriter was Dean Holloway, his longtime tour-bus driver.

### Interview with MERLE HAGGARD (singer, guitarist, and cowriter)

**MERLE HAGGARD:** In July 1981, when my tour bus pulled into the driveway of Britannia Studios in Los Angeles, we knew we had a rough two days ahead of us. I had just signed with Epic Records, and they wanted me and my band [the Strangers] to record twenty-three songs in forty-eight hours, giving them enough material for two albums. When we finished on the second day, I went out to the bus to check on Dean Holloway, our driver and my lifelong friend. For whatever reason, my timing was perfect: Dean was ticked off.

Dean and I had known each other since grammar school in Bakersfield, where my parents had moved from Oklahoma during the Depression. Dean and I met when we were thirteen years old at a little theater where Roy Rogers and Gene Autry used to perform. Naturally, the first thing we did was fight. Once we got up off the ground, we became best friends and were inseparable.

Growing up in the farmlands of California, Dean was the best driver I ever rode with. When we were teens, there was never a question about who was going to drive. He drove and I played guitar and that's the way it was. So in '66, when my career took off and I started touring longer distances, I asked Dean to drive my bus, and he did.

From then on—until the '90s, when he retired—Dean drove our bus. He had amazing instincts and reflexes. I remember coming out of Nashville one time in '66. We were in an old Flxible going at a good clip on a two-lane road with no shoulders. When we came over a rise, in front of us were two cars just sitting there—one behind the other. They were waiting for a wide truck to pass coming from the other direction.

I was sitting behind Dean rehearsing "Swinging Doors" and saw what lay ahead. I thought, "Wonder what old Dean's gonna do now?" There wasn't time to stop without crashing into those cars. So Dean sailed to the right of them. As we passed within inches of the first car, I could see two little girls in the back through their rear window. The bus leaned terribly to the right as we flew past and Dean managed to put that bus gently on its side in the grass. Dean saved those little girls, no one on our bus got hurt, and there wasn't even a scratch on the bus once the tow truck set it straight.

Getting back to Los Angeles in '81, when I headed out to check on Dean, he wasn't happy. Buses then didn't have much air-conditioning, and ours had been sitting in the heat for hours with the engine off. Dean was sitting there minding the bus when I asked how he was doing, Dean said, "I hate this place. I'm tired of this dirty old city."

As a songwriter, I instinctively listen and watch for interesting ways people put things at bars and diners and on billboards. "This dirty old city" sort of caught me. I said, "Mr. Holloway"—that's what I always called him—"I can see you're upset, but why don't we take that anger out on a piece of paper?" I climbed on board, and Dean handed me a pad and pen that he had with all the other things he kept near his seat.

Whenever I work on lyrics, I hear the music as I write the words. The two go together for me. On the bus, the lyrics came real good, and their feel sort of dictated the melody. I took Dean's "dirty old city" line and began to build a story. The feeling resonated, because it was a time in America when things were breaking down, especially in cities. I thought about Detroit and the problems the car industry faced after the gas shortage of '79. I imagined a family leaving Detroit and happy to be getting out.

I mixed in some lines about quitting a job so there was a reason to leave the "dirty old city." But for the chorus, I needed a place where the person in the song wanted to go. I said to Dean, "You're in the middle of Los Angeles now. Where would you rather be?" Dean said, "If it were up to me, it'd be somewhere in the middle of damn Montana." Well, with Dean on a roll, we had that song done in about ten minutes.

When we finished, I moved a bunch of lines around so they'd sing right, tore the sheet out of the pad, and told Dean, "I'm gonna run inside and record this thing before I forget the melody." Inside, the band was packing up. I said, "Hold on, let's do one more. I just wrote something and want to get it down." The band shrugged and said, "All right, if that's what you want to do." I ran down the song's melody and words for the band and told them the feel I wanted. I gave them the chords and told them where I wanted the others to join me on the vocal.

Before we started, I told Jimmy Belkin, my fiddle player, who had spent many years with Bob Wills and Ray Price, to give me a good, strong intro. He hadn't rehearsed anything—what you hear is what he played after I hummed the melody. Then Norm Hamlet came in with his steel guitar. I didn't play any guitar on this one— Roy Nichols did. I just sang. We didn't have an ending, but the band came up with one they thought I'd like and ran me off as we wound down.

While all this was going on, producer Lewis Talley had gone off for a jug, thinking the session was over. When he returned to the control room, we were in the midst of recording "Big City." Lewis was my mentor, and I could see that look on his face. He really liked the song. At the end, he hit the talkback switch and said, "Fix one bass note and you'll have a No. 1 record." We fixed it, and while I listened back to the tape, all I could think was, "Man, Dean-o just wrote a hit song."

The engineer ran off a tape reel of the song, and I took it out to the bus. I had a big player mounted in there, and I cued up the tape. I said to Dean, "I want you to hear something—this hasn't been written a full hour yet." I punched "play" and said, "Listen to our song, Mr. Holloway." Well, Dean's attitude went from the floor to the ceiling. I said, "You and I just wrote a hit." He was white around the mouth.

Dean said, "Damn," and he kept saying that as we listened. I said, "Yep, those words we wrote earlier are already a record. This was your inspiration, so we're splitting it down the middle." Dean was a plain old boy and was never the same after that. He wasn't in my tax bracket—he was a regular guy making a regular salary, and this thing transformed him.

I'm sorry to say Dean died in 2009. But a few years before he did, I had a chance to ask him how well he did with "Big City." Dean said, "Hell, that song made me a half-million dollars." I felt good about that. Dean was my best friend. For the rest of his life after that record came out, he talked to himself about what we had done.

Cyndi Lauper at a miniature golf course in Los Angeles in February 1984.

*Chris Walter/Getty Images*

# 43: Time After Time
**CYNDI LAUPER**
*Released: January 1984*

When MTV began broadcasting in the summer of 1981, the music-video channel added a powerful new visual dimension to rock and pop. By featuring musicians in video interpretations of their songs, the cable channel stimulated a demand for pop music not seen since the mid-1960s. Before MTV's launch, rock and pop were solely record and radio affairs, with concerts and occasional appearances by artists on TV variety and talk shows. After MTV—or at least for as long as record labels were willing to pay for the production of videos—rock and pop stars were in household living rooms, twenty-four hours a day, acting out the drama and humor in the lyrics of their latest hits. The music and videos were free, as long as parents paid their cable bill.

British pop artists seemed particularly adept at the new video format, from their bold fashion statements to their knack for poking fun at themselves. Within a year of MTV's launch, a significant number of MTV videos by U.K. pop artists had led to a second British Invasion in the U.S., with music marked by a liberal use of synthesizers and booming drums. Thanks to MTV, British bands such as Culture Club, Madness, Spandau Ballet, the Human League, Naked Eyes, and Duran Duran bypassed radio and gained early access to the U.S. market. By 1983, American artists, including Madonna, DeBarge, Toto, Lionel Richie, and Hall and Oates, had followed with synthpop hits and arty music videos.

One American artist who was perfectly suited for MTV was Cyndi Lauper. Lauper's eccentricity, bold thrift-shop fashion statements, and cartoonish voice made her a gentle role model for young women struggling to create an identify for themselves. Her single and video for "Girls Just Wanna Have Fun" were released in September 1983—a month before *She's So Unusual,* her debut album. But it was Lauper's video for "Time After Time"—her second single from the album, released in January 1984—that captured the imaginations of viewers. Where "Girls Just Wanna Have Fun" was a bouncy tribute to the female spirit and 1960s girl groups, "Time After Time" was a heart-wrenching ballad tailored to a generation of girls coming of age. For the video, the song's lyrics became a tribute to female individualism and independence, and the song went to No. 1, while the album *She's So Unusual* went to No. 4 and remained on *Billboard*'s chart for ninety-six weeks. "Time After Time" was covered by Miles Davis in 1985, thanks largely to the urging of Cicely Tyson, Davis's wife at the time.

### Interviews with ROB HYMAN (keyboardist and cowriter) and CYNDI LAUPER (singer and cowriter)

**ROB HYMAN:** In the fall of 1982, I was performing with the Hooters at New York's Bottom Line when my friend and college roommate, Rick Chertoff, called. Rick was about to produce an album for a singer named Cyndi Lauper, whose band, Blue Angel, had broken up a year earlier. She needed musicians, and he wanted to bring her down to the club. The Hooters played a lot of reggae and ska that night, and Cyndi liked that. Then we hung out and talked music. She made an instant impression.

In the months that followed, Cyndi came down often to Philadelphia to "the Ranch," the band's name for the warehouse where we rehearsed. Throughout the winter, Cyndi, [Hooters cofounder] Eric Bazilian, and I recorded rough demos of the songs Rick wanted for her album on a four-track Portastudio cassette recorder.

By the early spring, we were ready to record at New York's Record Plant. Cyndi was a tough taskmaster. She knew what she wanted and what she didn't—though that could change as we dug deeper. When we finished recording the songs in June, Rick said what we had was great but that he could use one more good song for the album.

Honestly, I felt a bit of dread. I didn't have a song kicking around, and we were exhausted after being in the studio for months. The next night, Cyndi and I went into the larger studio, which had a Steinway concert grand.

**CYNDI LAUPER:** I wanted to write some of the songs for the album. I used to write songs for Blue Angel with the keyboard player, but Rick wanted me to focus on singing. I was so happy when Rob wanted to write together.

We started by putting together a list of song titles. I thumbed through a *TV Guide* magazine. One movie title seemed good—a sci-fi film called *Time After Time* from 1979. I never meant for it to be the song's real title. It was just supposed to get me thinking.

**HYMAN:** At the piano, I had this repetitive melodic idea and started playing the four chords. They became the chorus you hear on the record, but at the time I was playing the music faster, with a bouncy, upbeat, reggae vibe. Cyndi and I sang "time after time" as a placeholder.

**LAUPER:** While Rob played, I stood next to the piano and danced, kind of free form. Moving around like that to the music helped me figure out how the song should feel. I wanted to catch a vibe off what Rob was doing.

Rob had just the chorus—a good melody but no words. As I danced to what Rob played I started thinking about up and down, lost and found: "If you fall I will catch you, I will be waiting/Time after time" and "If you're lost you can look and you will find me/ Time after time." The words sounded odd at first, but when I sang them, I realized that what I was talking about were pieces of my personal life.

**HYMAN:** As Cyndi sang, she and I realized the song was darker and more intense than a bouncy, happy song. When we slowed it down, the song became heartbreaking. There was suddenly so much emotion in the song. I was going through some relationship issues and Cyndi had similar experiences, so we both felt it. Even though we slowed down the music, the chorus retained a clipped calypso-type melody, which worked perfectly.

**LAUPER:** In the days that followed, the first verse I wrote was, "Lying in my bed I hear the clock tick/and think of you." That was about my life. I had a clock that I got for my birthday that I kept up on my loft bed in my one-bedroom walk-up apartment on 77th Street near York Avenue. Dave Wolff, my boyfriend and manager at the time, had climbed up to sleep, and the clock fell and smashed. I loved that clock.

Dave went and got a windup clock from his mother's house. But when we set it up, it was so loud. I climbed down and put it in the tub and closed the curtain. But I could still hear it ticking from the bed. I remember lying there and thinking about all this personal stuff I had gone through.

The second verse—"Then you say, go slow/I fall behind/The second hand unwinds"—was inspired by Rick [Chertoff]. At some point in the studio, his watch came in contact with something and became demagnetized. Its second hand was going backward, and he was saying, "Look, look, my second hand is unwinding." I loved that line.

**HYMAN:** With the chorus and two verses in place, we still needed a third. We came up with the last verse over the phone when I was back home in Philadelphia.

**LAUPER:** Rob called me, and the verse I came up with—"After my picture fades and darkness has/Turned to gray/Watching through windows"—was about my past relationships. I used to sit up on that loft bed and look out the window and watch darkness turn to gray, thinking about them.

When Rob came back up to New York, he played and I sang the song in the studio. I felt the verses had to have soul. As a painter, you're supposed to live in the moment and paint that moment. I studied the Impressionists, who painted their emotions. I did that with my vocal. We taped everything we did and then played it all back, picking the best parts. It all came out of a trance. We had tranced a lot of mumbo jumbo, listened to it, and figured out what worked.

**HYMAN:** The song took two or three nights working this way. We had agonized over the album's other songs and recorded multiple demos—trying this and that. This song had to happen much faster. Since we didn't have time to record a four-track demo, Cyndi and I just put the parts together. Then Cyndi went into a booth as I played my Roland Juno-60 synthesizer, which I had plugged directly into the board in the control room. I used an organ pad—a drony organ sound that functions a bit like strings. I played the pad the whole way through, giving the song a thick keyboard bed. It would act like superglue and hold together everything else we added later.

The track Cyndi heard through her headset also had a Roland TR-808 drum machine going. Eric [Bazilian] did a lot of the drum programming. Anton Fig added real drums later in a few places where they were needed. Cyndi singing to that organ pad was magical. Then Eric added guitar lines to the recording. Another keyboardist, Peter Wood, added the synth-horn sound on the bridge.

**LAUPER:** My repeating "time after time" as a fading whisper at the end just happened. I had fallen into a trance and came out of it like that, singing softly. I wanted it to sound hushed, like my voice was trailing off into the distance.

**HYMAN:** The craziest thing was when I overdubbed a harmony as Cyndi sang the melody line in the chorus. I added my voice just as a reference for another singer—a male-female dialogue thing, as if they're singing to each other. When Cyndi listened back, she liked it and said, "We're keeping it." If you listen carefully, you'll hear that the song has no bass until each chorus—"If you're lost you can look and you will find me." The song had to lift off there, so I added a synth bass.

Just as we were wrapping up in the control room, I sensed someone behind me. When I turned around, there was Roberta Flack—she was probably recording at the Record Plant. She said, "Wow, that's cool! That sounds great, guys." And then she was gone.

**LAUPER:** A lot of people I knew were in the song's music video. My mom plays my mom, and my brother is sleeping on a bench at the train station. I wanted the video to be like a picture book for me later.

The tear that rolls down my cheek at the end on the train was real. I didn't think I could do it, since I wasn't a trained actress. But when I picked up the duffel bag to get on the train, I choked up. Years earlier, when leaving home, I had a similar bag, so that got to me.

One day in 1984, a guy named Joe pulled me over when I was visiting Rick at Columbia. He told me that Miles Davis had recorded "Time After Time" for an upcoming album. Joe played it for me and I thought, "Oh wow, that's really nice."

Sometime later, I ran into Cicely Tyson, who had been married to Miles in the 1980s. She told me how much she loved *She's So Unusual* and how she had insisted Miles listen to "Time After Time." She played it for him, and he loved it, too.

Miles's version was a big inspiration. I had cowritten a song and this great jazz artist loved it. It was a nod, you know, that I could write beautiful songs. His recording said to me, "Go ahead and just do it."

Bonnie Raitt performing in Baden-Baden, Germany, in June 1992.

*Courtesy of Everett Collection*

# 44: Nick of Time
**BONNIE RAITT**
*Released: March 1989*

Rock artists and bands that played the blues fell on hard times in the 1980s. Thanks to MTV and the proliferation of music videos, synthpop surged in popularity, compelling artists to grow comfortable with role-playing, fashion, choreography, drama, and other visual and theatrical arts. Most blues rock artists, however, found it difficult to be anyone but themselves. Authenticity was baked into the music and its performance. While established blues legends such as B. B. King, Albert King, Buddy Guy, and Albert Collins did well in the 1980s, many young blues rock headliners resisted playing to the camera and didn't fare well, since the essence of their music depended on their sensitivity, humility, and artistic integrity.

Musicians such as Stevie Ray Vaughan, Robert Cray, and the Fabulous Thunderbirds toured moderate-sized venues in the 1980s and were nominated or won Grammys for blues recordings. But without Top 20 hits on *Billboard*'s pop chart or MTV videos, these artists weren't able to become household names, and their albums tended to reach only the high double digits on *Billboard*'s album chart. A turning point in terms of visibility for Vaughan came in 1989, when he appeared on *MTV Unplugged*, a showcase for musicians playing acoustic instruments. But his fame was short-lived. In August 1990, Vaughan was killed in a helicopter crash. After his death, his album, *Family Style*, hit No. 7 on the *Billboard* chart.

One of the best-known blues rock artist today is Bonnie Raitt. The daughter of John Raitt, a popular Broadway musical and film actor and singer, Bonnie Raitt began studying piano as a child, adding the guitar at age eight. After her family moved to New York from Los Angeles in the early 1960s when she was fifteen, Raitt became fascinated with the blues, and her interest grew as she came in contact with legends such as Mississippi Fred McDowell. The 1970s were a fruitful period for Raitt, but a series of personal and professional setbacks in the early 1980s rattled her confidence. She needed an emotional time-out to regain her balance and shake off bad habits. In 1988, a year after becoming sober, Raitt wrote "Nick of Time," a soulful mid-tempo ballad about aging and rebounding. When her album *Nick of Time* was released in early 1989, it climbed to No. 1 on the *Billboard* album chart, where it remained for 185 weeks, while the single, released later that year, reached No. 10 on *Billboard's* adult contemporary chart. In 1990, Ms. Raitt won two Grammys for the album, which became a major turning point for her as an artist. The album was inducted into the Grammy Hall of Fame in 2015.

### Interview with BONNIE RAITT (singer-songwriter, guitarist, and pianist)

**BONNIE RAITT:** By the end of the 1980s, I was closing in on forty and decided it was time to really reevaluate my health and lifestyle. When I looked around, I saw what my peers and I had been getting away with—indulging in eating and partying without exercising. None of it was wearing well.

My downslide started around 1983, when Warner Bros. Records dropped me just as I finished a new album. That decision forced me to cancel a much-anticipated tour with Stevie Ray Vaughan. Then a romance I was involved in ended badly in '84. Though I stayed on the road and released an album in '86, I was mad and hurt, and I internalized everything, relying more and more on alcohol and drugs to numb the pain.

By early 1987, I'd had enough. With the help of some good sober friends, I was able to stop drinking, lose weight, and get in shape.

I didn't expect sobriety to be such a profound change, but almost immediately I felt like I'd had a spiritual awakening and physical rebirth. I felt optimistic for the first time in years.

In 1988, I went away for a week on retreat in Mendocino, California. I just wanted to kick back and reflect on all the changes of the past year and maybe write some new music honoring how grateful I felt to have made it through. I wasn't writing for an album, per se. It was simply therapeutic, to get away and be inspired by all that beauty and nature.

Sitting in that cabin, looking out at the Pacific, I began thinking about the most poignant aspects of my life for a song. That's when the first verse of "Nick of Time" came to me. A dear friend had told me a painful story over the phone that echoed what several of my other friends in their late thirties were going through. A lot of them wanted children and it either wasn't happening or they hadn't met the right guy yet. Time was running out.

My friend's experience was heartbreaking. At one point she said she saw babies everywhere she went and would just burst into tears in the grocery store. I wrote a verse based on our talks: "A friend of mine, she cries at night / and she calls me on the phone. / Sees babies everywhere she goes / and she wants one of her own."

As I wrote the lyrics, I tried to capture the essence of what my friends were dealing with and what was real for me at that point in my life. I never felt cut out to be a wife or a mother. Growing up, I had two brothers and was a tomboy. My family lived at the top of Mulholland Drive, away from most other houses, and I didn't have after-school babysitting jobs, nor did I hang around kids. But I could relate.

The idea for the second verse came soon after. It was inspired by a car trip I had taken a few years earlier with my dad, John Raitt, to visit my brother. I was driving and my father was in the passenger seat. At some point, he dropped the seat back and dozed off. My father was a great actor and singer on Broadway and in film and such a leonine man—a big guy, handsome, with terrific stature and athleticism, even through his eighties.

As I drove, I looked over and noticed how different he seemed when he was asleep. Most of us don't get to see our parents sleeping until the end of their life, when they're in the hospital. This was one of those really tender moments. In his vulnerable state, I could see he was getting older and could really feel what it was like for a body to age. This whole idea of time and it being more precious as you age, I realized this would be what I'd write about.

After my week in Mendocino ended, I was driving back at night to Los Angeles on Route 5. As I drove, I was trying out different lyrics in my head when a dust storm hit. The wind was so strong it blew my car into the next lane.

These were the days before you could dictate into a cell phone. So I pulled over, and in the dust storm, on the side of the road, I wrote the second verse: "I see my folks are getting on / and I watch their bodies change. / I know they see the same in me / and it makes us both feel strange."

By the time I reached L.A., I had written nearly all of the lyrics. The third verse had more to do with my recent journey out of that angry, heartbroken place. "You came along and showed me / I could leave it all behind. / You opened up my heart again / and then much to my surprise / I found love, baby, love in the nick of time." The "you" in there wasn't about any one person in particular. It was about a bigger, more universal love.

When I had been up in Mendocino, I brought along my Yamaha portable electric keyboard. I also had my guitars and a little four-track Fostex cassette recorder. I hung a mike off a lamp and set up the keyboard on a chair without a back. I sat in a big swivel chair in front of the fireplace and maneuvered the lamp stand to hold the recorder. I rigged up the gear so I could see the fireplace and the ocean and trees outside.

For a beat, I used a Roland TR-606 Drumatix, a compact drum machine from the early '80s. It had range of preset synthesized grooves, and because the unit was from the disco era, some of them had sound effects built in. From the start I knew the song needed a mid-tempo beat. Singing the song as a slow ballad would have made the lyrics too heavy and not fit the message.

Unfortunately, the "Philadelphia Soul" beat I liked on there had syndrums built in. Syndrums sounded like the original *Entertainment Tonight* theme, with those high-pitched electronic "pewww-pew pewwws" shooting off [Ms. Raitt sings the TV theme and the sound effects]. So while I was recording myself playing and singing, the effects kept darting in and out. It was pretty funny.

Back home in L.A., as I was singing and playing the song, the last line—"I found love, love in the nick of time"—came so effortlessly. It was one of the most amazing experiences of my life. That night, I think I felt for the first time the incredible power and mystery of how a song can come through. I knew then that "Nick of Time" would be the title of the song. The double-edged meaning was apparent: "nick," as in just in the nick of time, and also the wear and tear of time and the nicks it leaves on the body and spirit. It was an incredible moment.

Soon after I returned, producer Hal Willner called to ask if I'd record "Baby Mine" from the movie *Dumbo* for a Disney tribute album called *Stay Awake*. He said he wanted to team me with the group Was (Not Was) and asked if I knew them. I said, "Are you kidding? I'm a huge fan."

When I met Don Was, one of the group's cofounders, I was surprised that he was completely familiar with my music and had been a fan since the beginning in 1971. We became fast friends.

After I signed with Capitol in 1989, I wanted Don to produce my first album for the label. I told Don about this song I had written, and he asked to hear the demo. When I put it on, the groove was there but so were those hilarious syndrums. But being a soul music guy himself, he loved the song and understood immediately that cool soul inspiration. He also felt the song might be the cornerstone of the album.

We recorded "Nick of Time" at Ocean Way Recording in Hollywood. The song's arrangement was the same one I had used on my demo, except we used Ricky Fataar on drums, Hutch Hutchinson on bass, Mike Landau on guitar, and I played the keyboard.

Ricky is an astonishing drummer. He got a kick out of the demo with the disco effects, but he knew exactly how to translate the basic elements I had written to an updated organic feel. At some point, we wanted to add that heartbeat pulse you hear on Marvin Gaye's "I Heard It Through the Grapevine," but we didn't have a hand drum. So Ricky picked up a burlap sandbag used to hold down mike stands and put it on his lap. They miked the bag and he played the heartbeat of the song with his hands. More percussion and background vocals were overdubbed later.

"Nick of Time" came from a part of me that hadn't yet seen the light of day. I wanted to dig deep and honor the changes in my life. Writing it gave me a sense of confidence and self-awareness that helped me break through some stifling self-doubt. While writing the song, instead of comparing myself to greats like Jackson Browne and Randy Newman and then giving up, I was just writing for myself, as a gift for the miracle that had happened.

At the Grammy Awards in 1990, I won two for "Nick of Time" and Don Was won for producer of the year. My father was there with me. After winning the first one, as I got back to my seat during a commercial break, my dad stood up to hug me. Our arms were wrapped around each other and I could feel him start to lose it. [Ms. Raitt begins to cry and pauses to regain her composure.] My dad was choking up. He knew what the album and the recognition meant to me, and I knew what it meant for him to see me not just doing well in the business but also the changes that had happened along the way. We never said a word. For us, in those few seconds, it was a beautiful moment.

Alternative rock's R.E.M. in Los Angeles in August 1994, from left—Peter Buck, Michael Stipe, Bill Berry, and Mike Mills.
*Kevin Cummins/Getty Images*

# 45: Losing My Religion

**R.E.M.**

*Released: February 1991*

As pop bands gained national exposure in the 1980s through videos, rock artists began to sound bland and formulaic. Albums by mainstream rock bands seemed devoid of the kinds of songs that many high school and college students depend on for confidence and to help them explain why they are different and unable to fit in. During the 1980s, many mainstream bands seemed to spend more time polishing their image and maximizing their exposure than producing work that explored the dark corners of young people's hearts and minds. By default, many young listeners began turning to the music of alternative rock bands that sang about defiance, anxiety, and existential issues that didn't always have neat answers.

The affordability of the personal cassette stereo, pioneered by the Sony Walkman, certainly contributed to alternative rock's growing popularity in the 1980s. The portability of recorded music allowed fans to listen more carefully to music and lyrics through foam headphones. As a result, music became a more intimate experience, and fans developed deep personal attachments to bands, particularly ones that addressed what they worried about most. Alternative rock bands such as Hüsker Dü, the Dream Syndicate, the Replacements, Sonic Youth, and Jane's Addiction filled a need that mainstream rock had abandoned. But alternative rock as a genre remained on the fringes throughout the decade.

The turning point came in 1991, with the release of R.E.M.'s album *Out of Time* and their single "Losing My Religion." Formed in 1980, the band from Athens, Georgia, spent the 1980s sticking steadfastly to its brand of angst-driven message songs and minimal instrumentation. "Losing My Religion," an unrequited love song about romantic uncertainty and self-doubt, quickly became R.E.M.'s biggest-selling single. It reached No. 4 on *Billboard*'s pop chart in June 1991 and won two Grammy Awards, while *Out of Time* climbed to No. 1 on the album chart and also won a Grammy. The success of "Losing My Religion" over the summer of 1991 primed the market for grunge's breakout in the fall and created a model for today's independent rock bands that strive to succeed without selling out.

**Interviews with PETER BUCK (R.E.M. guitarist and cowriter), MIKE MILLS (bassist and cowriter), MICHAEL STIPE (singer and cowriter), and BILL BERRY (drummer and cowriter)**

**PETER BUCK:** By the end of 1987, the band was exhausted. We had been out on the road performing for much of the year and we needed a rest. At home on my sofa in Athens, Georgia, I taught myself to play the mandolin. I had bought a strange-looking boxy model in New York several months earlier, and used it to write two new songs for *Green*—the album we were about to record later that spring.

At some point during those sofa sessions, I had the Atlanta Braves on the TV with the sound down and a cassette recorder going. I was strumming the mandolin like a guitar when an entire series of chords just fell out. They became the basis for "Losing My Religion."

I didn't have lyrics or a melody in mind—Michael [Stipe] would provide those later, along with his lead vocal—nor did I have a bass line or drum part. I simply had chord changes that sounded pretty good. But instead of rushing the song for *Green*, I held on to it for the album that would follow—*Out of Time*, which we wound up recording in mid-1990.

I also came up with a riff that lightly echoed Ryuichi Saka-moto's theme *for Merry Christmas, Mr. Lawrence*. I had seen the movie, and the riff stuck with me. It was perfect for connecting the song's descending chords, which shifted from minor to major.

In the summer of 1990, I brought the chords to the band at our rehearsal studio on West Clayton Street. By then, I had bought a traditional Gibson Flatiron mandolin. Drummer Bill Berry, bassist Mike Mills, and I ran down the chords a few times and recorded a rhythm-track demo that was pretty close to the way it sounds on the recording.

**MIKE MILLS:** Typically, we'd rehearse a song three or four times until each of us figured out what we were going to do on the record-ing. In this case, though, we had to rehearse the song more times than usual. I had a lot of trouble figuring out what I wanted to do with the bass line. There was a lot of sound to fill at the bottom, since the mandolin was in the upper register, but my line couldn't overcome the mandolin.

Eventually, I asked myself, "What would [bassist] John McVie do?" I super-admired Fleetwood Mac, and John's lines were always simple but melodic. They lift songs rather than hold them down. Thinking about John inspired me to come up with a line that locked down the bass part. Once the three of us finished the demo, we gave the cassette to Michael [Stipe].

**MICHAEL STIPE:** As a songwriter, I've always worked best when I can walk in large circles. I'm hyperactive, and walking around and around puts me in a meditative, trancelike state, freeing me to write without constraint or too much thought. In Athens, Geor-gia, I had set up my house to allow for that.

When the guys gave me the cassette, I put it on my stereo and walked around and built a melody while singing and capturing lyric ideas and anything else that came to mind on a handheld Sony recorder. Mike's bass lines helped dictate the melody and my vocal cadence. I love bass, and it's a natural anchor for voice. The song's melody came easy to me.

For the lyric, I knew I wanted to write an unrequited love song, like the Police's "Every Breath You Take." In writing the lyric, I wanted it to be unclear whether the relationship in the song was real or a figment of the protagonist's imagination. I created a character so shy and insecure that he questions every one of his moves and choices. He's yearning for love and acceptance.

I was never much of an autobiographic songwriter. I'm more of a storyteller. But I could draw from my own experiences and use details or observations from life to help bring resonance to the song's character. Within the details of the story, I hit upon a universal feeling that everyone has experienced—one of terrifying uncertainty and an almost teenage desire for acceptance.

"That's me in the corner" is a wallflower, shy and frightened and not able to speak up. "That's me in the spotlight" was initially "That's me in the kitchen," but "spotlight" had a harder consonant and worked better. It also flips the narrative. "Choosing my confessions" fit the atmosphere of uncertainty, in a near-religious, ecstatic context. The use of ecstatic or epiphanic moments is something I learned from my great friend and mentor Patti Smith.

The song's title came from an old Southern phrase—"I almost lost my religion"—that I heard growing up in the South. I changed it to "Losing My Religion," which sounded better for the song. The phrase is a gentle way of saying that you're at wit's end over something stressful that's out of your control.

**BILL BERRY:** After we heard Michael's melody, lyrics, and vocal, we rehearsed the song during preproduction at John Keane Studios in Athens. There, we created the blueprint for how we were going to record the song. Then each of us lived with a cassette copy for about two weeks. This let each of us mull over what we had done and any changes we might want to make before recording it.

**BUCK:** We decided to record "Losing My Religion" at Bearsville Studios near Woodstock, New York, where we had recorded *Green*. Bill liked the large space for the sound of his drums, and we wanted to get away from Athens so we wouldn't be disturbed or distracted.

**BERRY:** If you record in a large enough studio, you can use enough mikes to get a thick sound out of the drums. A pair of mikes were set up at different distances from my drums to create a tiny delay, which adds texture to the sound. One set was placed ten feet away and the other was twenty feet away. When I hit the drum, I got this longer, meaty sound.

Also, if you listen carefully you'll hear that on the second and fourth beats, I'm hitting the snare drum and tom-tom at the same time. That's a Mick Fleetwood trick, particularly on Fleetwood Mac's "Dreams." The tom-tom muffled the hiss of the snare and added more punch without drowning out Peter's mandolin.

**BUCK:** Acoustic guitarist Peter Holsapple, who had played with the band in concert, recorded with us in the studio. The mandolin produces a high, thin sound, so Peter's rhythm guitar filled in the mid-range below. As I played the mandolin riffs, Peter continued playing chords, which created a velvety curtain behind my notes. On the recording, I wasn't planning on having the mandolin ring at the end like an alarm or warning. I just wanted the sound of the instrument to decay so we wouldn't need a hard ending. Once the basic instrumental track was done, Michael recorded his vocal track.

**STIPE:** When I came in to John Keane Studios to record the vocal, I kicked everyone out of the room except our producer Scott Litt and engineer John Keane. I went into the isolation booth and sang to the instrumental track on my headphones. Problems emerged immediately. The bass was too loud at one point, or there was too much reverb or compression on the vocal. Then the drums were dropping in and out—there was always something wrong. Finding the correct mix to sing to was nearly impossible, and frustrating. In that moment of presenting a new lyric for the first time, everything that goes wrong feels seismic and mountain-sized.

I recorded three takes, barking out orders to fix what I didn't like in my headset. I was really annoyed. At one point, I took off my shirt. It was really hot—or I got hot. I also remember feeling frustrated with the process of trying to get the vocal down on tape. During the session, I finally arrived at a point where I made it work, and I completed the vocal in one take.

When I finished, I put on my shirt and stormed out. The next day, when everyone listened back to the song, the band and Scott loved the lyric and the melody. It was strange and filled with emotion. Adding strings was Peter Buck's idea, but I agreed with him. The song felt so big during the playback that we felt it could handle the color.

**BUCK:** The strings were arranged by Mark Bingham and added later. The band talked about it, and we decided to try something different. None of us owned synthesizers, and we weren't going to tour with the album. By then, we were making a bit of money and realized we could hire some strings from the Atlanta Symphony Orchestra. Violist Paul Murphy assembled the small string section.

Mark arranged the strings so they mirrored the bass and my electric guitar, which I had overdubbed to thicken the mandolin's notes. We didn't want a huge orchestral thing, just enough for color. We were in the control room when the classical musicians recorded and I remember feeling vaguely embarrassed, since I felt we were so far beneath them musically.

"Losing My Religion," like the rest of the album, was mixed at Prince's Paisley Park Studios. We were all big Prince fans and thought it would be cool. We tended to move around a lot, from studio to studio. I had friends in Minneapolis, so I knew I could catch up with them after long days recording.

Paisley Park was a nice room, but kind of rigid in terms of hierarchy. We told the studio manager that if Prince wanted to come by and listen, he was welcome to. The manager said that wasn't going to happen. We were also told that if Prince showed up, we weren't to look at him or talk to him.

When *Out of Time* was done, we wanted to release "Losing My Religion" as the album's first single, before the album came out. It was a different-sounding song for us, and some people at the label thought a mandolin-driven single wouldn't work on the radio. After a series of back-and-forths with label executives, "Losing My Religion" became the consensus choice.

**STIPE:** Even when the song was released, it wasn't supposed to be a big deal. It was just supposed to be the teaser track—the first song that would get us played on MTV and therefore introduce the album. Then we would release what was supposed to be the big hit—"Radio Song," featuring rapper KRS-One. It was a great track and a great plan, but soon after "Losing My Religion" was released, it became our biggest-selling song worldwide.

The song's success was a complete fluke. None of us thought that "Losing My Religion" had much potential. There's no traditional chorus, and the lead instrument was a mandolin. The video was unusual and groundbreaking—super-pop, super-homoerotic, and hypercharged. In the video, I lip-synced for the first time. But it all connected, and fans responded to the song's realness and emotional urgency.

My desire as a musician, if I ever had one, was to write a song of the summer, like the Rolling Stones' "Miss You" or Pharrell Williams' "Happy." Having a huge international summer hit is the biggest goal you can achieve as a pop artist. Nothing about "Losing My Religion" should have made it that kind of hit. But that's what the song became for us in 1991.